HAVING HER SAY

*A compilation of articles by and about Dr. Rosie—
Timekeeper, Almanac, and Scorekeeper for Black America.*

Dr. Rosie Milligan

Copyright © 2017 by Dr. Rosie Milligan
Los Angeles, California
All rights reserved
Printed and Bound in the United States of America

Professional Publishing House
1425 W. Manchester Ave. Ste. B
Los Angeles, California 90047
323-750-3592
Email:.professionalpublishinghouse@yahoo.com
www.Professionalpublishinghouse.com

Cover design: TWASolutions.com
First printing February 2017
ISBN: 978-0-9983089-2-0
10987654321

No part of this book may be reproduced, stored in a retrieval system or transmitted in any form or by any means without the prior written permission of the publisher—except by a reviewer who may quote brief passages in a review to be printed in a newspaper, magazine or journal.
For inquiries contact: drrosie@aol.com

Dedications

I dedicate my literary work to my late father, Simon Hunter. He told me at an early age that I was a genius. I believed every word that my father had spoken, and in my Ebonics language, I will say it like this; "And here I be, a genius." My father was always reading something. My father often offered me $5.00, if I could be quiet for five minutes, and that was back in the day when $5 was a lot of money. I never got the money. But ironically so, I am getting paid today for talking. I am happy that I did not allow him to shut me up from my God-given talent and gift. My success today is due to the fact that my father taught me how to counter negativity with a positive.

One day, I came home from school crying because the children were teasing me about being tall. They asked to what African tribe did I belong. My father sat me on his knees and said these words to me: "It's good to be tall. When you go back to school and they start teasing you, you tell them that you like being tall because if something is up high, you can reach and get it. And if something is low towards the ground, you can stoop and get it, but for those who are short, they can only get what's low to the ground."

From that day forward, I stood tall proudly, and I was happy to tell the teasers that my height gave me an advantage that they did not have. Since then, turning a negative into a positive has propelled me to reach higher heights in my personal and professional life. My father's spirit continues to live on within me.

To my mother, Florine: I did not get to know too much about you. I do remember at the age of five, I was holding on to your dress as you were pressing my baby sister's hair when you collapsed with a heart attack. I was told by everyone that I look so much like you, and I was told how smart you were, so I give you credit for my being a genius. Thank you, Mother, for always showing up in the corner of my room, as an angel, whenever I was at a low point in my life.

To all the ancestors who continue to watch over us, I thank you. I feel your presence.

Acknowledgments

To all my children, who have always supported what I chose to do in life. Your love and good behavior have allowed me to follow my dreams. Thank you, Pamela Milligan-McGee, M.D. You are the best daughter, mother and wife that the world could ever have—you are so loved and you bring so much joy to others. To my son, John Sherman Milligan, Jr., the great musician—thanks for feeding the family whenever I was too tired and too busy to cook. Thank you for playing that soothing music when we needed to be comforted. To my son, Cedric Andre Milligan, the entrepreneur and my business partner. Thank you for being such a great Dad to Little Cedric and a role model for other single Dads. I love you all so much.

To my godchildren, Rita Hall, Dejuana Butler, Dorotha Steed, Yolanda Mills, Delana Cagnolotti, Ruby Maxwell, Sharron Johnson, Georgia Horton, Gayle Dickerson, Jacqueline Thomas, and the rest of you who refer to me as godmother. I love you and you mean a lot to me. The love you have shown to me has helped to sustain me in my endeavors.

To my sisters, the late Willie McCou, and my sister-mother, Owen Nelson, who has allowed all her sisters and brothers to share her home and who has been a mother for so many non-family members. To my sister, Margaret Hoskins: thank you for being the glue that keeps all the family members in contact with each other and for spearheading the family gatherings. To my sister, Kenyaka Beckley, the spoiled one, who continues to keep us all conscious as to who we are and to connect to our African roots. To Attorney Clara Hunter King, my sister-friend and co-author. Thank you for being an example as to how we should look out for those who are not able to look out for themselves. Your works continues to inspire me to do more.

To my brother, Leroy Hunter; continue being an entrepreneur role model for the family. To my brother, Robert Earl Hunter; your accomplishments in life as a pilot and your trade skills have been encouragement to the family.

To my friends and business associates, Ernestine Dixon, Barbara Lindsey and L. C. Green, Jr., Donald Spears, Dr. Maxine Thompson and John Sherman Milligan, Sr. Thanks for being there for me in all my business endeavors—you have made a difference in my life.

To my pastor, Sylvester (Scuffie) Shigg, and first lady, Alyse Shigg; I thank you so much for your friendship and spiritual guidance. Thank you for leading by example and for taking the church to the people outside of the walls of the church house.

To my godson, Bishop Edward Turner; thank you for your love, friendship and for "doing" church versus "-having" church. Thank you for hosting Community Day for the community.

To Dr. Claud Anderson, Dr. Joann Anderson and the West Coast Supporter of the Harvest Institute, Opal Young and Thomas Sampson; I am inspired and motivated by your love and hard work. Your encouragement is what pumps me up daily.

To all my friends and supporters, I appreciate you. If I did not mention your name, please know that I thank you for whatever role you played in my life and for the works that you have done.

About the Author

Dr. Rosie Milligan—a woman who knows no limits. She is a Minister, Registered Nurse, Author, one of Los Angeles's Renowned Financial Gurus, a seasoned Senior Estate Planner, Business and Credit Consultant. She also holds a Ph.D. in Business Administration. She has always been an achiever. She is sought after nationwide for her business and financial coaching services. Every career or business she's been involved in has included helping other people accomplish what they wanted in life. Her motto, *"Erase 'NO,' Step Over 'CAN'T,' and Move Forward With LIFE,"* has been a motivating influence for hundreds to whom she has been mentor and role model.

Milligan is the most versatile speaker on the circuit today. She is a sought-after speaker by religious organizations of all denominations, as well as by corporate and social groups. Dr. Milligan lectures nationally on economic empowerment, and male/female relationships

Dr. Rosie Milligan is a critically acclaimed, *Essence®* and Black Board Bestselling author, and an expert in the publishing industry, with thirty years' experience. She has authored and co-authored twenty-four books, and under her publishing house, Professional Publishing House LLC, she has published more than three hundred titles. Her books, *Creating a New You in Six Weeks*, *Starting a Business Made Simple*, *Getting out of Debt Made Simple*, and *Understanding Credit made Simple* have helped many across the country.

Dr. Milligan owns the largest and fastest-growing African American female publishing house in the nation. Many authors she published were signed by mainstream publishers and have taken their places on numerous best-seller's lists across the country. Using her expertise, she has set up independent publishing companies for twenty-five of her clients. Additionally, she assisted Dr. Maxine Thompson, a top literary agent in Southern California, launch her literary agency business.

Dr. Rosie Milligan

A successful motivational speaker and trainer, she has appeared on numerous television and radio shows, and she is a regular guest on *Stevie Wonder's KJLH Radio*. She is also the host of a weekly live Internet talk show, *EXPRESS YOURSELF HOUR*, and she is founder and director of "Black Writers on Tour." Contact her at: 323-750-3592; drrosie@aol.com; Drrosie.com.

Table of Contents

Introduction 1

Section 1: General Articles 3

Section 2: Words of Wisdom to Bite and to Chew On, and
    Healthy Food for Thought 101

Section 3: Articles and Letters Regarding Family Affairs 117

Section 4: Health Issues 157

Section 5: Articles and Thoughts on Sex and Sexuality 167

Section 6: Letters and Articles to and About Ministers, Political
    Leaders and NAACP 185

Section 7: Media Profile Media Sagas 207

Section 8: Other Articles by Dr. Rosie Milligan 221

Introduction

Today, we live in a society of entitlement. We often talk about what is owed to us. We often talk about our rights. But we don't talk enough about what it is that we owe the world and our responsibilities versus our rights. We should deposit back into humanity some of what has been sowed into us, be it talent, money, or good deeds. At the age of seventy-one, I have had a lot deposited and sowed into my life—and for that I am grateful. For that reason, I feel the need to show my appreciation via giving back, especially to my people. I say my people, meaning Black people.

I have been accused of loving Black folk too much and have been told that if I did not give so much time to Black folks, that I would have much wealth. My response is this: I have had people from other ethnic groups to help me along the way, and I am thankful to them. However, it was Black folks who supported my business down through the years, and because of their support, I was able to survive and sustain my family being a business owner, even during economic hard times. I was able to help educate my children with the monies that came from the hands of Black folks. Black folks have been my cheerleaders, therefore, I love me some Black folks, and I will not apologize.

I have paid attention as I traveled this road called LIFE AVENUE and HELL BOULEVARD. I have seen the lightning flash and I, too, have heard the thunder roll, I have felt the hatred from some white folks, who tried to conquer my soul. I have been knocked down, but I was able to get back up, I have been bent but not broken. I am like a tree that is planted and rooted so deeply that I can echo the hymns of the old, "I SHALL NOT BE MOVED, and I AIN'T GON' LET NOBODY TURN ME AROUND." My soul is anchored by the voices and the strength that I gather like stones from my ancestors.

As an ex-cotton picker, a pea picker, a farmer, a hog slopper, I know hard times, and I have also learned that trouble and hard times does not last always.

Whatever you are confronted with, or by, know that—THIS TOO WILL PASS. I contributed my measure of success to my faith in God, my works, determination, patience, persistence, and perseverance. Having faith alone is not enough. You must do the works, too. A good example is this: if your leg has been broken, and you now believe you can walk again, the work is for you to get up and take the steps. You cannot just sit at the "Wishing Well" and hope that something will happen for you because you have the faith. Faith is executed by your works.

You must be determined to reach your goals in life. You must have the patience to wait until the right time to make a move. Life is life. It includes cycles such as the four seasons, and you must learn to operate in seasons as the farmer does. You must know when to plant and when to pluck. You must be persistent; you must stay focused, unwavering and unmovable. You must persevere, regardless as to what it looks like or what it feels like. You must not allow your present circumstances to influence your thoughts or behavior. Always know that your current condition is no reflection of your tomorrow.

I do not have wealth to leave you; I have shared my finance along the way. What I have I gladly leave it to you. I leave you hope, I leave you wisdom; I leave you knowledge through the many articles and books that I have written, and books that I have published for others. I leave you the courage to fight to change things that should be changed. I leave you the desire to love and to respect each other. I leave you self-determination. I leave you a thirst for knowledge for knowledge is the key that unlocks the doors that holds on in every type of bondage.

As you read my articles and my books, you will note that I have given you information that I have gathered along life's highway. My articles are like dining at a smorgasbord; there is something for everybody. If you eat from my literary plate of knowledge, you will gain strength to endure your ride down LIFE AVENUES and HELL BOULEVARDS.

While some of my literary foods may not taste good or feel good, eat all of it and share it with your family and friends. It will do the body, mind and spirit good. With the much love I have given you all, this is my legacy. I want to be remembered by what I have given versus what I have taken. Enjoy the ride to the HOUSE OF KNOWLEDGE CENTER! You will find articles about every aspect of life. Make sure you take something back home with you from the HOUSE OF KNOWLEDGE CENTER and share it.

SECTION 1: GENERAL ARTICLES

I HAD A DREAM ABOUT AFRICAN-AMERICANS

In 1992, I had a dream about African-Americans. This dream inspired me to write the book, *Negroes, Colored People, Blacks, and African Americans in America*. In my dream, I saw the bones of African Americans scattered in a valley called "The Valley of the Dry Bones." In the dream, I was the only person alive. I was so afraid. I lifted my hands up in the air and cried, "Father, can these bones live?" A voice answered, "Yes, if you can connect the parts together the way they were." I found all the bones of the lower extremities, from the toes to the hip bones, except the ankle bones. I found all the bones from the hip bones to the head bones, but the chest bones were missing. I found bones from the shoulders to the fingers, but the wrist bones were missing. Flesh covered the body parts as they were discovered. I tried but was unable to stand the body erect because the ankle bones were missing. I could not put the heart in place because the chest bones were missing. I could not put the hands on because the wrist bones were missing.

I left the scene to search for help, hoping, by chance, that there might be someone else in the valley. I met a car driving backward down a steep hill. The driver had no flesh on his bones. I asked why he was driving backward and he said he was trying to see where he had been so that he could get a grip on where he could go again. I immediately woke up and heard a voice say, "Write what you saw—the problem and the solution."

I interpreted my dream thusly: The inability to stand the body erect represents succumbing to the images depicted by the Eurocentric media. The inability to place the heart represents loss of love, care, and support for Black businesses. The inability to attach the hands represents the lack of self-determination.

Dr. Rosie Milligan

STOP WORRING ABOUT PRESIDENT ELECT—DONALD TRUMP

This is Dr. Rosie Milligan, self-appointed Mayor of South Central Los Angeles
Stop worrying yourself about the president elect. It's going to be all right because those who were in their coma state are coming alive. You know sometime it take an Earth Quake to wake folks up. Get Trump off your brain and out of your mind.

I suggest you read Philippians 4:8-- Finally, brothers, whatever is true, whatever is honorable, whatever is right, whatever is pure, whatever is lovely, whatever is admirable — if anything is excellent or praiseworthy — think on these things. DONALD TRUMP IS NONE OF THESE THINGS, SO STOP THINKING ON HIM!

Y'all act like Big Momma and God just died. What's wrong with y'all? God is alive and well. Let me conclude by saying this: YOU ARE IN GOOD HANDS RIGHT NOW---YOUR OWN HANDS AND MOST OF ALL YOU ARE STILL IN THE HANDS OF GOD—SO SHUT UP, STAND UP, PIECE UP (MEANING WORK TOGETHER) AND CHILL. LET'S NOT DISCUSS TRUMP FOR THE NEXT SEVEN DAYS; YOUR IMMUNE SYSTEM WILL BE ENHANCED. I AM JUST SAYING. Holler if you hear me!

THE HARRIETT TUBMAN'S TOWN HALL MEETING WILL BE SCHEDULED VERY SOON—SO GET READY.

Having Her Say

WARNING LETTER FROM A BLACK ELDER

Dear African-Americans, Negroes, Colored People, and Blacks,

The light of hope had faded within many Blacks. Many were able to see a sparkle when Obama was elected the first African-American president of the United States of America. What does having a black president mean to Black? The following are responses to a survey I conducted: 1) It means that my son can one day become President. 2) It means that Americans are now color blind. 3) More doors will be opened to Blacks. 4) Blacks will be respected more all over the world.

Fact: Obama being President gives false hope to Blacks. I believe that Obama becoming President was a move of God to neutralize the hate and destruction of the American people.

Fact: We should aspire to have Black children learning to read, becoming bilingual, pursuing a trade, career, or vocation where doors are opened to them based on their skills and not the color of their skin or from which side of the tracks they are from We should steer our children to become business owners versus job seekers and beggars we must lead by example, by letting our children see us going out of the way to do business with Black people.

Let me tell you what Obama cannot do for you and your children. For you, he cannot make employers hire you. He can't stop police from profiling you. He cannot change images that the media and movies portray of you. He cannot change the lyrics or the words rappers write for and about you. He cannot change the disparity in the healthcare system for you

Sincerely yours,
Dr. Rosie Milligan

Dr. Rosie Milligan

BLACK AMERICA, WHAT'S BEYOND THE JUBILATION

There is a time for all things. On November 4th, 2008, when the newscasters announced that Barak Obama was the President Elect of the United States of America—the first African-American President—this was certainly a time for jubilee. Jubilation, yes! It was like a woman, who was told that she was barren, hearing the words, "You are pregnant!"

Waiting for the election outcome to be announced was like waiting for the outcome of a plane crash and you hear the words "They all survived!" What we heard on Tuesday, November 4th, was more than *good news*; it was the **Best News!**

I recall, as a child, how excited my siblings and I would be at Christmas time after receiving and opening our gifts. However, the next day or two following the celebration and excitement, my father, Simon Hunter, would say, "Okay; now put the toys up. It's time to go chop wood!" Meaning, it was time to go back to work. Well folks, we have cried, shouted, and danced; now it's time to go back to work. Hope without work is like faith without works—it's DEAD!

Come on people; roll up your sleeves—we've got cotton to pick.

Blacks take lead in the following areas: infant death rate, adolescent morality, and homicidal rate. They also lead in many chronic diseases. Black women lead in the *never to be married* category. Black men lead in the incarceration rate. Black children lead in the category of children who are least likely to be in a two-parent home, and they lag in literacy. Indeed, we have work to do.

Unemployment among Blacks has hit astronomical numbers. The official national rate is 35 in Detroit, the rate is 48%, Baltimore is 48%, Pittsburgh is 49%, in New York City the Black male unemployment is 51% and the national unemployment for Black youth is 89%. Even these statistics are under-reported because of they do not include the long term unemployed who no longer collect unemployment compensation or are so discourage they are not actively searching for work.

Blacks have been infused with a spirit of hope, and they are feeling a sense of validation. We must seize the moment to carve a path that will change the dismal plight of Blacks all over the world—not just those of the United States of America.

Obama's win of the presidential election demonstrates that courage has no *color*. Obama has brought us to the well, but we must draw our own water. So let's get to work!

Obama cannot do the following: (1) make our children read books versus watching television, (2) make our young men pull up their pants and stop sagging, (3) make our sons and daughters stop making music that disrespects themselves and our women, (4) make you or your children stop buying such degrading music, (5) make parents set proper priorities for their family, (6) make you spend your money when possible with black-owned businesses, (7) make you open businesses and dominate those industries in which you frequent regularly, etc.

Here is what we must do: (1) we need an equity ownership in our community, industries, and services that Blacks dominate. We must open those businesses or boycott those that provide the service and force them to partner with us, (2) divide our cities in regions and appoint a mayor for each region. Every church, school, and business within the set region must collaborate to make that region safe and viable. Every church must adopt a school and a foster care home in its community.

We must develop a Council of Elders for each city. We must get involved with senior citizens in planning.

There is much to be done. In my book, Black America Faces Economic Crisis: Solutions Made Simple," I have committed to you a reconstruction plan for each of us. Let's do the work. The harvest is plentiful—we need laborers **NOW!**

Dr. Rosie Milligan

NO LONGER A FAIRYTALE FOR A BLACK MAN TO BE PRESIDENT

On November 4th, 2008, at approximately 8:00 p.m. (Pacific Standard Time), a fairytale became a ***truth***. A year ago, past president, Bill Clinton, said these words, "A Black man becoming President of the United States of America is a fairytale." Well, as I reflect backwards, being anything other than a slave or a good house Negro was, **a** fairytale for Blacks in the minds of Europeans.

Let me just name a few of the things once thought of as a fairytale. For Blacks, being a Black female, and becoming the most influential talk show host in the world—Oprah Winfrey. **A** Black man invent**ing** Blood Plasma—Dr. Charles R. Drew. In the early 1900s the first Black female, **Madame C. J. Walker**, became a self-made millionaire, **as** founder and owner of **her** haircare and beauty products company. Additionally, there was Bass Reeves, the **Black United State Deputy** Marshall; Hermon Grimes, Sr., invented the Folding Wing Aircraft which was used in World War II, Korean and Vietnam Wars and are still used in today's military services—this is just to name a few. I recommend you visit www.911forblackamerica.com—click on the link Black Inventors.com. **I, also, recommend you** read the book Hidden Secrets about Black History, Volume I, by Francella Henderson.

Xenonia Clayton, founder of the "Trumpet Awards," she showcases annually Black Americans who have affected and made an impact on the nation/world and those who have done, or are doing things that were once thought of as a fairytale.

The old folks used to say, "The cat is out the bag now!" What they were saying is "The truth has risen to the surface for all to see." The Bible tells us in John 8:32, "*and ye shall know the truth, and the truth shall make you free.*" It is without a doubt that many Americans have embraced such truth that God created all equal and that intellect and talent is in every race. In this historical 2008's presidential election, **we** witnessed these truths as votes were cast for Barack Obama.

The world took note of the fairytale phenomenal. They waited with the anticipation of a child who placed his tooth under the pillow awaiting tomorrow's fulfillment of his wish. When newscasters broadcasted Barack as the President Elect, it was likened unto a baseball game; whereas it was the last ending, the scores were equal. The bases were loaded, the last batter was up, **he had hit two foul balls**; and the pitcher was preparing to throw his final ball. The world held its breath as its heart raced. The pitcher threw a curveball; yet, Obama hit a home run. Crowds in every country went wild, cheering, and tearing. Like the commercial about gas pain, "How do you spell relief?" It's not *Rolaids*, but indeed it's getting the Republicans out of the White House.

Never before has the world taken such notice in the presidential election of the United States of America. This fairytale coming true, made the world stand still; the stars twinkled, moon became full, the sun had gone down, but I'd bet you it peeped. I believe there was an eclipse; we missed it due to the excitement.

May this historic moment of the first Black president of the United States sends a message to all, that with God's help even fairytales come true and may you keep hope alive and continue to dream.

Remember, the sky is not the limit; there is much beyond the sky. Today I feel more of a American than ever before. I am cog**nizant** of the fact that Obama alone cannot change America but with all of us working together, yes we can.

Dr. Rosie Milligan

BLACK FOLKS NEED TO SHUT THE HELL UP!
From Dr. Rosie Milligan's Desk—The Elder, Mayor of South Central

Dear Black America:

Hear me out. Stop worrying yourself about Donald Trump, Hillary Clinton and the White House. They will be okay—but what about you and your black house? Find something worth talking about that can help you going forward. Stop all the chat-chatting and come to a still place and focus on what you can do to improve your life, your family life and the lives of people in your community, if you cover that square mileage, you will see a greater impact.

The Trump children, the Clinton children and Obama children, they will be okay if they choose to be okay. But what are the choices for your children based on your current financial condition? Come on think. Do not engage in any conversation regarding the election and turn off the news for the next two week and watch how your life will take a new turn. It's time for you to start planning for 2017. Trump and Clinton already know what they are going to be doing in 2017. What about your plans?

If you following my instructions and you find yourself without anything to do, I suggest you read Dr. Anderson's book, PowerNomics, A Plan To Empower Black America. My books Nigger, Please, Creating A New You In Six Weeks, Black America Faces Economic Crisis, Getting Out of Debt Made Simple. Jim Clingman's books, BlackOnomics. I will continue to suggest books for you to read. I would also suggest you visit PowerNomics web site and check our all Dr. Anderson's books and tapes. My books and tapes are on Drrosie.com.

As your self-appointed Mayor of South Central, I will call a Harriett Tubman like Town Hall meeting very soon to discuss our plan of escape from the debtor's, economic, and social Prison. And if you are scared, don't bother to come---just keep waiting on the White House and elected official to save you. Your made up mind, your faith, your works and God is your only hope. "I AM JUST SAYING." SO SHUT YOUR MOUTH FOR THE NEXT TWO WEEKS.

IF YOU WANT TO BE INFORMED OF THE CLOSED DOOR HARRIET TUBMAN TOWN HALL MEETING—EMAIL ME AT DRROSIE@AOL.COM. I AM NOT PLAYING, IF I WANTED TO PLAY I WOULD GO TO THE PARK AND GET ON THE MERRY-GO-ROUND. IT'S TIME TO GET SERIOUS

Dr. Rosie Milligan

BACK DOWN MEMORY LANE FOR BLACKS IN LOS ANGELES"

I suggest that we reflect in our mental mirror and compare where we have been and where we are today. We must remember to never forget the **Past**—for the **Past** serves as a compass that will tell us when we are headed in the right direction. There was an era in history when hope in the unborn had died. We must not allow our youth to revisit that past era of history of living without hope for themselves and their offspring.

We slept during the political fight to take prayer out of the schools—and we have seen the devastating effects from not standing up for what we know is right. Let us not go to sleep behind the wheel ever again.

We went to sleep at the wheel when we were tricked into voting for the *"Three Strike"* law. The voters were deceived; they were unclear as to the ramifications of this law. Most people thought it was designed to incarcerate hardcore criminals, such as carjackers with guns, murderers, those who participated in drive-bys, etc.—certainly not for someone who steals a piece of pizza. We must ask ourselves this question: What came first—the increase in building more prisons or the increase in crime? It does not take a rocket scientist to see that the laws were put intact to guarantee the justification for building the *"New Slave Ship,"*—prisons—the ship that does not sail.

It is not enough to enslave the adults—our children are now being tried as adults! It sounds like good economics to me—for those who profit from the sweat of the incarcerated.

Our children were not always unmotivated about attending school, and they were excited about going to college. They had summer jobs and training programs. They felt safe playing in their neighborhood parks. There was no such thing as *"drive-bys"* or *"selling drugs,"* and they could wear any color without the fear of being identified with a gang. Many of them worked in their family-owned businesses. During integration, many Black-owned businesses were abandoned, which forced them to close. Blacks became more interested in having their children work for white folks rather than helping to build their family businesses.

Forty years ago, when you mentioned the word *"minority,"* it was synonymous to saying *"Coloreds," "Blacks,"* or *"African-Americans."* Today, however, when you say *"minority,"* you are including *everyone* except the white male. It's like a pie where before, Blacks shared one-half of it. However, now, that same one-half portion of the pie has to be shared by four or five other ethnic groups/nationalities.

Let me take you back down memory lane. I want to remind you of what it used to be like for Blacks in Los Angeles so that you may gain a better perspective on what must be done to change the conditions for Blacks in our city.

Following the *1965 Watts Riots*, we had training programs and corporate work partnership programs for our youth and young adults. We had programs—*CETA, WIN, STEP, MDTA*, and summer programs at churches and parks for our youth. Do you remember? Moreover, our youth were not killing each other, neither were they selling drugs. They were not dropping out of school, becoming nonproductive citizens. They were literate and college-bound. Even a blind man can see what happened back then, and what needs to happen today!

Do you remember that prior to the *1965 Watts Riots*, if a person got shot or otherwise critically injured in South Central Los Angeles, that person would be taken to the *Big County General Hospital,* on Soto Street, in East Los Angeles? Many bled out and died en route. The *Watts Health Foundation/Medical Clinic*, on 103rd Street, near Alameda Street, and the *Dr. Martin Luther King Jr. Hospital* came into existence to fill the needs of Blacks for healthcare. Then, Blacks constituted most of that demographic population. Do you remember when Black doctors' offices were plentiful in our community? Do you remember when Blacks owned many of the businesses in South Central? *Where are all these today?*

In addition, do you remember the *Morningside Hospital*, on Harvard, off Manchester Avenue, near Western Avenue—*Kennedy Hospital*, on Manchester, near Figueroa, just under the (110) Harbor Freeway—the *Bonaire Hospital*, on 120th Street, near Broadway—the *Broadway Hospital*, on 96th and Broadway—the *University Hospital,* on Vermont, near Exposition—*View Park Hospital*, on Stocker, near Don Felipe Drive—*Dominguez Hospital*, in Compton? *Where are all these today?*

Looking back is a good thing when it helps one to trace his steps to where progress began in years passed. Remember, if you know where you have been—you *can* go back there again. There is a strategic plan to wipe out an entire generation of Black people—via an inadequate public school system. As you very well know, miseducation leads to incarceration, and poor healthcare leads to early death.

Legislation that was passed to not provide public assistance for a mother's new birth has caused an increase in abortions among the economically challenged, which only adds to our problems today. The rate of incarceration for Blacks, coupled with all the above, will provide us with a bleak future if we do not wake up and devise a plan to save **"US."** Make no mistake, *we will be history*.

Let's look back, gain a proper perspective, and do the right thing.

Dr. Rosie Milligan, author of *Negroes, Colored People, Blacks, and African-Americans in America.*

JENA 6
RESURRECTED BLACK DRY BONES

The response of Black folk from across the country to the injustices suffered by our young Black males in the Jena 6 Trial has resurrected and revitalized a new spirit, hope, and determination in Blacks worldwide. I believe that our youth will now gain a new respect for us and will gain a renewed sense of security, because we have demonstrated our outpouring of love and support for them "big time."

History bears witness that Black men during slavery in America were denied the right to defend their families. Black men were not able to protect their wives and children from being sold into slavery. Even today, 2007, we witness a modern-day, high-tech slavery movement called the "Prison Industrial Complex," which is bent on enslaving young Black males. Our youth are still considered economically beneficial to the new slave masters. They are more suitable for hard labor, which yields higher productivity. They are ripe for the picking. In addition, although not surprisingly, our Black youth and Black men are being enslaved during their prime reproductive years. *Is this genocide or what?*

Black men have remained passive, having the faith to change their conditions, but they are emotionally paralyzed when it comes to applying the work/activity necessary to make their faith work for them. But now, these "dry bones" have come alive and are ready to accept the responsibility that we are indeed our brother's keeper. We also realize that when one of us hurts, we all hurt. We know that it may be my child today, but it will be *your* child tomorrow, if we fail to protect *any* of our people.

I believe this movement of Blacks being bused from across the country in support of Jena 6 will serve to empower Black folk all over the world. It gives us all a sense of power and security, knowing that none of us are alone in our fight for justice. It empowers us to take a stand whenever unrighteousness prevails.

I have launched a Web site—www.911for blackamerica.com—to serve as a vehicle to connect Blacks worldwide to information that impacts their lives and, survival. I pray that our next movement will be an economic movement to connect black businesses, domestically and globally. If mainstream society can do business globally, surely we can coordinate with Black-owned businesses across America and internationally.

When I learned of Jena 6, I recalled a dream that I had in 1992. This dream inspired me to write the book, *Negroes, Colored People, Blacks, and African Americans in America*. In my dream, I saw the bones of African Americans scattered in a valley called "The Valley of the Dry Bones." In the dream, I was the only person alive. I was so afraid. I lifted my hands up in the air and cried, "Father, can these bones live?" A voice answered, "Yes, if you can connect the parts together the way they were." I found all the bones of the lower extremities, from the toes to the hip bones, except the ankle bones. I found all the bones from the hip bones to the head bones, but the chest bones were missing. I found bones from the shoulders to the fingers, but the wrist bones were missing. Flesh covered the body parts as they were discovered. I tried but was unable to stand the body erect because the ankle bones were missing. I could not put the heart in place because the chest bones were missing. I could not put the hands on because the wrist bones were missing.

I left the scene to search for help, hoping, by chance, that there might be someone else in the valley. I met a car driving backward down a steep hill. The driver had no flesh on his bones. I asked why he was driving backward and he said he was trying to see where he had been so that he could get a grip on where he could go again. I immediately woke up and heard a voice say, "Write what you saw—the problem and the solution."

I interpreted my dream thusly: The inability to stand the body erect represents succumbing to the images depicted by the Eurocentric media. The inability to place the heart represents loss of love, care, and support for Black businesses. The inability to attach the hands represents the lack of self-determination.

The dry bones blinked an eye at the Rodney King beating; they opened their eyes in response to the overlooked Katrina victims. Enough is enough! These dry bones finally got up when hearing of the injustices concerning the Jena 6. Now, *that's* what I am talking about!! Doing the *right* thing.

Having Her Say

Oftentimes, incidents occur that get wide media coverage. But months, and even years, later, the question is asked: whatever happened to the outcome of this case or that case? Many people are left in the dark. If you know of such cases and are wondering about the final outcome, contact us and we will research it and place it on the Web site www.911for blackamerica.com. Stay tuned to the naked truth that is brought to you by *Los Angeles Truth News*—news you can trust.

HOW REVISITING THE BLACK MAN'S HISTORY CAN IMPROVE THE RELATIONSHIP BETWEEN THE BLACK MALE AND FEMALE

I believe that we must revisit history as we examine the family structure of Blacks in America. An absentee father was the norm for the African-American family. Families were separated by force! Slavery severely impacted the lives of the Black family. Considering the fact that our physical exodus from slavery has only been 140 years, that's not a long time, and we are still experiencing its effects.

Blacks were forced to produce offsprings, not for themselves, but for their master's economic gain. Today, Blacks are not forced to produce babies; however, because of the residual effect of slavery on the Black family, their offsprings continue to be an economic product for the modern-day master called "PRISON." Today, in 2005, Black males in prison are paid less for their labor than they were paid 140 years ago.

Black men were not socialized as other men, that is, to be accountable or responsible for his family. In order to understand why the Black man and Black woman are having such challenges in their relationships, you must understand how their experience and living conditions in America have impacted their lives and the lives of their family.

When a Black family needed assistance from Social Services' programs, the father had to remove himself from the family in order for his wife and children to get assistance. Black men have a long way to go to get back to their African roots of being a provider and protector. Black men have come a long way, and they will get back to their God-Created-Nature, with the help of God, Almighty, and with the understanding of their past.

The Black man, his wife, and his children all had to look to the white man for food, clothing, and shelter. In essence, the wife and children provided for themselves, they worked side by side with the Black man in the field from sun up to sun down. The Black man could not protect his family. The white man impregnated his wife and daughters and there was nothing that the Black man could do about it, if he wanted a place to live and if he wanted to live.

The white man positioned himself as the surrogate parents for Blacks giving them the illusion that he was their caretaker, while he abused them, molested their children and raped their women. He, the white man, was in charge. If the Black man did something to his wife and she felt he was out of order or which she considered was not proper treatment, she would tell the white man on her husband and he would talk to, punish or beat the Black man. As you can see the Black man could neither provide for nor protect his family.

When Blacks were so-called freed from slavery, there was no economical provisions made for him to provide for his family. Therefore, many of them had to continue to be beholding to their masters under the same harsh conditions. Some families were able to leave the plantations and move up North with family members to start a new life.

Many men left their families behind; they left to secure a job and then sent back for their families. Men who resisted the abusive treatment or who refused to be treated as less than a man, he had to flee, find work and send back for his wife and children. The pain, the heartache and the financial struggle was so much to bear; therefore some of them never looked back, went back nor sent back for their family.

The Black man had to always pretend about something, he was not free to express his true emotions. He had to grin and pretend that he was happy in the presence of his master, because being unhappy was disturbing to the master. Being unhappy equated to one possibly thinking for himself or just thinking of running away. The Black man could not show his feelings towards a woman for fear that the master would ship him or her to another plantation.

You see, the white man knows the value, power and strength of being or having a sense of family unity; therefore, he did not want to see Blacks socialized to be an intact family unit. After all, being an ideal family for Blacks was not good for the white man's economy. The Black man was not brought here to start a family; he was brought here for economic profit, to work for free and to produce as many babies by as many women as possible, so that he could deliver more workers for his master.

Feelings and emotions were almost beaten out of the Black man. In fact, it was detrimental for him to express feelings and show emotions. He was safer when he was a man of few words, for he knew the consequences if he was misunderstood when communicating. Black fathers passed their behaviors and experiences down to their sons as a safety precaution. Black men could only show emotions and feelings at church or at a funeral service, and during the time of intimacy with his woman or wife.

During slavery, sex and family was the only enjoyment that was within economic reach for the Black man. Even today, 2005, sex is the only form of gratification for the average economically challenged Black man. He cannot get on his yacht, or take a cruise on weekends, etc. He cannot buy expensive toys to play with; he does not have a get-away home.

Therefore, sex becomes the only reachable pleasure for him. Sex becomes his pleasure, his tranquilizer, his drug, etc. As an escape from the pain, racism, and injustice, sex is like a safe haven. It's like returning to your mother's womb where there is comfort—where you are free of the cares of the world and no one can hurt you there.

Black men's emotions, feeling and dialogue are still guarded even in his relationship with his wife, because if either is misinterpreted, he is placed in the "dog house" and the one thing that he cherishes the most, "sex," is taken away from him; and he does not function well without it.

Most Black men really want to be with their families and children. What they need is someone to be a father-like figure for them. A Black man needs guidance. Most of them are trying to be something or somebody that they have never seen or experienced, and must be taught that. The woman's ideal of what a man is supposed to be is distorted because she too has not experience a father in her life.

You see, a father is a role model for his son and a father gives definition to his daughter as to what a man is. A mother is a role model for her daughter and she gives definition to her son as to what a woman is. 70% of Black households are headed and ran by a female with the father most times being totally out of the picture. The sons and daughters are both confused about male/female responsibility.

The son sees the mother as a nurturer and the provider. All of his life he has been provided for by a female—his mother, grandmother, both females. Being cared for all one's life by a female is a familiar comfort, and this familiar comfort is what makes it easy for a male to allow and to feel comfortable having his woman/wife to take care of him, because that has been his experience.

The daughter of the broken-home-experience her mother as the sole-provider; therefore, she takes on the role of her mother and she will accept a man into her life who does not have the means to provide for himself and she will have a baby with him. When the responsibility of providing becomes overwhelming, she lashes out at the one who she perceives as the blame—her man/husband.

The male is now frustrated, insecure, and unsure of what to do. He now feels that she got what she wanted from him—a baby—and now that is the only person who matters to her. He now begins to feel like the outsider, the insignificant intruder. When he can no longer take the pressure, he leaves or she leaves him or puts him out since she has the baby.

The drama is on. He could not provide the help needed, when they were together and now he has to provide for himself shelter and she now expects more monetary support from him, than he could give while living with you. In the first place, you knew his financial status, and secondly, she made the decision to have the baby without his consent or permission.

He is no longer allowed to have any relationship with his child. If he is allowed to participate in his child's life, it must be on her terms **only**. When it becomes unbearable, he leaves the woman and the child behind. The real victim is the child.

I am not casting blame on the Black woman. I am only pointing out the facts that are hindering the progress of the Black family. I believe that if we could get a perspective of the Black man, as related to who is who he was before coming to America and what America has made him become, then we would have a better understanding of our family dynamics and we can embrace each other and begin to value ourselves and our children again.

BLACK AMERICA, YOU OUGHT TO HEAR AND LISTEN TO SOMEBODY!
From An Elder, Dr. Rosie Milligan, Part 1 of 3

Black America, I admonish you to listen, hear, and obey words of wisdom. We must create a better financial path for our children. Our parents and their parents worked hard, fought hard, and made many sacrifices to free themselves from slavery. While many of them had no, or very little, education, they understood the value and importance of education and made sure that their offspring got a good education. Today, Black parents have far more education then their children. It used to be that parents had to live with their children when they became old, but nowadays, their children and their children's children have to live with their parents and grandparents. Our grandparents lay away a little something for their children's and grandchildren's education, and they had an insurance policy on their children and grandchildren. They had an insurance policy with a cash value for a college fund, and they all had a burial plan for themselves.

Our grandparents understood the value of ownership. When they migrated from the South, as soon as possible, they bought homes, duplexes, and apartments. They instructed their children not to ever sell the family home and to keep it as a homestead so that no one in the family would have to be without shelter. They paid off their home as soon as possible. They viewed having many children as a blessing and not as a curse. The old folks knew that God could feed twelve as well as He could feed two. They believed His Word, and they took God at His Word. They had faith, and they had the works to back up the faith. They did not hurry their children from their homes. In fact, when their children got married, many of them stayed in the home with their parents even after having children of their own. This was good because it gave them a longer period to gain wisdom from the elders and to be given instructions on how to be a husband, wife, and mother.

Many grandparents reared their grandchildren so that their children could go North to pursue a better education, job, and life. Until their parents got settled, in most cases, the grandparents continued to rear the grandchild, and there was no such thing as these children feeling abandoned—but, of course, there were no psychiatrists around putting labels on folks back then. The only way that most of us were able to escape the South was because one of our relatives allowed us to come and live with them. They could even leave their money on stop of the dresser or in the dresser drawer and no one took it.

Let's fast-forward the tape to this generation. This generation would rather have a $50,000 car and a closet full of clothes. It takes them thirty minutes to decide what to wear. They would rather have an expensive car then a home. And they hurry their children away from their home. This new generation is so selfish. They do not have time to have babies or to rear them—one is enough, and two is too many. If they got pregnant for the third time, even their family and friends would question their sanity. They will not welcome their loved ones into their home even when they are struggling. Instead, they make statements such as: "I don't want anybody in my house; I might just decide to want to get up and walk around in my house naked." Yea, right!

Many make no preparation for their children's education so if their child does not get a grant, loan, or scholarship, they have to forfeit a higher education and try to find work with limited education and skills. The salary that's earned by those who have limited education and skills is just enough to keep their heads above water, as the old folks used to say.

When their child gets married, he/she usually marries someone in the same predicament—someone whose parent or parents have the same behavior and attitude about family, finances, and responsibilities. You add a child to this equation and expenses multiply. Now, what do you have here? In most cases, you have a family that is relegated to poverty. And quite often, they will treat their children the same as how their parents treated them—no support, no provision for education, and "Get out of my house as soon as you turn 18 years of age, and I am not going to help you with your babies cause I raised mine and you're going to raise yours!"

This generation does not plan for life or death. They have no burial plans; therefore, if they or their children die, the community has to raise money to bury them. Children do what they see. And remember this. I quote, "Children see what we do long before they understand what we say to them." These irresponsible behaviors have perpetuated from generation to generation, and because of this, we are now an underclass in numbers and in economics. In the county of Los Angeles, the numbers for Blacks is approximately 8.7 percent and Latinos 40 percent, with Whites 29.1 percent, and our business ownership and median income is far less than the other ethnic groups. With this being said, our only hope is to pull together in every way. There is no room for division. We are outnumbered in every way.

BLACK AMERICA, YOU OUGHT TO HEAR AND LISTEN TO SOMEBODY!
From An Elder, Dr. Rosie Milligan, Part 2 of 3

Black America, I admonish you to listen, hear, and obey words of wisdom. We must create a better financial path for our children. Our parents and their parents worked hard, fought hard, and made many sacrifices to free themselves from slavery. While many of them had no, or very little, education, they understood that "If we collectively come together—we can accomplish anything!"

Dr. Anderson uses graphic descriptions and time lines to show how nearly 100 percent of this nation's businesses, wealth, resources, and political power were distributed into the hands of the dominant society, and that Blacks will be locked into the lowest level of a real-life Monopoly game. He said that by 2010, Blacks would become a permanent underclass. It is now 2012. Did we listen?

Black America, we are in a critical baseball game like position. We are in the last inning, the bottom of the 9th, and the game is tied. The bases are loaded with two outs, and the last batter is up to bat. The umpire has called three balls and two strikes. As the pitcher winds up to throw the ball, the crowd is yelling, "Let him walk you!" The batter's instinct is telling him to hit a home run. Which voice will be heard and listened to? The batter is in the old fork-in-the-road position.

Our problem is not that we do not have enough religion, churches, and political leaders. We have more than enough. Our problem is that we have left our first love—God, and we are neither cold nor hot. Our other main problem is that we have not pursued economics in the way we should have. We are suffering from economic anemia, economic hemorrhage, and economic paralysis. We display a failure to do for self and failure to support Black-owned business. We still suffer from the White man's ice is colder than the Black man's ice. Here is what others who came before us have said about economics and self-determination:

Booker T. Washington said to us, *"Now is the time, not in some far-off future, but now is the time for us as a race to prove to the world that we have the ability and the inclination to do our part in owning, developing, manufacturing, and trading in the natural resources of our country. And if we let these golden opportunities slip from us in this generation, I fear they will never come to us in like degree again. Let us act … before it's too late, before others come from foreign lands and rob us of our birthright."*

Let's see what Mr. Booker T. Washington had to say about politics, shall we? *"We did not seek to give the people the idea that political rights were not valuable or necessary, but rather to impress upon them that economic efficiency was the foundation for every success."*

Dr. Martin Luther King Jr. said these almost exact same words: *"The emergency we now face is economic."* We must believe that it is our birthright to partake of the riches of the world, and this is the faith that we must hold to. Dr. Martin Luther King Jr. also said, *"Faith is taking the first step even when you don't see the staircase."*

Let the words of Malcolm X ring out in your mind: *"By any means necessary."* Let's not retreat. Our forefathers did not retreat, which got us as far as we did. We must not be afraid; we must not fear. Harriet Tubman once said, *"I can't die but once."* We are in a war, and in every war there will be casualties. Sister Rosa Parks said, "I have learned over the years that when one's mind is made up, this diminishes fear, knowing what must be done does away with fear."

Frederick Douglass had the following to say: "Without a struggle, there can be no progress." So stop talking about you being tired of fighting the system and asking why we have to fight so hard to get what's due us. Don't get tired; ask God for more strength to fight. Frederick Douglass also stated, *"If there is no struggle, there is no progress. Those who profess to favor freedom and deprecated agitation are men who want crops without plowing up the ground; they want rain without thunder and lightning."*

W.E.B. DuBois had the following to say: *"To be a poor man is hard, but to be a poor race in a land of dollars is the very bottom of hardship."*

Can we be saved on this side of the river?

The biblical characters Sampson and Hezekiah pleaded with God for another chance, and God granted them their requests. He can do the same for us if we come together in prayer, works, and faith. God is the same today as He was yesterday. II Chronicles 7:14 tells us, "If my people which are called by my name, shall humble themselves, and pray, and seek my face, and turn from their wicked ways, then will I hear from heaven, and will forgive their sin and will heal their land."

Here is what we must do: We must reflect back on what Mama Dem did. What the new generation did was this: Since they could not embrace everything about their parents/grandparents, they threw the baby out with the bathwater and started anew. They tried to bake a new cake leaving out all of Grandma's ingredients. When they got to the fork in the road, they did not want to travel the roads that Grandma had traveled. They took a new path—and here we are tore up from the floor up, in a ship without a sail, in a boat without a paddle, in the dark without a light.

We must move from being consumers to being producers. We must endure being inconvenient via going out of our way to do business with Black folks or with folks who hire Black folks. As Dr. Claud Anderson has said, "The drain of wealth and disposable income from the Black neighborhood will destabilize the neighborhood."

BLACK AMERICA, YOU OUGHT TO HEAR AND LISTEN TO SOMEBODY!
From An Elder, Dr. Rosie Milligan, Part 3 Of 3

Black America, I admonish you to listen, hear, and obey words of wisdom. We must make family restoration a priority. We must teach and instill a sense of pride in our children. We must teach them our true history. We must restore family and cultural values. We must take control of our children and community. We must reach out to our young folk, teach and show them the proper way to live in America where all odds are stacked against them, and let them know that if God is for them, He's more than the entire world against them. We must immunize, vaccinate, and inoculate our people with the words of truth about their history. They are not just descendants of slaves but indeed, ascendants of kings and queens. We must give them their booster shot along the way to protect them from vicious racism and from the media's attack of demonization that has depicted them as being less than human.

When our children are told that Blacks do not have the ability to do math, tell them about Dr. Charles Drew who invented blood plasma; Granville T. Woods, an engineer who patented the telephone transmitter as well as over 150 electrical and mechanical inventions; and Lewis Howard Latimer who was a pioneer in the development of the electrical light bulb, just to name a few. You cannot do those things if you have not mastered the skills of mathematics. Tell them to Google Black inventions and Black patents or read Francella Henderson's book, *Hidden Secrets About Black History*.

If they tell you that Blacks don't know how to run successful businesses, tell them about Little Black Wall Street which was likened unto a mini Beverly Hills where Blacks had created a successful infrastructure and dollars circulated 36–100 times and sometimes took a year to leave the community. This town was in Tulsa, Oklahoma, and it was destroyed by White mobs in 1921, leaving 3,000 African Americans dead and over 600 successful Black businesses destroyed. Tell them that this Black enclave community without SBA loans had 21 churches, 21 restaurants, 30 grocery stores, 2 movies theaters, a hospital, a bank, a post office, libraries, schools, law offices, six private airplanes, and a bus system. Keep giving them booster shots against miseducation and misinformation and inoculate them with the truth.

Last but not least, we must teach our children about God and get them involved in a holistic church, a church that ministers to the whole person's needs, not just his/her spiritual needs. We must pray with our children and teach them how to pray. We must pray before going to bed and pray with them daily before sending them out in the world. Ask God's blessings and protection for them. We must teach them a heart of gratitude. Teach them to bless their food before eating and to thank people when they do things for them; to say please when asking for something from others.

Even though we are far off course economically, we can fix the situation by accepting full responsibility for rearing our children. We must postpone immediate gratification and make child rearing a priority and make decisions for our children based on the future and not the present. We must forego purchasing new automobiles. Buy a used car and fix it up. It will run, and you'll have less car insurance payments. If your car is not paid for, as soon as you pay it off, put the amount you were paying into a savings account. Save that money instead of spending it. Don't buy any more clothes until the ones that you have are worn out or are no longer usable. Have your purses and shoes repaired versus buying new ones. It's cheaper, and you'll save money. Shopping in thrift stores can save you lots of money. Read the book by Helen Pearson, *Thrift Store Diva: Spending Pennies and Looking like a Million Dollars*.

Teach your young child about finances. Open a savings account for your child when he/she reaches the age of 13; teach them how to manage money. Make a family budget and have family participation. Save 10 percent of your earnings, buy life insurance for yourself and your children prepay your burial plot or crypt or cremation if that's your choice. Start a savings account for a college education for your children or work with them to keep their grades up so they can get a scholarship.

Make plans financially for your retirement. Social Security is a supplement, and that's all it is. It will not be enough to sustain you in your latter years, and in most cases, your children will not be able to help you. Have family prayer time and hold a family meeting weekly. Prepare a Living Trust if you have real estate so that your property that you worked so hard for does not go into probate. Attorney fees and probates eat up what should be left for your loved ones. You decide who gets what's in your estate so that the family does not have to fall out with each other because if there was ever a time that we need each other it is *now*, so prevent future division by proper planning now. Get rid of your credit cards accept for one and do not use it unless it's totally necessary.

We can turn this situation around if we take heed. Elders, you need to step up to the plate. You have an obligation to offer wisdom and to teach your loved ones. And the adults and children need to listen to their elders. The older generation has been where you are trying to go. They may not know how to use a computer or surf the Internet, but they know enough to help you to be better and to live better if you listen. As elders, we learn from you and you can learn from us, so let's go for a marriage. Our forefathers shed a great deal of blood and fought too hard to be delivered from the hands of slavery and because for that reason, we should fight to not return to slavery conditions—economic slavery. At this time, we are close to returning if we are not mindful of how we treat God and our finances.

STATE OF EMERGENCY FOR BLACK-OWNED BUSINESSES

I have witnessed the rapid demise of Black businesses. Black businesses are closing at an alarming rate. In fact it's a state of emergency for Black businesses. Do you see what I see? Is anybody paying attention? Does anybody care? Is there anyone awake in the village?

I am the chairperson of The West Coast Supporters of the Harvest Institute, supporters of Dr. Claud Anderson's economic empowerment plan. We sponsored "Get on the Bus Tours" in 2009. We took 40-50 people to three Black businesses on a Saturday; one business was a sit down restaurant. Our purpose for the tour was to expose the community to these businesses in hope that they would return and would tell others about the businesses and to give those businesses an economic boost. Many of these businesses have since closed their door. However, these businesses locations were reopen by Hispanic business owners. Remember Granny's Soul Food near 60th and Crenshaw, Cultural Affairs Restaurant & Arts, and The Wafer House on Vermont where the old Kitz restaurant used to be—they are gone and now owned by Hispanic.

Jobs come from business ownership. According to SBA, small business accounted for 65% of new jobs created between 1993-2009.

I hope you can see the correlation between business ownership and the unemployment rate of different races. Jobs that left this country are not returning no time soon. Those jobs are gone, and other races are hiring their own—so what is the Black man/woman to do? It does not taka genius to find a solution. Entrepreneurship is the basis for economic empowerment for Blacks. Have you noticed when you visited the court house, city hall, county and state facilities, doctors' office, dentist office and even hospitals? There are very fee Black employees.

Starting a business is no longer a luxury, it is a necessity. This truth is what led my sister attorney Clara Hunter King and I to co-author the book, "What You Need To Know Before You Start Your Business" It is important to have the right information so that you can make adequate decision for your business. You need to know the different ways to own a business and the pros and cons of each.

The most critical component to the survival of Black is for Blacks to make a conscious decision to support Black businesses by any means necessary. Be willing to pay a little more for product or services, go out of your ways if necessary, tell others about the Black businesses that you know about. It is important for Black businesses to survive! Every time a Black business closes a family suffer, employees loses jobs. It was a time when a Black business owner would say, "I am going to close my business and go back to work for corporate America, this is not an option today, there are no jobs to go back to.

Black business owner must seek Black businesses to patronize also. Many of them always hollering about Blacks not patronizing their business and at the same time they themselves do not frequent Black businesses when they need products or services. Even when dining out they choose non-Black restaurants. Black business owner must align themselves with other businesses they can network with on a referral fee for service system.

When a Black family owned business close, it impacts several households—that's really traumatic. I thank God that I had other business ventures and my R.N. license to fall back on when the books and herbs store started suffering a loss a year ago, many bookstores have closed their door. The message that I am send is that nothing is guaranteed, there is no security in any business or service, so bottom line is always have a plan B. To sum it all up, what I am saying is Saving Black businesses is everybody's business.

YOU WILL NEED A FINANCIAL LIFE JACKET SOON!

If you pay attention, you will notice how tough times are. Times will become tougher for those who just sit and stare, talk about it, pray about it while still sitting, watching, waiting with high hopes and doing nothing. Does this sound like you? If you were warned that a flood was coming, you would gather sand bags immediately. If you were warned that a large rain was coming, you would carry an umbrella. If you were warned that Wall Street was going to crash, you would rush to pull your money out. Middle-Class Americans are facing a financial flood, rain, and Wall Street Crash and we had better carry our own parachute.

If you have only one source of income coming into your house, that's not good. If the Federal Government withheld your checks, including your Social Security check for one month—would your life be impacted? What if, you went to your job tomorrow and were given a pink slip? What if you were in a serious accident and could not work on your job or your business—would your unemployment or disability insurance cover your basis needs? Think.

Most of my business associates who started out with me 30 plus years ago, their businesses have closed. I am still here because I have always had multiple streams of income and I still do. Look around and you will see that many of the conventional jobs are no longer available. Therefore, it's imperative that we look towards alternative means of earning income. I have mastered such skills and I am willing to show you how. Whether you are an employee or an employer, you need to explore new means of earning residual income—that's income that you receive from other people's efforts. I can share with you multiple choices and I am certain that one of the options will be right for you. There is an old adage, *"When the horse is stolen, the fool locks the door."* The moral to this statement is, be proactive and not reactive.

MONEY IS LIKE INSURANCE, DON'T WAIT UNTIL YOU NEED IT TO TRY AND GET IT!

A BLACK WOMAN WHO KNOWS NO LIMIT LAUNCHES LITERARY EMPOWERMENT MOVEMENT

By Maxine E. Thompson
http://www.maxinethompson.com

It is said that Harriet Tubman was so spiritually guided that she often knew when not to down the wrong path, because the run-away slave catchers would be there. Due to her being so spiritually attuned with her Creator, Harriet Tubman was able to say before she died, (in regards to her work on the Underground Railroad,) "I never lost a passenger." Just think of it. Without a compass, without a map, and with only God as her guide, as history tells us, she successfully led over three hundred slaves to freedom.

However, we don't have to just look back to history to find African American examples of phenomenal leaders. Today, right within our midst, we have an unsung hero—a modern-day Harriet Tubman, so to speak. Her name is Dr. Rosie Milligan. What she is doing for the African American literary community parallels what Harriet Tubman did for African American people in bondage.

To illustrate the point, one only has to look at how Dr. Milligan is leading many African American readers/writers out of the bondage of under-representation through the freedom train of her bookstore, Classic One Books, and her publishing company, Professional Publishing House. The ride has a two-fold benefit.

Just as The Underground Railroad was the freedom train for enslaved Blacks, self-publishing or independent publishing has become the new "freedom train" for unpublished Blacks. This process helps authors to retain a sense of ownership of the material, as well as to retain control over the process. Of course, there's the money, too, for those with marketing savvy. But the real reason we gain freedom is that literature and books are the repositories of our culture. African American readers and writers are led to "Freedom"—the freedom of choice. The freedom to have our collective voices heard. The freedom to read and write about our stories, which are about the unique journeys of the African Diaspora here in America.

As such, Dr. Rosie Milligan is a Black woman who knows no limits. Her motto, "Erase No, Step Over Can't, and Move Forward With Life," is a motivating influence to numerous people who see her as their mentor and role model. Upcoming on April 19, 2014, she will be celebrating the eighteenth Annual Black Writers on Tour Conference, where writers come from across the country to learn the publishing industry and how to market and sell their books. (www.blackwritersontour.com).

Not only is Professional Publishing House the fastest-growing, African-American female-owned publishing house in the country. Dr. Milligan is an expert in the publishing industry. Under her publishing house, Professional Publishing House, she has published more than three hundred and fifty titles. Many authors she published were signed by mainstream publishers, and have taken their places on numerous best-seller's lists across the country. Using her expertise, she has set up independent publishing companies for 35 of her clients. Additionally, she assisted the top literary agent in Southern California, launch her literary agency business.

Part of the secret of her success can be attributed to the fact that Dr. Milligan is willing to take risks and go where traditional mainstream publishers fear to tread. Many writers with political stories, unpopular genres, (such as historical fiction,) and poetry books from all over the country, and even as far as Africa, are now beating a path to 1425 W. Manchester, in South Central Los Angeles where Professional Publishing House is located. Stories that would have been squashed are now being published through Millligan Books.

The Los Angeles community refers to her as "Our Modern Day Harriett Tubman/community empowerment activist." Authors across the country refer to Dr. Milligan as the "Mother of the Literary Empowerment Movement," from authors nationwide. Her quantum leaps are due to her networking ability, as well as her rapport with nationwide bookstore owners, distributors, radio talk show hosts, newspaper editors, and talented editors. Taking full advantage of modern technology, she has showcased the authors via national radio talk shows.

The freedom train has become unstoppable. Now, instead of leaving a slew of remaindered and out-of-print-books, the next generation will have a legacy of Black literature and information to pass on.

The main point is that Dr. Milligan's books have taken readers to a new level. Instead of just offering "girlfriend, boyfriend," books, readers can now choose to read about African Americans' unwritten history. Because these new works are more empowering and enlightening, readers are developing a healthy appreciation for literature and nonfiction books without mainstream censor. Moreover, by providing consciousness-raising or historical fiction books, the readers are entertained as well.

These are just some of the highlights of books published by Professional Publishing House.

Professional Publishing House re-issued out-of-print book by radio-TV celebrity, Mother Love, *Mother Love: Forgive Or Forget*. In October 2002, Dr. Milligan published a groundbreaking work about professional Black women in the work place, *A Piece of America: Black Women In The Work Place*. This book tells how Black women in corporate America are breaking the code of silence. Edith Gonsal, Ph.D. authored this scholarly work derived from her dissertation.

Dr. Milligan published *Why?*, the story of John Carlos, the athlete who held up his fist in the 1968 Olympics. For more than thirty years, Carlos's legendary tale of the greatest silent protest in history against racism was not told. Obviously, mainstream publishers did not want to tell his side of the story.

The New Slave Ship, written by Melvin Farmer and published by Professional Publishing House, is a landmark book. Farmer holds the distinction of being the first convict sentenced under the three-strike law in the state of California. The *Los Angeles Times Newspaper* and other national newspapers, magazines, radio and television talk shows nationwide have interviewed Melvin.

Even white writers, who were rejected by mainstream, have found a home at Professional Publishing House. This includes Elizabeth Anderson, who re-told the story of Frederick Douglas, *My Bondage and My Freedom,* and Richard Daniel Davies, the author of *The NBA'S Dirty Laundry*.

In 1998, Professional Publishing House reissued historical fiction novel, *The Ebony Tree*, which was touted in the Washington Libraries "... as a great read for Black History Month in 2002." Written in 1995, *The Ebony Tree* was a forerunner in historical fiction, along with second novel, *No Pockets in a Shroud*, which dealt with family secrets, now beginning to be depicted in mainstream books.

In addition, Dr. Milligan has begun to publish young writers, who are launching their entrepreneurial businesses and seeing the publishing industry as a viable way to make a living. These writers include Miya and Meryl McCurry, at the time of publication, age 10 and 12 respectively. They are both writers and illustrators. Their book titles are *The Foods* and *The Sea Monster's Darkest Night*. Marquis Cormier, age 8, the author of *I Am Not A Problem Child!: How an even-year old Black male child fought against special education placement*. In 2013, she published an anthology of children ages 10-15 from La Salle Elementary school, South Central Los Angeles, book title, *"Let The Children Speak."*

Dr. Milligan has published physicians, including renowned Los Angeles based cardiologist and speaker, Dr. James A. Mays's novels, *Mercy is King* and *Trapped*. Although both books are period pieces/medical thrillers, they address what it was like for the Black doctors in the medical profession from the 1950's to the 1980's. *Mercy is King* deals with the untold story of the founding of Martin Luther King Hospital in Watts, California. Dr. Lenore Coleman and Dr. James R. Gavin, III. *"Healing Our Village."* Dr. Danny Colton, an autobiography, *"From Hard Life to Heart Surgeon,"* This is a book that surpass the Dr. Ben Carson's story.

Dr. Milligan has published ministers, Bishop Will Wheat, Reverend Dr. Elfleda J. Tate, Rev. Tracy A Liggins-Brown and Bishop Frank Stewart, who is the author of *Together, We Stand Stronger*. This book urges the Black churches to become more involved in economic empowerment for their members.

Dr. Milligan published works by attorneys and judges such as: a most-sought after book by Attorney Joe Hopkins, "I Will Not Apologize", a groundbreaking work for examining the behavior of youth that land them into the Criminal Justice System. Attorney Clara Hunter King, "This Is Not Cool: Legal Lessons For Youth And Their Parents, Volume I and Volume II. Judge Paul Brady, *"The Black Badge: The Life of Deputy United States Marshal Bass Reeves"* a story destine to become a movie.

From the prison to the pulpit, many Black writers have found their voices. Dr. Milligan is at the helm of a social movement, which is encompassing America like a tidal wave. Just as there was the anti-slavery movement, the women's right movement, there is now a literary economic empowerment movement—one which will be greater than the Harlem Renaissance Movement of the 1920's,

1930's. This time, the writers will own the rights to their intellectual property and their financial status will be perpetuated to the next generation.

According to Dr. Milligan, "This is a new form of reparations—by taking charge of your creativity and paying yourself through making a living from your talents. We are no longer waiting for mainstream to validate our voices."

Dr. Milligan has written and published eighteen books of her own and co-authored six books. However, at the same time, she has provided a means for writers such as Victoria Christopher who was among the first to write Christian fiction books, Murray, Dominique Grosvenor, Patricia Phillips, Patricia G'Orge-Walker, Dr. Roland Jefferson, Annetta P. Lee, and Parry Brown to become mainstream authors. Her literary agency landed book contracts with one of the most prestigious publishing houses, Random House

Dr. Milligan packaged and helped one of the most renowned/long standing secular music group in the nation to birth their book baby---The Famous Whispers.

So what motivates the woman who knows no limits?

"I left Mississippi and came west to plant a new kind of crop," says Milligan, the daughter of ex-farm owner. "I learned from my father, Simon, the importance of owning your own. All the children worked for Simon. There's something special about having your own. It gives one a sense of pride, confidence, and a sense of purpose."

When I ask if she ever gets tired—a natural question to a woman involved in so many successful ventures—she says, "Tired? What's that? I cannot fix my mouth to say the word when I think of all the real hard work that our forefathers had to do that we could have these opportunities that we can now partake of. No, I am no ways tired."

When asked for the secret of her success, Dr. Milligan modestly says that she is on a mission, and God has guided her to fill this need, since it wasn't being met in the African American community. Today we salute Dr. Milligan for her vision and courage to help build an infrastructure for Blacks in the publishing world. She is founder of Black Writers on Tour, which sponsors conferences and workshops for writers nationwide. Dr. Milligan answered questions for writers across the country in her *Dear Dr. Rosie* column in the national magazine *Black Issue Review* for three years. She has hosted a cable TV show for writers called, "Express Yourself Literary Café." She is a radio personality, and she host her own live Internet Talk Show every Tuesday at www.Drrosie.com from 10 to 11am, PST. She is also a nationally sought-after speaker. This woman truly knows no limits.

After all, as Dr. Milligan says, "Who will tell our stories? You cannot tell it from the grave." As she constantly tells those who ride the "freedom train," these stories will become the blueprint for the next generation.

URGENT CALL FOR BLACK AMERICA! YOU WILL NEED YOUR OWN PARACHUTE

Often times we talk about what is owed to us, but seldom do I hear people talk about what we owe—we owe someone, too. In these critical, financial, hard times, we owe it to ourselves, our families and community to get out of debt and to restore our credit so we can financially empower ourselves to a position of strength versus a position of economic deprivation. We cannot leave our children in such deplorable conditions.

I am asking you to tell everybody you know about the importance of being credit worthy and the high cost of having less than good credit. Can you imagine what our community could do if we had no debts and if we were not paying the high cost of interest for the things we purchase? COME ON NOW, our family, community and our churches are suffering badly because of our poor financial conditions. What does this speak about our awesome and powerful God, who we claim to serve? Think.

Stop paying attention to what the media is saying about the job market and employment rate and just look around you and note what you see for Black folks from your own eyes. Black Americans had better get out of "Debtor's Prison." The Mayor of Los Angeles stated on a talk show that 60% of the homeless in Los Angeles are African Americans. We know the percentage is higher—nobody is going to save us, but us. Were you aware that when applying for Section 8 and low income housing, you are subject to a criminal background and credit check? Therefore the jobless and homeless rate for blacks will continue to rise. Many of those who will be released from prison early will also join the homeless and jobless population—you must have good credit in order to rent a house/apartment—the future is bleak for Blacks in Los Angeles until we learn to do for self.

Remember this: If we do not provide jobs for our future generation, most of them will be jobless—just look at what you see right now—check out who is working in City Hall, courts, hospitals, doctor's office and on constructions sites. Somebody had better hear me "UP IN HERE."

The Crenshaw Baldwin Hills area, the 90008 zip code, has the highest number of Blacks living in that area—78%. Take a look at who is working on the Crenshaw Corridor—you will see a Black person working every now and then. Who's paying attention, or shall I ask, who cares?

The deplorable conditions will not change for Black Americans until Black Americans take full responsibility for changing their own educational and economic status. It's a disgrace to our race that we do not own a supermarket in Los Angeles, especially in the areas where 70% or more Black folks live—shameful. I am calling on Black America to cease buying furniture, clothes, and automobiles for the next six months and to set aside $100.00 a month for the next six month to place in an escrow account for investing in a super, Black-owned market.

Please do me a favor and stop talking about how few times the dollar circulates in the Black community. Just stop and think for a moment; how can the dollar circulate in the Black community if Blacks don't own the businesses? You should also know that jobs come from businesses, and as long as Blacks do not own businesses, Blacks will not have the jobs—it does not take a rocket scientist to know this. Come on Black Folk and let's save ourselves. If you are in need of credit restoration and want to learn how to get out of debt, I have a program that can help you do it.

BLACKS HANGING ON LIFE SUPPORT

Blacks must fund their own economic liberation. How long will Blacks depend on others for economic oxygen? We must learn economic CPR and resuscitate ourselves. Almost every major event held by Blacks in Los Angeles, California, was cancelled last year due to a lack of funding/sponsorship from non-Blacks. If it were not for White folks' money, the NAACP and other groups would not be able to hold their events.

I had to cancel Black Writers On Tour last year for lack of financial help. I have funded a large amount of this event's cost from my personal funds. I am at retirement age, and I cannot continue to do so. Via these writing conferences, I have helped authors from age 7 to age 95 tell their stories, because Literacy Is Everybody's Business. I have helped 275 Black authors see their books in print and have helped more than 30 authors start their own publishing companies. I helped launch a major literary agent's career on the West Coast, Thompson's Literary Agency. Our forefathers took their stories to their grave because they had no one to help them tell it. History will repeat itself if we do not learn from their experience. When we fail to record what we did, others will come along and claim those honors; and if we are not mindful, we will be written out of history. Instead, we will be remembered by the pages written by a one-sided player-hating and insensitive media.

I hope and pray that even after my transition there will be someone whom I have touched who will carry on the legacy of assuring that our stories will be told. Mary McLeod Bethune stated in her will, "I leave you hope, I leave you love, I leave you a thirst for knowledge." I want to leave you a thirst for knowledge, and I challenge you to continue to make literacy everybody's business and to see to it that *our* stories, not *his-story*, is passed on to the next generation. I challenge you to leave no Black child behind when it comes to reading and writing. Our stories may not be televised, but they can be written in the pages of history.

Haven't you noticed that it is our Black children and adults who lag behind in reading and writing skills? So, then, who should be concerned? As a publisher, I see poorly written manuscripts with three hundred pages containing no paragraphs, without proper nouns capitalized, and many more major mistakes. If you don't believe me, ask your child, even your adult child, to write a one-page topic on any subject and you be the judge for yourself.

The days are gone when one could just call a meeting to discuss, face-to-face, a grievance, complaint, etc. Instead, you are asked to "put it in writing," and a poorly written communiqué will get no response in most cases. Be it politically correct or not, people tend to judge one by the way they write and speak—so we must do better.

I need you to financially help me to keep this venue alive and well. I am reaching out to you so that you will not be able to say what people often say when things go south, "What happened to that business/organization?" I need your help. It's not for me; it's for those that I am concerned about. You can go to www.Blackwritersontour.com and make a donation via PayPal, or you can send your donations to Black Writers On Tour, 1425 W. Manchester Avenue, Los Angeles, CA 90047. 323-750-3592

Thank you in advanced for your assistance. You may have friends who want to help. Inform others about this noteworthy event. It is a tax-deductible donation.

BLACKS MUST MAKE A RADICAL CHANGE NOW...OR ELSE!

Don't get it twisted because you see a few Blacks doing well, such as: Oprah Winfrey, Steve Harvey, a few athletes, actors, and entertainers—they are also on the White man's "Life Support Machine." And when he pulls the plug, they too will need resuscitation.

Blacks must fund their own economic liberation. How long will Blacks depend on others for economic oxygen? We must learn economic CPR and resuscitate ourselves. Most Black cultural events slated for Blacks in Los Angeles, California, were cancelled this year due to a lack of funding/sponsorship from non-Blacks. If it were not for White folks' money, the NAACP, the Urban League, and other groups would not be able to hold their events.

Time is of the essence, and we must act right now. Here is what we must do: We must make literacy and reversing our economic status top priorities. It's important that we patronize those businesses who advertise in souvenir programs for Black events. This will encourage these businesses to continue to support our endeavors. Blacks must support venues where Blacks are exhibiting their product or services, and if you are not able to make a purchase on that day, collect business cards, and remember these businesses when you are in need of the product or services that they offer and be sure to tell family members and friends about these businesses.

Black America must create a new awareness and a new consciousness regarding supporting Black businesses by any means necessary. I am the founder of Black Writers On Tour. We showcase over one hundred authors and vendors at our annual conference. I observed that many of the exhibitors did not leave their booth to take a look at what other vendors were offering for sale. My thought is this: If you take a look at what other Black businesses are offering, you can make a mental note and patronize them at a later date.

What amazes me most is how Black business folk complain about how other Blacks do not support their businesses . . . and at the same time, they are not supporting other Black-owned businesses—what's up with that? Even Blacks who own a food eatery do not think of another Black food eatery when they are considering going out to dine. We *cannot* continue business as usual if we are to change our dismal economic plight around the globe. It's important for us to supports Black vendors because many of these businesses are not in a traditional business setting due to the overhead of doing business in a "normal" manner. Many Black entrepreneurs came about as a result of corporate downsizing and layoffs, etc. and this is their only means of economic survival—and they *need* our support. Your support could save a marriage, as well as keep a mother/father and their children working and supporting themselves.

In the new two weeks, I will have placed a list of the authors, vendors who were exhibitors at the Black Writers On Tour conference, and the advertisers on our Web site www.blackwritersontour.com, and when you are shopping for a book to read, a product, or service, please consider these businesses.

We must be willing to suffer a few inconveniences to empower Black businesses. (We do not want to put up with or suffer any inconveniences to help our people, and that is why other cultures bring their businesses next door to where Blacks live because they know our behavior—we want something right around the corner—as though we are walking to the business—how insane!). Think of the hardships our forefathers suffered so that we may have the opportunities that we do have today, and as I write, many of these opportunities are being snatched back from us and given to other cultures and diversities. You had better wake up and tap your Black self on the shoulder, look into the mirror, recognize that you are Black no matter the shade of your skin, and make a run for the economic survival for you and your family.

BLACK WRITERS ON TOUR MAJOR MERGE

"Whereby we are weak standing alone, pulling together, we become mighty and strong." These are the words that the Spirit spoke to me, and to the Spirit I listen. I started a new venture—Southern California Black Business Expo. And for the Nineteenth Annual Black Writers On Tour, these businesses have merged. Authors and black businesses are so excited about the merge. The energy and momentum is going through the roof this year. I wasn't sure how this coming together would be received, but God told me to do it and I did. One thing I have learned over the years and that is—God will not push you out there and leave you hanging—now the devil, he will do just that.

It's the start of something big! Black Writers On Tour and The Southern California Black Business Expo showcasing all under **one roof**. We have only a few exhibit spaces left for the 2015 event. This will be the most financial successful event ever for vendors because we do not have more than two businesses in each category except for authors. We have businesses such as jewelry, cosmetics and clothing who have registered for 2016 to secure their place.

Saving Black businesses and helping them to thrive versus merely survive is more critical now than ever before. It is business ownership that will secure an economic future for our next generation. We have started a $50.00 spending day with black owned businesses campaign. We expect more than 3,000 attendees this year. We are asking for 1,000 people to spread the word and to email me at Drrosie@aol.com, expressing your commitment to spend $50.00 on Saturday April 18, 2015 at the conference/expo. We will keep tally of the commitment. Can you imagine the economic shot in the arm that will be for black business owners and writers?

Why we merged: It has been two years since Los Angeles has hosted a Black Business Expo. Showcasing Black Businesses is more critical now than ever before. It is important that black businesses survive and thrive— jobs come from businesses. Every time a black business closes its doors, another black person and in many cases, his/her family members who were employees for the family business suffer. Years ago, when one's business failed, he/she could say, "Well, I guess I will have to go back to work for someone else again." Today, this is not often an option—it's more critical than you think for black folks. Poverty and illiteracy hurts us all in one way or another.

The late Muhammad Nassadeen slated the month of April as black business recognition month—wow, I miss him. As a way of keeping his endeavor alive, we have incorporated showcasing black owned businesses with the Black Writers On Tour. Having limited funds and sponsorships, this gives greater exposure for both. The ***coming together under one roof*** creates a win-win situation for black businesses and for those in the publishing industry such as: writers, authors, graphic designer, printers, illustrators, web designers, social media experts etc. When authors need a product/service, they know how to find a black owned business; the black business owners can purchase a book for themselves and their children directly from the author/publisher—the author makes more money. When the business owners need a web designer, business cards, promotional materials, a printer, marketing person etc., they will know how to locate a business that provides that service. Many businesses that you frequent for products and service, you will discover that there are black owned businesses that provide such products and services. America has become the "Great Melting Pot" and every race must take some responsibility for its own welfare and economic existence—**REAL TALK. ALL ROADS MUST LEAD TO THE CARSON COMMUNITY CENTER ON APRIL 18, 2015—MAKE IT YOUR BUSINESS TO SPREAD THE WORD AND TO BE THERE!**

DEBT AND TAXES OWED MUST BE PAID FROM YOUR ESTATE

Debt can follow you to your grave and can continue to eat away at what you had intended to leave for your loved ones. As a Sr. Estate Planner and Credit Consultant, I have continued to admonish my people about the importance of perpetuating wealth legacy via proper estate planning and debt elimination. One of the most common errors that are made in settling one's trust is: The successor trustee is anxious to start the distribution of the trust, and the beneficiaries are anxious to get their share of the trust. A word of caution—it is the successor trustee's obligation to pay the trustor's valid debts and to satisfy any tax liabilities owed.

It has been said that "All you don't know won't hurt you." Let me put it like this: "All you don't know can certainly cost you—*BIG TIME*. For the last two years I have been conducting seminars/workshops on "Putting Your Financial Personal and Business House in Order." I was motivated to do so because I was tired of seeing Christians as well as non-Christians trying to wash enough cars to pay for a funeral; I witnessed people not getting the assets they thought they would inherit from an estate due to debts and taxes owed by the deceased.

A client of mine shared this account with me: "My sister died and left two houses in a trust for her husband. He took the property out of the trust and prepared no trust or will. He died two years later, leaving behind five adult children and a six-year-old. The husband had not filed his federal income or state taxes for four years, and they both had made an assessment as to what he owed based on his profession and the number of dependents he claimed in prior years. The taxes were assessed at $35,000. He had an electric/water bill for $19,000; he owed a friend $7,000, who presented a claim in probate court and was paid. There were others debts owed as well. From probate settlement of $270,000, there was $112,000 left to distribute among his loved ones. I did not believe her—until she brought me the paperwork, and like the old folks used to say, "I saw it with my own eyes." How shameful!

Bottom Line: Pay your taxes and get out of debt, and if the debts that are showing on your credit reports are not your debts, inaccurate, or should be deleted based on the statute of limitation, then you should have them removed and seek to restore your credit *now*. You will not escape debt owed for taxes or to your creditors—even after death—you still pay.

Credit will impact four areas in your life: Housing, banking, employment, and insurance. Having bad credit can cost you over $200,000 during a lifetime. Below is an example of two students paying a student loan of $8,000 with different interest rates. Karen's interest rate is 7.25%, her monthly payment is $234, and her total interest paid in ten years is $8,175. Joyce has bad credit; her interest rate is 13.25% on an $8,000 loan. Her monthly payment is $302, and her total interest paid in ten years is $16,189. Joyce's penalty for having bad credit is $8,013.

LET'S STOP THE ECONOMIC HEMORRHAGES NOW!

Black America suffers from *economic anemia*. We are about to bleed out due to high unemployment rate. (Pay no attention to the statistic regarding unemployment rate for Blacks, it's a false report. The unemployment rate for Blacks in most major cities is 40 to 50% and for Black youth, it's approximately 80%.) How many people do you know, even among your family members, who are unemployed or their wages are so low they feel unemployed after being paid? At least 60% of the homeless population in Los Angeles is African Americans. Blacks lost one-third of their real estate, which included Black churches during this great depression. W.E.B. DuBois said, "*To be a poor man is hard, but to be a poor race in a land of dollars is the very bottom of hardship.*"

It's bad when one hemorrhages from the cut/puncture from the hands of another, but when one hemorrhages from the cut/puncture from the hand of self via inappropriate behaviors/and spending patterns, that's more than pitiful. Blacks can stop the hemorrhaging by doing the following for the next six months: Make literacy a top priority, access every member of your family for literacy—it's never too late get help when needed. If you own real estate, prepare a Living Trust—we are losing too much real property due to no estate planning. Restore your credit—stop paying higher interest for all your purchases, which would be a large savings. Get an insurance policy for yourself and children.

Be prepared to make a sacrificial sacrifice like not shopping where your people are not working (drive the distance if you must). Ask businesses that you frequent if they have Black workers. Do your own nails, purchase no hair or wigs, only buy clothes and shoes when needed. (Most people have enough clothes to last six months. If you must buy clothes, buy from thrift stores, Goodwill, etc. Remember, it's about a sacrifice. Save the money from these savings and put it in savings accounts. If you are renting, move in with a parent, sibling, relative, friend or share an apartment/home. If your child moves in with you have them pay some rent and check frequently on their savings. If you have extra rooms in your home, rent rooms and save that money. Make no purchase for any holidays, including Christmas—this is a good time to start teaching your children how to sacrifice in order to accomplish a goal. Cook at home, teach your children how to prepare a family meal, take your lunch and stop eating out on weekends. Last, but not least, we must demand from the government what's owed to us: Reparation, Funds from the 1866 Treaty, and money owed to Black farmers. Do not vote for anybody who does not include such on their political agenda. Let's make it better for the next generation, please!

HAVING GOOD CREDIT WILL BECOME AN ABSOLUTE NECESSITY IN THE NEAR FUTURE

The Internet—Superhighway is where billions of dollars are spent on the purchase of numerous products and services. Billions of dollars for payments of bills are also paid via Internet. Spending money on the Internet Via credit cards will become a way of life for many. Not everyone have access to a traditional credit card due to poor credit (FICO). Most people who do not have a traditional credit card, they have a Debit card connected to their bank account. It is time to become proactive about credit because the time is coming, and that time is sooner than you think, when debit cards will no longer be an acceptable form of payment. Today it can be challenging when attempting to use a debit card for car and hotel rental.

Due to the economic depression, high unemployed rate, businesses failure at an alarming rate, unemployment benefit running out with no extensions, many will no longer have access to a bank account or debit card. **Now What Are Your Options?** You are back to keeping money in your house; you are cashing your checks at cash checking outlets, purchasing money orders and postage stamps to pay your bills. **Why Is Having Good Credit And Credit Cards Important Today?** Good credit can gain you access to capital, and we know that lack of capital is primary reason for business failure. Having the ability to utilize credit can get one from point A to point B while waiting for point C to come available, in other words it can keep you afloat and prevent you from financially drowning when there is a cash flow challenge.

The Most Prudent Thing To Do Is: Get out of debt and stay out. Restore your credit now. There is a quote: "Don't wait until your horse is stolen from the barn to lock the door." Restore your credit today. Just as big businesses were bailed out of their financial crisis, there is bail-out for consumers under the Consumer's Protection Laws and via Debt Filtration—having your debts cancelled---LEARN HOW NOW! You can build your credit in 90-days and get back in the GAME and living the life you so deserve. We conduct free weekly seminars on Credit

Restoration. We offer an educational system that will help you to better understand the credit world and how the new credit system has changed many lives.

You will need to improve your credit score immediately if:
1. You are job seeking
2. Plan to purchase a car or home and want a decent interest rate & lower monthly payment
3. Your auto lease is expiring soon
4. You are looking to rent a house, apartment/ car
5. You want to lower your car insurance.
6. You are due for an employee review on certain government jobs.

THIS IS REAL TALK. IT'S ALSO LEGAL FOR CERTAIN JOBS TO RECHECK YOUR CREDIT AFTER YOU ARE EMPLOYED—AND THEY CAN FIRE YOU IF YOUR CREDIT IS BAD—LET'S GET SERIOUS! IT'S NO JOKE.

Dr. Rosie Milligan

CAN A MARRIAGE BE RESTORED AFTER BEING SHATTERED TO PIECES FROM INFIDELITY? ... LIZ TELLS HOW

"Love covers a multitude of sins," 1 Peter 4:8

As this is the month of love, bringing up the matter of infidelity in marriage might sound like a damper on Cupid's Arrow. But inasmuch as we live in an imperfect world with imperfect people, infidelity plagues more marriages than people are willing to admit. We see it from the White House to the pulpit. But the good news is that marriage can survive infidelity—if a couple is willing to work at repairing their relationship.

Liz Williams, a once broken woman/wife/mother, shares the personal and intimate experience of her marriage with the world in hopes that ordinary families can be restored. In her book, *From Fairytale to Forgiveness: One Woman's Journey*, you will learn what a husband must do to restore the marriage and rekindle the passion. You will get it first hand—the thoughts and feelings of the children, when infidelity strikes.

What you will glean from the book is this: Infidelity unsuspected is more devastating than infidelity suspected. The author stated, "I had no clue. My husband was the perfect husband and a perfect father. We had a fairytale marriage. He was so good to me. He was loving and available for me and the children in every way. I never had to pump gasoline for my car during the 24 years of marriage. My husband was the kind of man women dream of having.

"I was like many unsuspecting wives—with a fairytale marriage. I did not catch my husband cheating. My husband came to me and told me that he had been unfaithful and that he had a child who was now 5 years old. My world crumbled faster than the New York World Trade Center. Was I in a plane crash, ran over by a train, shot in the heart by a bullet or stabbed with a sword? I was mentally and emotionally dead."

Whether you're married one year or twenty-four, as in the case of the author, infidelity can be devastating. For the hurt partner, adultery can be likened to a death—the death of the innocence the relationship once shared when it was thought to be monogamous. Just think about it. In the early stages of love, one feels like he or she is in a Garden of Eden, a paradise, so to speak. However, when that perfect life is lost, a wife/husband may never feel like she(he) will ever love the offending partner again.

The discovery of adultery sends a person through the same grief process as one undergoes who has experienced the sudden death of a loved one—Denial, Anger, Bargaining, Depression, Acceptance. In time, one reaches acceptance, sometimes forgiveness. However, even in forgiveness, most of the hurt partners never forget. As the author says, "You can forgive and still choose to leave. I chose to stay, though."

In *From Fairytale to Forgiveness*, the author takes you through the journey of healing from that ultimate betrayal—other woman and a child. As the author goes through the story of their innocent childhood sweetheart relationship to their twenty-four year "fairy tale marriage", you will laugh, you will cry, and you will rejoice in their love, when it weathers the storm.

Throughout the emotional roller coaster you go on with Liz and her husband, you will see that healing and complete restoration is possible. From reading this book, men will learn what it takes to bring complete healing to their wives after the affair.

This book is more than a tell-all, controversial book. It is a must read for all married couples and anyone who expects to be married one day.

IT'S TIME TO BE DELIVERED FROM THIS FINANCIAL ECONOMIC BONDAGE—LEARN HOW NOW—
Saturday July 12, 2014. THIS IS A FREE EVENT

Hello, this is Dr. Rosie Milligan. I have been made aware of a growing problem that is impacting the masses. As I began to interview people, I discovered that so many people have already been challenged severely by the credit system and their credit score (FICO). America herself is deeply in debt above her head. However, the American people are held hostage and placed in a position of what I call Financial Economic Bondage—a slave to lenders and financial institutions—and for many, it's no fault of their own.

The American people did not vote to ship our jobs overseas; we did not make it so unbearable for large businesses to be able to run a successful business in America or some states, causing businesses to relocate to other states/countries. The American people did not vote to have large corporations hire in-house prison inmates, who are given extremely low pay for their labor, to perform the work that was once performed by the general population. But, yet, we are paying a debt that we did not incur.

The Bible says in Hosea 4:6, *My people are destroyed for lack of knowledge.* This scripture goes on and tells the consequences of rejecting knowledge—read it for yourself. I am concerned about the position/condition that we are leaving our next generation in.it's a shame, and it's pitiful. The Bible says in Proverbs 13:22, *A good man shall leave an inheritance to his children's children.* I am not trying to preach to you—it's just a teaching moment right now.

Did you know that it's legal to deny a person a job opportunity because of their FICO score? Furthermore, no one cares about what happened to you to cause your credit score to be poor. Many people's scores have been lowered due to high medical bills, job lay-offs, unemployment benefits running out, having disabilities with no benefits, a deceased spouse, school loans, Pay Day Loans, divorce, etc. There is no end to this list, but who cares other than your mother/father and God?

Did you know these facts? A poor credit score can: 1) prevent you from getting the job you want and deserve. 2) Increase your insurance rates. 3) Cause you to get rejected as a renter on a house/apartment you can afford. 4) Cause you to have to put up *three times* the security deposit when renting compared to someone else. 5) Lock you out of the banking system. 6) Cause you to pay a higher interest rate on all your purchases such as: automobiles, credit cards, etc.

WHAT IF YOUR CHILD GRADUATED FROM COLLEGE WITH A 4.0, AND HAS A SCHOOL LOAN AND MISSED A GREAT JOB OPPORTUNITY DUE TO A POOR FICO SCORE?—THIS IS REAL TALK. IT'S ALSO LEGAL FOR CERTAIN JOBS TO RECHECK YOUR CREDIT AFTER YOU ARE EMPLOYED—AND THEY CAN FIRE YOU IF YOUR CREDIT IS BAD—LET'S GET SERIOUS! IT'S NO JOKE.

AFRICAN AMERICAN FEMALE ENTREPRENEUR URGES BLACKS TO EMBRACE THE NEW WAVE OF TECHNOLOGY AND MEDIA COMMUNICATION

Maxine Thompson, Los Angeles based business woman, author/publisher, former social worker for the county of Los Angeles and Detroit, Michigan, developed a love for reading and writing at an early age.

Thompson is a trailblazer—one who dares to dream. She is among the first in many categories. She was the first Black to integrate St. Francis, an all-white Catholic High school in Traverse City Michigan in 1967. In 1968, through writing for the school newspaper, she spearheaded a movement to bring Black History and Black Literature to her high school in Oak Park, Michigan. Later, in 1989, she entered Ebony's very first writing and, out of over 3,000 entries, won $1,000 for her short story, "Valley of the Shadow."

In 2000, she became one of the first African American female publisher to offer e-book selling/publishing through her electronic on line store. In March, 2002, she became one of the first African American females to host an on-line radio talk show on www.voiceamerica.com called "On The Same Page." She has interviewed radio/television celebrities such as Mother Love and Cultural Icon, Haki Madhubuti, founder of Third World Press, who was recently inducted into the Arkansas Hall of Fame. Using technology, she has interviewed guests as far as Paris, France on the same date she interviewed guests from different parts of Northern America.

This literary guru owns a publishing company, Black Butterfly Press, Maxine Thompson's Literary Services, and Maxine Thompson's Literary Agency. She is the author of two novels, *The Ebony Tree* and *No Pockets in a Shroud*, and a Short Story Collection, *A Place Called Home*. She is also the author of an ebook, *How To Promote, Market and Sell Your Book Via Ebook Publishing*. She has published an ebook, *Sister Betty Goes Hollywood*, by Pat G'Orge Walker, and an anthology, Saturday Morning, for the Saturday Morning Literary Workshop.

In addition to Thompson acting as a role model and mentor to many writers, she works with other publishing companies and literary services. She utilizes her professional social worker's skills to bring balance, perspective and harmony among competing literary businesses via demonstrating the cooperative effects and joint ventures as a win-win for all.

Through her Internet-based literary services, Thompson offers story editing, literary coaching, and ghostwriting for writers. She has guided many through the maze of moving idea and stories from the computer to the book market. Maxine Thompson's Literary Services has been a catalyst for many who have gained entrance into mainstream publishing houses. These authors include Pat G'Orge-Walker, Patricia Phillips, and Annetta P. Lee. Even though Maxine believes in self-publishing and maintaining control, she recognizes that self-publishing is not for everyone. She has also assisted independently/self-published authors who have been on bestseller's list such as Sybil Avery Jackson *(Degree of Caution)*, and nominee for a Gold Pen Award, Yolanda Callegari Brooks *(First Love)*.

In an effort to shrink the digital divide between Blacks and white, she has supported black authors through writing columns on www.bwip.org, www.theblackmarket.com, www.doenetwork.com and book reviews on www.netnoir.com, among other sites, as well as conducting author interviews on www.maxinethompson.com . Black Expressions, one of the largest Black Book Clubs in the United States, has written her up as" a key promoter of African American writers." She conducts writing workshops nationwide and through the Internet. As Thompson says, "If you do not fear change and technology, you will never be left behind."

When asked for the secret of her success, Thompson says, "When I was six, my mother, (now deceased,) walked me to the local library in Delray and opened up new worlds for me. Seeing the lives depicted in the books, which were so different from my world, showed me 'possibility.' When parents don't have money, they can enrich their children's lives through reading and using their public library. Reading is the key."

As a social worker, Thompson learned her motto: "If you don't write it down, it didn't happen." She feels this is why African Americans lost so much of their unwritten history. Although there was an oral tradition, for years, Blacks were forbidden to read and write. This is why she is committed to seeing that as many writers write their stories down as possible. She sees this as part of her God-given calling.

Although she wrote her first story at age eight, Thompson feels that the delays in her writing career prepared her to be able to work with other writers and assume a leading role in this new Renaissance of Black Writers. She sees this movement as one which will be longer lasting and greater than the Harlem Renaissance because of more African American publishers/writers taking control. She is a firm believer that the power of the pen can lead to a revolution of thought, social change, and attitudes.

Recent Titles: *Saturday Morning*, An Anthology, *A Place Called Home*, Short Story Collection. Non-Fiction writing: *Everything I Need to Know About Writing I learned as a Social Worker*

BLACK AMERICA THERE WILL BE NO GAIN WITHOUT SACRIFICE! PART I

Dear Black America,

I love you and I am shedding tears as I write this article. There is a price for every inch of gain that we seek. There will be no gain without sacrifice. I want you to think about what it is that you want for yourself, your children, community and your race as a whole. Then, I want you to pledge what you are willing to give up in order to get what you want. We must become long distance runners in the race for success. We must develop a *"Lay-A-Way"* mentality. With a lay-a-way mindset, you will learn that instant gratification can be delayed when it's in your best interest—this, you must learn and teach to your children.

We give lip service about what we want, yet we are not willing to make any changes in our thinking, behavior, shopping patterns and we are unwilling to be inconvenience. Other races will go out of their way to patronize their people while many Blacks will not. Blacks have the "Ho's" shopping mentality, *I don't care who I shop with as long as I get what I want*—that's being self-centered. History has taught us what to do to make gains. Did you forget the Montgomery Bus Boycott? It wasn't for one week, Black Friday, nor Christmas. It went on until something changed drastically for Black people. I can tell you this, if we don't change our ways, we will remain a permanent underclass as a race. Is this what you want for the next generation? If we make just a one-year sacrifice, we will be able to measure our economic potentials. We could save enough money to invest in a major supermarket.

I am calling on all Black Americans to purchase food and water *only* for the next three months, no clothes, gadgets, or new cars. If you cannot make this sacrifice, you are satisfied in your condition and your offsprings will not be able to purchase the things that you are unwilling to sacrifice and not purchase at this time. Did you know that 60% of the homeless population in Los Angeles is Black people? And there are so many more that are not counted among the homeless because they are living with a relative or friend.

Stop sitting around, talking about what other races have and what they are doing and how they are coming up economically, etc. They are not spending their precious time talking about you—the proof is in the pudding. Let's start talking about what we can and must do. We talk about others, who won't hire Blacks, yet we see Blacks who won't hire Black and we keep eating and shopping in their establishments. We want to hold everybody accountable to us except Black folks—what's up with that? We have power and we need to demonstrate it. Here is the plan: In our community, we are going to boycott one supermarket chain, one franchise food chain and one hotel chain at the same for three months. Let's see if we "MATTER." I will be calling for a town hall meeting for planning. Holler if you hear me! Let's stop the economic hemorrhage now!

TAKING BACK OUR BUSINESSES/COMMUNITY BY ANY MEANS NECESSARY

Dr. Rosie Milligan, along with the West Coast Supporters of the Harvest Institute, under the leadership of the renowned Dr. Claud Anderson, launched a powerful economic empowerment movement—"Get On The Bus Black Business Tour."

Milligan told participants, "It makes absolutely no sense for Blacks not to own 75% of the dry cleaners, the wig shops and the beauty supply business. We must plan our takeover." She further stated that the only reason for non-Blacks owning businesses is that we (Blacks) support those businesses and Blacks have not developed the mindset to takeover.

Dr. Rosie held her gun in the air as she went on to say, "This gun represent the seriousness of compelling Blacks to do the right thing." The crowd nodded in agreement as they clapped for approval.

Rosie told the economic freedom riders, "We can no longer brag about being one of the largest consumers, with a spendable income of 650 billion." She admonished the riders that, "Unless these dollars are placed in a Black person's hand, it means nothing for us, but so much to others."

"I do not want to hear another Black person quote the ethnic spending pattern again, as to how many times the dollar recycle in communities. What is your point and what is your comparison, huh? So think next time before you speak or quote stats.

"We owe it to our children to leave them the kind of community that others are able to experience. How do we reclaim our community? Inch by inch. It does not take a rocket scientist's strategic planning to do it. I have a 5 year plan that can drive the majority of non-Black businesses from our community and replace them with Black owned businesses. I will disclose it at our Black Business summit. I am not against anybody, I am for including my people and myself.

"In conclusion, we must come to grips with truth. The truth is, we must become economically self-sufficient and competitive. Another truth is we must improve the employment rate for Blacks in order to reduce crime. When I say we, I mean that Blacks must be in position to employ more Blacks. If we do not do it for ourselves, no one else will do it for us. We can do it. Revisit history, and revisit Black Wall Street in Tulsa Oklahoma in 1923. Do the right thing and Get On The Bus!"

When asked what must we do by riders, Milligan stated, "We must come together and pool our monies. We must be financially ready to close some businesses down. When the rain pours down we must have our bucket in place—not looking for a bucket."

Queen Sierra was almost in tears as she thanked the riders for their economic boost when they visited Al's Market & Deli. She further stated, "I know my business is in a depressed area, however, Dr. Anderson warned us to go into those areas and clean them up because our people deserve such."

The businesses visited were:
Express Yourself Books   Al's Market & Deli
1425 W. Manchester Ave.   7512 S. Hoover
Los Angeles   Los Angeles
(323) 750-3592   (323) 750-3963

Coley's Caribbean Restaurant
300 East Florence Avenue
Inglewood
(310) 672-7474

The riders are anticipating the next "Get On The Bus." The group will identify the Black owned dry cleaning businesses next. Riders came from as far as San Diego, California.

POVERTY IS NO PREREQUISITE FOR HEAVEN

Poverty is *not* a prerequisite for entering the Kingdom of God—so do not get it twisted. The Word of God is clear as to what God wants for us. 3 John 1:2 states, *"Beloved, I wish above all things that thou mayest prosper and be in health, even as thy soul prospereth."* It's time to read God's Word and to ask for *wisdom* and *understanding*. We have become so disempowered simply because we have misinterpreted and misquoted the scriptures. Some people seem to think that food stamps, run-over-shoes, poor housing, being broken down in spirit, being a victim with the "poor-me syndrome" is a sure ticket into the Pearly Gates.

A Christian woman said to me one day, "Child, the Bible said that the poor you will always have with you; that is why I am not worried about having wealth." I asked her to show me that scripture and she did. In Matthew 26:11, Jesus said these words, *"The poor you will always have with you, but you will not always have me."* Do me a favor and please read the *entire* context of that scripture and be clear about what Jesus is saying. Anyway, I said to her, "Yes, I see what it says. It says the poor you will always have with you; however, it did not say poor Rosie Milligan you will always have with you, so it's not referring to me, therefore, and I choose *not* to be the poor." You see, I love helping people, and I love helping to build the Kingdom, and it takes money to do that. Can poor people help also? Absolutely yes, and we *all* have choices as to what level we want to be helpful.

Our financial prosperity speaks nonverbally about our God and communicates that He *can* and He *will* provide. Many do not choose Jesus because they see the powerlessness of the so-called people of God all around them. Wealth is required to position, maintain, and to advance the Word of God that men and women might hear the Word and come to Christ. I know many people who pay tithes and give offerings, and yet they struggle financially. My question is this: If God wants you to be blessed financially and you want to be blessed financially, then what is the problem here? Could it be lack of knowledge about God's Word, listening to misquoted scriptures, misinterpretation of the scripture, and not reading the Bible for ourselves and merely acting upon what we have heard others say?

I suggest you Google each quote below and read, reread, and study the scriptures from the quotes that we hear frequently such as:

1) God said take no thought for tomorrow. (The point Jesus was making was not that a Christian should adopt an attitude of apathy or laziness as a way of life but rather that worry is totally unnecessary for those who are cared for by God the Father.)

2) Money is the root of all evil. The LOVE of money is the critical factor in determining if money is used for good or evil, from God's perspective.

3) It's easier for a camel to go through the eye of needle than for a rich man to enter into the Kingdom of God. (God is not anti-money or anti-wealth, He is anti-money *worshipping*.)

4) Ain't nothing wrong with being poor 'cause the Bible says the poor will be with you always.

Okay, to each his own.

I am concerned about how our young generation will view God and His love for Black America. Will they see Blacks as God's stepchildren, the children who do not receive equal distribution of the inheritance of wealth? The ones who are given the least amount of attention, and the ones who have to struggle the most—even their children's children? My point is this: Black America, now that we have been afforded the opportunity to learn how to read, let's read the Bible for ourselves and teach your children the same, and let's read other books about money and daily living. And if you only read the Bible and understood everything it says, you will be able to live a balanced life in every aspect, such as: family matters, money matters, social matters, wives will know how to treat their husbands and husbands will know how to treat their wives, parents their children and children their parents, employers their employees and employees their employers, spiritual leaders their followers and followers their spiritual leaders.

If we follow the Word of God, there would be less poverty because families would not have to start their life in the basement of the economic building. The Bible teaches us to leave an inheritance for our children's children—please take heed. W.E.B. DuBois had the following to say: "To be a poor man is hard, but to be a poor race in a land of dollars is the very bottom of hardship." Let's do better and watch God work on behalf of you and your offspring when you do what's right. Remember, God wants you blessed in *every* aspect of your life. You can enter the Kingdom having plenty of money. God needs people to serve Him who have money. Will *you* be one of them?

THE WORST IS YET TO COME—PREPARE FOR IT!

The 2016 political climate may usher in a period of unrest. This should give us more reasons to think outside the box. As I listen to people these days, I sense a feeling of insecurity due to the uncertainness about what box. It's more critical now than ever to have residual income via network marketing or investment income working for us. Think about this for a moment . . . If your income from your job ended, or your business failed to earn enough revenue for you to keep the doors open, what would happen to you and your family?

If the news story read, "There is a flood storm approaching," one would start gathering sandbags. Well, there is an economic flood storm approaching your house and the house of your loved ones, therefore, we must all start making preparation to protect ourselves. There are many social programs in the process of being cut, such as: assistance for the elderly—making it impossible for the elderly to survive at home alone because of fewer hours for in-home support. This will force the elderly to have to be placed in an extended care facility and upon their demise, the home that had been intended to be left as an inheritance for their loved ones becomes the state of California's property. It becomes reimbursement for medical care paid on your loved one's behalf if they were receiving any type of state assistance, such as Med-i-Cal benefits, in-home support, etc. The loved one's heirs, under certain circumstances, may have to sell the home or reimburse the state for benefits paid on the deceased's behalf.

It's important that we cut our spending and find ways to earn all the money that we can in order to make some kind of investment this year. In 1916, we will have a new president with a new direction, and we do not know how the scale will be tilted. But one thing that we do know is: If we don't find ways to help ourselves, there will be no help for us. So, let's make a serious move right now and improve our economic status. We must stop relying solely on the income from our job and create other means of income.

We must make an economic change immediately. Every family needs a budget. My book, *Getting Out Of Debt Simple*, provides a sample budget, along with seventy-five ways to save money, and much more. We must find a way to save money, even if it means renting a room to have extra money. Gone are the days when you can live in your big house by yourself. Your child or grandchild may need a place to stay—and you should open your doors to help them. Please, don't start talking about, "When I was coming up, we did not have to move back home with our parents." Stop that kind of talk! As an elder, I could tell you lots of things about how it used to be. However, those days are long gone, so get with the new wave and help your children and family members when there's a need. Thank God that it's others who are in need versus you who are in need. I would rather have my children come to live with me versus me having to go live with them. You had better know how to count blessings.

Starting in June 2015, I will start conducting "*Getting Your Financial House In Order*" seminars in the Altadena/Pasadena area. The first one will be held on Sunday, June 14, 2015, from 10 to 12 noon at Altadena SDA Church, 2609 N. Lincoln Ave., Altadena, CA 91001, 626-794-3953. Join us.

REFLECTIONS OF A BLACK FARMER AND A FOURTH-GENERATION DESCENDANT OF A SLAVE

The experiences of Blacks in America are so painful that it causes one to totally blot out from their consciousness different pieces of their history. While history has served others well, it has been bitter with not much sweet for Black Americans. Dr. John Henrik Clarke said, "History is the clock that tells time." Understanding this statement, I now know and understand why many Blacks do not know what time it is—they have consciously blotted out pieces of their personal and family history.

I, like many, hail from the South and was a farmer. We came through an era where whites were taught to hate Blacks and conversely, Blacks were taught to love whites. Our folks were so focused on teaching us to love whites that they forgot to tell us to love Blacks, which is where the problem lies today. I guess they thought that it was a given that we would love each other. In spite of the ill-treatment we received from many whites, I am thankful that our parents taught us love versus hate. I am thankful because I've witnessed the metastatic cancerous effect hate has had on our nation and the world. A child asked the question after 9/11, "Why do they hate us?"

To love is a conscious decision that one must make for him or herself. There are many reasons to choose hating, but loving serves us best. Let me give you many reasons why Blacks could hate.

The Black man could hate the white man for the following reasons:

1. Taking him away from his homeland (Africa) and bringing him to America to be a slave.

2. Separating him from his wife and children.

3. Stripping him of his native language.

4. Beating him for trying to learn how to read and to write.

5. Working him from sunup to sundown without pay.

6. Making him look down when talking to a white man.

7. Making him say, "Yes, sir," to the white man's minor children.

8. Beating him if they thought he looked at a white woman.

9. Causing the Black man to have to escape by night with his family after having an altercation with a white man. There were times when he had to leave his family, his land, and possessions behind.

10. For working him and his family all year long, only to be told that he almost got out of debt and not being given a receipt when purchasing clothes, food, and seeds on credit, then being beaten if he questioned the amount he owed.

11. Refusing to let him and his family try on clothes and shoes before purchasing them.

12. For selling his wife/children to another slave master.

13. For raping his teenage daughter and his wife.

14. For entering his house and having sex with his wife while he's out on the porch helpless to do anything.

15. For beating him in the town square for white folk's recreation.

16. For beating him in the presence of his wife and children.

17. For depositing his white seed into his wife and daughter and then denying his own child provisions.

18. For the degradation of knowing that the children he claimed as his were really the seed of a white man.

19. For forcing him to have to leave his wife and children in order for them to have food to eat via getting on public assistance.

20. For refusing to make him a farm loan and causing him to lose his land and farm.

21. For denying him the right to plant cotton on his own land.

22. For plowing up his crops if he planted more than what was allowed, regardless of his family size.

23. For prohibiting him from taking his farming products to the marketplace for public sale.

24. For having to take his cotton to the cotton gin early in the morning, yet having to wait until after all the white farmers, who arrived much later, took care of their cotton weighing business first.

The Black woman could hate the white man for the following reasons:
1. Taking her from her homeland (Africa) and bringing her to America to be a slave.
2. Separating her from her husband/children.
3. Stripping her of her native language.
4. Beating her for trying to learn how to read and to write.
5. Working her from sunup to sundown without pay.
6. Making her look down when talking to a white man or woman.
7. Making her say, "Yes, sir," to a minor white child.
8. For causing her husband to have to leave her and her children behind after have an altercation with a white man.
9. For refusing to allow her and her family to try on clothes and shoes before purchasing them.
10. For selling her husband/children to another slave master.

11. For disrespecting her husband, walking into their home, making the children go outside while he had sex with her while her husband was sitting on the front porch, feeling helpless.

12. For beating her husband in the town's square for white folk's recreation.

13. For beating her husband in her presence and her children's.

14. For depositing his seed in her without her permission time and time again.

15. For raping her daughters and leaving them pregnant with his seed.

16. The degradation of knowing that her husband was not the father of her children.

17. For beating and hanging her son/husband without cause.

18. For having to live as a single parent just to be able to feed herself and her children because her husband could not live in the home.

19. For making her have to hide her own husband when the social worker came around. For having to breastfeed the white woman's baby before nursing her own baby.

20. For having to return back to the field or her master's house to work a week after she delivered her baby.

21. Having to leave her infant at home with his siblings while she worked in the home of white folks, caring for, cooking, and cleaning for their children from sunup to sundown for very little pay.

22. For only being allowed to go to school during rainy season because of having to work the white man's field.

In spite of all the white folk did to Blacks, Blacks continued to love them. In fact, I really do think that Blacks love white folk more than they love Black folk. Our forefathers, who were slaves, drilled love and respect for the white man into our consciousness as a mean of protecting our lives. We were taught to smile, show all teeth when the white man was around so that he would think that we were happy. If the white man thought that the slaves were unhappy, he would watch them closely to make sure that they did not run away. If they looked sad or unhappy, he would think that there might be an uprising or that they were planning an escape, leaving his farm to ruin.

Even today, 2016, 151 years after the Emancipation Proclamation, Blacks still smile and show all their teeth when the white man is present. Case in point: Watch the Black teller in the bank the next time you visit the bank. Watch the behavior of the Black woman when she is servicing the white man versus the Black man. With the white man, you will see all teeth and smiles—check it out!

Well, I guess he who writes the script writes the best role and image for himself. He who defines words and language makes all that pertains to them good and perfect. An example: the word "white" denotes good and pure while the word "black" denotes bad and evil. Everyone wants to be good and pure, and no one wants to be bad and evil. Let's examine the psychosocial adaptation to the dynamics. You want to ascribe to the ways of the good ones, and when they accept you into their social and personal arena, you gain a sense of validation; your self-worth is higher esteemed. When other Blacks see you with the good, the pure, the white man/woman, you are more esteemed in their eyes. Now what do you have? You have a race striving to be a Caucasian clone. Subconsciously, you want to be with them, intermingle with them on every level. You want to eat with them, go to school with them, and marry them—it's a natural instinct to want to be with the best.

Let's look at how having the need to assimilate and being validated has cost us: It cost us our Negro Baseball League; it cost us the closure of Black hospitals and many Black businesses. Black bus companies, Black cab companies were forced to close due to integration. We are now seeing a shift in the Black church arena; Blacks feel more esteemed serving under white pastoral leadership.

Do we love non-Blacks more than we love Black folk? Most Blacks would answer with a resounding no, but the truth lies in the pudding. The truth is where the rubber meets the road. The truth rests in who we spend our money with.

In conclusion, we cannot even begin to fix our problems until we face the fact that we have a problem with loving others more than we do ourselves and our children. We support others. We keep their businesses open, help to provide a job for them and their children—even though they do not hire our children. Our patronizing their businesses helps to educate their children while we cannot afford tuition for our own children.

When Black folks start loving Blacks as much as they love other folk and when other folk start loving Black folk as much as Black folk love them, then the future for Blacks will be better. When Blacks come up, the nation as a whole will reap the benefit.

It does not take a rocket scientist to know what I have shared with you—it only takes an elder who has paid close attention and who has made real observations along the journey called life. Don't get mad; get busy changing the dismal plight of Black Americans, by any means necessary.

IT'S TIME TO BE DELIVERED FROM THIS FINANCIAL ECONOMIC BONDAGE—LEARN HOW NOW— Saturday July 12, 2014. THIS IS A FREE EVENT

Hello, this is Dr. Rosie Milligan. I have been made aware of a growing problem that is impacting the masses. As I began to interview people, I discovered that so many people have already been challenged severely by the credit system and their credit score (FICO). America herself is deeply in debt above her head. However, the American people are held hostage and placed in a position of what I call Financial Economic Bondage—a slave to lenders and financial institutions—and for many, it's no fault of their own.

The American people did not vote to ship our jobs overseas; we did not make it so unbearable for large businesses to be able to run a successful business in America/some states, causing businesses to relocate to other states/countries. The American people did not vote to have large corporations hire in-house prison inmates, who are given extremely low pay for their labor, to perform the work that was once performed by the general population. But, yet, we are paying a debt that we did not incur.

The Bible says in Hosea 4:6, *My people are destroyed for lack of knowledge*. This scripture goes on and tells the consequences of rejecting knowledge—read it for yourself. I am concerned about the position/condition that we are leaving our next generation in—It's a shame, and it's pitiful. The Bible says in Proverbs 13:22, *A good man shall leave an inheritance to his children's children*. I am not trying to preach to you—it's just a teaching moment right now.

Did you know that it's legal to deny a person a job opportunity because of their FICO score? Furthermore, no one cares about what happened to you to cause your credit score to be poor. Many people's scores have been lowered due to high medical bills, job lay-offs, unemployment benefits running out, having disabilities with no benefits, a deceased spouse, school loans, Pay Day Loans, divorce, etc. There is no end to this list, but who cares other than your mother/father and God?

Did you know these facts? A poor credit score can: 1) prevent you from getting the job you want and deserve. 2) Increase your insurance rates. 3) Cause you to get rejected as a renter on a house/apartment you can afford. 4) Cause you to have to put up *three times* the security deposit when renting compared to someone else. 5) Lock you out of the banking system. 6) Cause you to pay a higher interest rate on all your purchases such as: automobiles, credit cards, etc.

WHAT IF YOUR CHILD GRADUATED FROM COLLEGE WITH A 4.0, AND HAS A SCHOOL LOAN AND MISSED A GREAT JOB OPPORTUNITY DUE TO A POOR FICO SCORE?—THIS IS REAL TALK. IT'S ALSO LEGAL FOR CERTAIN JOBS TO RECHECK YOUR CREDIT AFTER YOU ARE EMPLOYED—AND THEY CAN FIRE YOU IF YOUR CREDIT IS BAD—LET'S GET SERIOUS! IT'S NO JOKE.

TALKING ABOUT DEATH AND INCOMPETENCY MAY NOT BE PLEASANT—BUT IT'S NECESSARY

We are all going to die, so we may as well embrace it and face it. And there is a strong possibility that many will become incompetent during their lifetime. (*Incompetent* means: being unable to make sound decisions for one's self.) People are living longer these days, and the elderly population is rapidly growing. Many of our elderly are medically challenged with dementia and Alzheimer's disease. These disorders cause memory loss and the inability to make sound decisions on one's behalf. Many persons who suffer with dementia and Alzheimer's disease have to be placed in a nursing home facility to be cared for, even though they may own real estate properties, have money, and other assets.

CHOOSING A POWER OF ATTORNEY IS A MUST! It is important for you to choose the person who you want to make health-care and financial decisions for you should you become unable to do so. If you do not make the choice, in many instances, the very person who you would not want to be in charge of your affairs—becomes the actual one handling your business on your behalf.

POWER OF ATTORNEY MUST BE SIGNED AND WITNESSED IN THE PRESENCE OF A NOTARY. The person who is giving someone else the power of attorney to act on his or her behalf should he or she become unable to function adequately or become incapacitated, that person must have a valid driver's license or passport as a form of identification in order for the notary to notarize the documents giving someone else the power to act on their behalf. Recently, I was asked to prepare an Advance HealthCare Directive and Durable Power of Attorney for Finance for a person's mother who suffers dementia and is in a nursing home. I had to refuse to prepare the documents because in many instances, the people suffering dementia or Alzheimer's disease are not competent in decision making. Furthermore, a savvy notary will not notarize such documents under these circumstances.

A NOTE TO SINGLE PARENTS If you died today, who would become guardian over your children? If you become incompetent, who will care for your minor children? If you died and you have minor children, who would be guardian over the money and property you are leaving for your children? **TAKE CARE OF YOUR BUSINESS WHILE YOU ARE IN YOUR SOUND MIND!**

Call Dr. Rosie Milligan, Senior Estate Planner, 323-750-3592 for an appointment to get your Living Trust, Advanced HealthCare Directive and Durable Power of Attorney prepared today. Bring this article and receive your discount.

This is Dr. Rosie, "AND I AM JUST SAYING" WE ARE ALL GOING TO DIE! SO WE MIGHT AS WELL PREPARE FOR IT!

Take a moment and think of all the people that you know who died last year—then think of the ones who had made no preparations and the financial hardship it caused their family at an economic critical time. I am not giving you any new revelation. You know that one day, you *are* going to die. So why not plan for your demise? It's a shame and a disgrace upon the family when parents or loved ones die and leave their estate unplanned. (An "estate" means the things you own, such as houses, cars, jewelry, antiques, collectibles, stocks, bonds, IRAs, 401Ks, furs, clothing, etc.)

Times have changed so much since yesteryear and family values have also changed. Selfishness and greed causes family members' behavior to be very ugly when someone dies leaving an estate. It has been said that "blood" is thicker than "water;" yes, it is, indeed, until someone dies and leaves something of value—then "blood" becomes "thin." Let's face it, in the past; estate planning was not as important as it is today. Remember, if your grandparent or great-grandparent told the oldest child or the most responsible child to distribute their estate a certain way, that person dared not tamper with their parent's wishes.

Your word was truly your bond, but of course, your word was all that you had during those days. I remember asking my father, Simon, "What do mean when you say that 'Your word is your bond'?" He explained, "The phrase means that your word is used for collateral for a debt or for bail." I now chuckle when I think about that old saying. If the truth be told, all most people had then was their word. They didn't own mansions, yachts, land, expensive cars, collectibles, antiques, IRAs, 401ks, and large bank accounts. Can you imagine today someone using their word as collateral to purchase a home or car? Please!

Families didn't fall out with each other during those days of yesteryear. In fact, they had to come together to help bury their loved ones and to help rear their children if they were not of the age to care for themselves. Remember that? Today, when someone dies and leaves an estate—the fight is on! Most of what should go the family members is eaten up in probate and large attorney fees. What a waste and a disgrace.

My cousin died twelve years ago, she did not have a Will or Living Trust. She owned a home in Mississippi and income property in Los Angeles. Her property in Los Angeles closed probate nine years after her death. Because my cousin did not have her business in order, it caused a family feud. If you think that this is not a common problem, I suggest that you make a visit to probate court in any city in the USA. It's real. If you read the newspapers or listen to the news on television, you have heard of the many horror stories even among superstars who fail to do their estate planning.

You may think that because you have a Will, you are okay. Yes, a Will is better than having nothing at all. A Will may or may not be right for you. It depends upon the value of your estate (meaning all that you own, including money in the bank). If what you own is valued at over $150,000, it must go to probate court. Probate and attorney fees can be very expensive. If your children or loved ones do not have enough cash to pay probate fees, they must sell your home or other properties to obtain enough money to pay the probate fees. They may not be able to keep the home that you left for them to enjoy—a place called home.

It's already time to take an inventory of your assets and start thinking about who you want to have what you have worked so hard for. So when it is time for you to make your transition and to connect with the ancestors, you can rest in peace, knowing that you handled your business on earth. And know that estate planning does not speed up your demise. And yes, you *will* indeed die! So you might as well plan and prepare yourself for it

Article: Living Trust
YOU WILL DIE! YOU MIGHT AS WELL PREPARE FOR IT!

I am not giving you any new revelation. You know that one day, you *are* going to die. So why not plan for your demise? It's a shame and a disgrace upon the family when parents or loved ones die and leave their estate unplanned. (An "estate" means the things you own, such as houses, cars, jewelry, antiques, collectibles, stocks, bonds, IRAs, 401Ks, furs, clothing, etc.)

Times have changed so much since yesteryear and family values have also changed. Selfishness and greed causes family members' behavior to be very ugly when someone dies leaving an estate. It has been said that "blood" is thicker than "water;" yes, it is, indeed, until someone dies and leaves something of value—then "blood" becomes "thin." Let's face it, in the past, estate planning was not as important as it is today. Remember, if your grandparent or great-grandparent told the oldest child or the most responsible child to distribute their estate a certain way, that person dared not tamper with their parent's wishes.

Your word was truly your bond, but of course, your word was all that you had during those days. I remember asking my father, Simon, "What do mean when you say that 'Your word is your bond'?" He explained, "The phrase means that your word is used for collateral for a debt or for bail." I now chuckle when I think about that old saying. If the truth be told, all most people had then was their word. They didn't own mansions, yachts, land, expensive cars, collectibles, antiques, IRAs, 401ks, and large bank accounts. Can you imagine today someone using their word as collateral to purchase a home or car? Please!

Families didn't fall out with each other during those days of yesteryear. In fact, they had to come together to help bury their loved ones and to help rear their children if they were not of the age to care for themselves. Remember that? Today, when someone dies and leaves an estate—the fight is on! Most of what should go the family members is eaten up in probate and large attorney fees. What a waste and a disgrace.

My cousin died twelve years ago, she did not have a Will or Living Trust. She owned a home in Mississippi and income property in Los Angeles. Her property is in probate court as I am writing and it has certainly caused a family feud. If you think that this is not a common problem, I suggest that you make a visit to probate court in any city in the USA. It's real. If you read the newspapers or listen to the news on television, you have heard of the many horror stories even among superstars who fail to do their estate planning.

You may think that because you have a Will, you are okay. Yes, a Will is better than having nothing at all. A Will may or may not be right for you. It depends upon the value of your estate (meaning all that you own, including money in the bank). If what you own is valued at over $100,000, it must go to probate court. Here is an example of probate fees: If your estate is valued at $250,000, the probate fees in California are 10 percent of the total value of your estate, which is $25,000. If your children or loved ones do not have enough cash to pay probate fees, they must sell your home or other properties to obtain enough money to pay the probate fees. They may not be able to keep the home that you left for them to enjoy—a place called home.

There are four essential "players" in a Trust. 1. The Trustor, the person who owns the property that is transferred into the Trust. 2. The Trustee, the person (or institution) that manages a Trust and the Trust property according to the terms of the Trust. The Trustee can be, and usually is, the person who sets up the Trust. 3. Successor Trustee, the person (or institution) that takes over as Trustee of a Trust when the original Trustee(s) has died or become incapacitated. 4. The Beneficiary, the person (or organization) named by you to receive your assets or property upon your death.

I am sure that if you had a choice, you would prefer your children and loved ones to receive all of your estate (property), rather than to allow a strange attorney and others to receive a large portion of it. Your better choice is the Revocable Living Trust. If you do not have any assets to leave in a Will or Trust, you still need a Durable Power Of Attorney and Advance Health Care Directive in order to avoid the possibility of having a conservator appointed on your behalf. If you have a stroke or become unable to make sound decisions for yourself, someone must make decisions for you. You can appoint someone you trust in the Durable Power Of Attorney to make those decisions. If you do not have your Power Of Attorney, someone will be required to go to probate court to become your conservator. You must pay attorney fees, court fees, and other fees. Make up your mind while you are able to.

We conduct Free Living Trust seminars for groups and organizations, such as churches, social groups, family groups, block clubs, senior citizen centers, etc. Visit our Web site for answers to the most frequently asked questions about the Revocable Living Trust. Understand the disadvantages of adding someone to the deed of your property. Learn about the pitfalls when placing someone on your house deed as joint tenant for probate avoidance.

This is the beginning of a new year. It's already time to take an inventory of your assets and start thinking about who you want to have what you have worked so hard for. So when it is time for you to make your transition and to connect with the ancestors, you can rest in peace, knowing that you handled your business on earth. And know that estate planning does not speed up your demise

YOU BETTER HEAR ME! AN ELDER SPEAKS

Hey, you Bible-totting Christians, what are you leaving for your children's children? The Bible says that you should leave them something. If you are going to eat from the Bible's plate—eat it all. It's shameful that each generation has to start out with nothing, especially in a society where money determines one's fate. Start today making money and family security a priority—Save something. When Jesus said, "The poor you will have with you always," He was not telling you to *be* poor. So get a grip and do what the Word said to do. I will post scriptures about money and what the Bible says about money each week. You had better read the Bible and do what it says and then your generation will be BLESSED.

Why are Black folks afraid to go after the money that's owed to us? We fight strong for everything but for the debt that's owed to us ... like reparation, Black farmers' lawsuit, the money due Blacks from the 1865 Treaty. Let's take the same united front that we took for the murder of Travon and the Jena Six Louisiana fight, get on the bus, hold rallies, press conferences, etc. Where are the fighting politicians and ministers when it comes to Black folks getting their money? Blacks have become an economic underclass, and this will become a permanent position unless we do something quick. We cannot change this economic status via just getting more education and working harder. Look at the current job situation, the increases in college tuition fees, business closure rates, and jobs that continue to be shifted to other countries.

In order for Blacks to come up from their dismal economic plight, we must demand the U.S. government pay us what they owe us. Money is not everything, but like following God and breathing oxygen, it's next in priority. Check your bank account. Thousands will die this year due to a lack of money to pay for medicine and/or medical expenses. Thousands will go to jail or prison due to a lack of money to pay for good legal representation, therefore leaving behind children who will enter the foster care system. Many times, these children will never be able to reconnect with their biological parents. Last but not least, there will be more divorces, more bedroom turmoil, and more will join the homelessness status—all because of a lack of money.

If you think it's bad now, fast-forward to when these folks who divorce during these hard times reach age 65 (retirement age). *If* Social Security is still intact, with the husband's and wife's check together, it will barely be enough to keep a roof over their heads, with nothing left for any form of recreational activities.

Let's get real. Years back, many people had jobs that offered a good retirement plan. In Los Angeles and surrounding areas, there were jobs like: GMAC, Good Year Tire, and many large aircraft companies, etc. Many Blacks worked for the city, county, state, and federal government—however, take notice that as the Blacks retired from these institutions/agencies, they were not replaced with another Black person. Don't take my word for it, go to any government building and look around and see who's employed. You won't see too many Black people, even in the courthouse.

What's due Blacks from the 1865 treaty is more than money. It includes: free education, free medical care, ownership of casinos, land, and much more. Unlike others who have received their reparations, we have to fight to get what's due us in the higher court systems. If and when we run out of money, the fight is over—and the system counts on us running out of money. We are in the Court of Appeal for the 1865 Black Indian Lawsuit, a lawsuit that has been funded by The Harvest Institute/Black Freedmen Foundation, and a few of Dr. Anderson's friends. I pray that the funds do not run out because we have come too far to quit now. If you care to help, please send funds to The Harvest Institute, 623 Florida Ave. NW, Washington, D.C. 20001 or e-mail:harvest623@aol.com.

In the county of Los Angeles, the numbers for Blacks is approximately 8.7 percent, Latinos 40 percent, with Whites 29.1 percent, and our business ownership and median income is far less than the other ethnic groups. With this being said, our only hope is to pull together in every way. There is no room for division. We are outnumbered in every way, numerically, in business ownership, and median household income. Therefore, it is critical now more than ever for Blacks to have a united front on economic issues.

IF WE LISTEN, THE ELDERS CAN TEACH US

Madlyn Richard, a resident of Altadena, California, pens her memoir, *On The Wings Of The Wind: A Long Journey To Clarity*. The old folks used to say, "Wisdom comes with time, so just keep on living." Richard has stood the test of time, and with 80-plus years, her eyes and ears have witnessed much. If we listen carefully, we can glean from the pearls and wisdom she shares.

There are many who have made their transition, which has left no impression or impacted family members or friends. This is not the case with Madlyn. Her children, her children's friends, and colleagues pay great homage to her.

In a recent political debate, much discussion has been generated about "Stay-at-Home Moms." Richard addresses this issue profoundly as she states, "We need to revisit how we used to value marriage and not see marriage as an oppressive institute, but instead, as something beautiful that's sanctioned by God." And she wants women to know that being a mother and a housewife is as important as any role held by women.

On The Wings Of The Wind is a literary guide that will motivate others to leave a written account of lessons learned on their journey that can benefit the generations to follow. You will clearly see how important it is to know the belief systems, family values, spiritual beliefs, and the deep secrets to their success.

This memoir is, in essence a blueprint—a life road map—and a lamp that lights the way for those who seek to get through the maze of "Life Challenges." As you cruise the pages of this book, you will gain a better insight on how to deal with the war on poverty, hunger and racism, economic crisis, etc. You will understand that we have traveled this road before as citizens of the United States, and we will get through it all if we stand together as one race—and that is the human race.

This is a must-read book for all ages. Reading this memoir is like sitting on the floor around the fireplace listening to your grandmother giving a present-day saga and a history lesson at the same time. You feel as though you were there with her back in time. It's like being guided by a tour guide who is walking ahead of you with a lamp, guiding you along the path of the unknown, but with the assurance that you will safely make the journey.

Mrs. Madlyn Richard helps us to connect to what is missing in most of our modern-day children's lives—some good old mother's wit.

THE COST OF NOT HAVING A POWER OF ATTORNEY

We made it. It's 2012, and God has given us another chance to get our affairs in order. I have sounded the alarm for many years instructing my family as well as the public of the importance of having a Living Trust, Advanced Healthcare Directive and a Durable General Power Of Attorney. As the bible tells us in Hosea 4:6, *My people are destroyed for lack of knowledge: because thou hast rejected knowledge.* Reject means to have been told and to take no action—sad. I have written many articles on how families are impacted when their loved one dies without having a Living Trust and when they have a Living Trust but fail to update when necessary.

However, in this article I want to only focus on the Power of Attorney. A Power Of Attorney is very important. With a Power Of Attorney you are appointing someone to act as your agent to make medical and financial decision for you if you should become physically or mentally unable to do so. I have witnessed so many cases where the person who is running everything for a disabled relative is not the one that person would have appointed to manage their affairs. Don't let that happen to you.

Let me provide you with three recent encounters that I am knowledgeable of regarding having and not having a Power Of Attorney.

(1) A 50 year old friend of mine was hospitalized, he asked me to become the number one agent for him on his Advanced HealthCare Directive and Durable General Power Of Attorney, he has a sister, who is his only relative in Los Angeles, California. By having Power Of attorney for him, I was able to pick up his last payroll check, take it to the bank and deposit it into his account, obtain a debit card for his account and to pay his storage bill; this action prevented his valuables from being auctioned off.

(2) A female client's mother had a stroke and was in a coma, she was told by the hospital administrator that she could not make medical decisions for her

mother without a healthcare power of attorney—she was the only child. The hospital was not going to assume the liability of having her to make medical decisions and later having to face a legal battle if other children showed up later. She had to hire an attorney to go to court to become the conservator for her mother.

(3) I know a man whose mother came to live with him and his wife, she had a stroke after being with them for six months. He told me that they tried to get her to have a Power Of Attorney prepared and to put him on her bank account but to no avail. After 100 days in a skilled nursing facility, being on Medicare, she would need another means for paying for her hospital stay. When the social worker applied for Med-i-Cal on her behalf, it was denied because she had $2,900.00 in her bank account. The man was told that when her funds had been spent down below $2,000.00, he could reapply. He could not spend down because he had no access to her bank account. He has obtained an attorney to go to court for him to apply for conservatorship.

I have provided you information that I hope will inspire you to GET YOUR HOUSE IN ORDER! I wish you more blessings than you can stand in 2012.

WHILE YOU ARE IN YOUR RIGHT MIND

I used to hear my father, Simon Hunter, say in his prayers, "God, I thank you for waking me up in my right mind." We children would laugh because we thought that everybody woke up in their right mind. Well, as years passed, I came to realize that many lie down at night and upon awakening, they don't know where they are, who they are, and the time or today's date. Some of the times their memory is lost for only a few moments, but other times, their memory is lost forever—just that quick.

In the old days, the church used to sing the song, "While the blood is running warm in your veins." We laughed at that song also; we did not understand the meaning of the words. Today, I understand my father's prayer and the old church song. There is now a face on the expression "while you are in your right mind"—it's called *competency*, and when you are not in your right mind, it's called *incompetency*—not able to make a sound decision for yourself. I know the interpretation of the song "while the blood is running warm in your veins." It means that when the blood is running warm, you are alive, and when the blood is cold in your veins, you are dead.

What I am I saying? We need to make decisions about how we want to live and die while we are in our right mind. We need to designate who we want to distribute our assets upon our death or should we become incapacitated. We need to designate the person that we want to make health-care and financial decisions for us if we are unable to do so. I promise you that if you do not decide these issues while you are in your "right" mind, the person who you would least likely choose may be the one taking charge of your health-care and financial affairs.

Dementia and Alzheimer's disease are affecting so many people. Just recently, it was announced that a coach from Tennessee, in her late 50s, had been diagnosed with early Alzheimer's. What's my point? For a power of attorney for health-care and financial concerns, these documents need to be notarized and witnessed. If a person is suffering from dementia/Alzheimer's disease, you may find it difficult to obtain a notary to notarize this document knowing of such a diagnosis. So do it while you are in your "right" mind.

The following is a very sad story. A month ago, I was made aware of a 79-year-old woman who rented a room to a male tenant. He befriended her and became her caretaker and gained her confidence. It was discovered this year by a relative that her Living Trust had been amended to add the tenant as a trustee and the sole beneficiary, deleting her only son who lives out of town from the trust. It was also discovered that a few years back, she had taken a reverse mortgage on her home and received $170,000 cash. No one knows what bank the money had been placed in, and she now no longer remembers and the male tenant no longer lives with her. This is what can happen when one is not in his/her "right" mind and when there is no one paying close attention to the seniors in their family.

I have been sounding the alarm for year, warning folks to get their personal and business affairs in order—and, yes, I am talking to *you*, so what are you waiting for? You need to handle your business while you are in your "right" mind and while the blood is running warm in your veins. Do the right thing for yourself, your children, and your family. I have articles posted on my Web site that you may want to read and share with others. Go to www.Drrosie.com and print them at no cost. These informative articles are: "Families Must Discuss Death & Dying," "How Are The Elders Faring?" "It's Time To Get In Your Children's Business," "It's Time To Get In Your Parents' Business," and many more.

UNSUSPECTING GAMBLERS—WOMEN

L. Lynn Hilliard, a reformed gambler, releases the most startling revelations about women who gamble. In her book *Gambling: The Pleasure Of Winning, The Pain Of Losing, Women Living Through The Pain*, she shares some of her experiences, and experiences she has seen through friends and family members who did not recognize the addiction before it ruined their lives and the lives of their family. Lynn makes herself transparent so that she may help those women who feel that they cannot quit and turn their lives around. She makes it clear that God is the source and power that can turn you from your path of destruction.

One of the most pathological diseases that's epidemic today is gambling addiction. The disease is a silent destroyer of one's mind, values, and families. When we think of gamblers, we usually put the face on a man; therefore, women are unsuspected victims. Women who gamble heavily are a new phenomenon. But according to recent research, women are fast surpassing men as casino customers and make up a growing number of problem gamblers.

During the cable television show A&E, which aired a program about compulsive women gamblers on February 23, 2009, it was noted that compulsive gambling among women is a growing problem. While 10 years ago only 3 percent of compulsive gamblers were women, that number is 46 percent or higher today. In the United States, about 2 million (1 percent) adults meet the criteria for compulsive or pathological gambling in a given year, according to the National Council on Problem Gambling (NCPG). Another 4 to 6 million (2 to 3 percent) can be considered problem gamblers, defined as people who meet one or more of the criteria and are experiencing problems because of their gambling behavior.

The author states: "These women will neglect and/or lose their children, husbands, homes, and their jobs due to their gambling addiction. They will pawn their jewelry, car, and anything of value. It is nothing for them to have 10 outstanding loans with the Payday Loan businesses. This mind-controlling disease is no respecter of person; it matters not the social and economic status. Gambling addiction is rapidly and silently destroying the lives of too many women and their families. It is my hope that people will learn and recognize the signs and symptoms of a gambling addiction and encourage men and women alike to seek professional help before they ruin their life and the lives of their families."

Suicides are increased with gambling addiction. This is due to the shame and guilt associated with: losing money saved for their children's education, losing their family home, embezzling money from their job, taking money from joint accounts with their parents, and inability to replace the funds, etc.

Excerpts from the book: *You don't know me. I am the grandmother, the mother, the daughter, the housewife, the real estate broker, the teacher, the doctor, the lawyer, the welfare recipient, the person living on a once-a-month pension, the person living from paycheck to paycheck. I come in all shapes, forms, and colors. I have no social or economic boundaries. I am the gambling addict; I am you, haunted by an unrealistic dream, caught up in the emotions of the moment, living for the pain and pleasure of gambling.*

Unlike substance abuse, society accepts casinos, card clubs, bingo parlors, horse racing, sports betting, and lotteries, all of which contribute to the legalized gambling addiction. Gambling is an addiction so crippling it takes away your identity. Something happens when you are in a gambling environment. You feel you'll never win enough. You tell yourself, "If I can get back what I've lost I'll leave." It never happens. You are hooked. You leave a loser. A sucker never wins, and a loser never quits.

According to an updated CBS News report on June 23, 2011, there is now casino gambling in 38 states, which use the revenue from gambling to help solve their bloated budget deficits. The main attraction at these gambling halls is now the new slot machines. There are close to 850,000 of them in the United States—twice the number of ATMs. Americans spend more money on slots than on movies, baseball, and theme parks combined. But with slots there is the potential for a dangerous side effect: gambling addiction. And more people are addicted to slot machines than any other form of gambling.

Hotels give you a slot machine card to track your points when playing the slot machine, and they give you a free hotel room when you play a lot. They also give you free meals and drinks to entice you to keep coming back.

If a female in your household is always broke when she should have money, if you are receiving notices regarding the mortgage payment when it should be paid, if you are constantly being lied to about the disappearance of money, if you notice lots of Payday loan slips around the house, if she disappears for long periods of time, if the children are unkempt, if she avoids eye contact when talking with you, if she appears to be hiding something most of the time, when these symptoms occur, most people think drugs. You may want to tune your antennas to gambling.

I interviewed Lynn a week ago, and the telephone lines were jammed with callers who are gamblers. One young woman called asking for help for her 82-year-old grandmother who gambles her whole Social Security check every month but states that she does not have a gambling problem. Gambling casinos are constantly being built across this country and commercial advertisements are becoming plentiful, appealing to the beginner gambler.

Your hole is never too deep that God cannot reach you. If you feel that you are drowning, God is a lifejacket. Catch hold of Him.

A CLOSE-UP LOOK AT HOW THE ELDERLY ARE FARING

The elderly population is one of the fastest-growing population segments in the United States. How prepared are *you* for your golden senior years? Your latter years should be your best years. However, for many, it's the opposite.

I can recall when our parents worked at one job until they retired, having retirement benefits and Social Security benefits. During their golden years, they were able to garden, fish, enjoy their hobbies, and spend time with their grandchildren or even babysit their grandchildren.

What happened? During the last 40 years, America shifted from a manufacturing industry to a service and information-based economy. This resulted in a heavy reliance on foreign imported products, and now, many American corporations (multinational) are outsourcing their work to a number of these countries. Take a look at any American port and you will see for yourself why the economy is struggling.

Sadly to say, jobs for the unskilled/laborers in industries such as automobile and aerospace, as well as others, have disappeared. This left the baby boomers, those born between 1946–1964, in a "canoe without a paddle trying to go upstream" state. They were left with small or no retirement benefits. Those who found work after our major industries shifted out of the U.S.A. saw their salary dropped by 50 percent or more, thus, yielding them a small Social Security benefit at their retirement age.

Social Security benefits for the average African American is between $500 to $1,000 a month, and this will not cover rent and utilities even in low-rent senior citizen housing. Now we are facing the plan to increase the minimum age for receiving Social Security benefits from 62½ years to 65 or 67 years.

Wow! What clever politician came up with this idea? I just don't know.

When I was growing up, I recall the grandmother and/or grandfather coming to live with their children and grandchildren. Today, it's the reverse; children have to move in with their parents. For many Blacks, the grandmother has to become caretaker for their grandchildren due to drug addiction or incarceration of their children. This brings into existence a new challenge for the elderly Blacks. Even though they are financially challenged, they cannot take advantage of senior housing because their grandchildren are living with them and children and teens are prohibited from living in senior housing.

As an elder, I am saddened as I witness the hardship and distress of our senior citizens today. I am saddened for their children who want to help their parents but cannot because of corruption and greed on the part of the "Haves" against the "Have Nots." I hear the cry of the elderly who did everything right, abided by the rules, got their education, and now find themselves in a position of barely surviving.

Many of them are depressed, and because of their depression, isolation, and loneliness, they suffer many health challenges. For many Black elderly, the only outlet they have is the church, and when they can no longer drive or catch a bus, there is no one to come and help them get dressed and take them to church even though their entire life and socialization has been the church. So sad!

It's time that we all start thinking, planning, and talking about our golden years. If the rapture doesn't come and your number is not called, you *will* get to be a senior! So become aware of political changes, new laws that come into effect, the global and nation economy that could impact your future as a senior. Keep up with your political representatives and monitor what they are doing to protect the seniors. Write letters to your politicians regarding elderly concerns, and encourage seniors to vote because they do make a difference. Let your political representatives know that their elderly constituents are many and they want their voices heard. Let's live life to the fullest, make preparations for becoming an elder, and our golden years will stay golden.

Being a senior citizen should not represent the ending of life but the beginning of a new one. If we plan ahead, we will have good reasons to look forward to our golden years. The scripture is right: "We perish due to lack of knowledge." Become knowledgeable.

SECTION 2: WORDS OF WISDOM TO BITE AND TO CHEW ON, AND HEALTHY FOOD FOR THOUGHT

THIS IS DR. ROSIE MILLIGAN, SELF-APPOINTED MAYOR OF SOUTH CENTRAL LOS ANGELES

Stop worrying yourself about the president elect. It's going to be alright because those who were in their coma state are coming alive. You know sometime it take an Earth Quake to wake folks up. Get Trump off your brain and out of your mind.

I suggest you read Philippians 4:8-- Finally, brothers, whatever is true, whatever is honorable, whatever is right, whatever is pure, whatever is lovely, whatever is admirable — if anything is excellent or praiseworthy — think on these things. DONALD TRUMP IS NONE OF THESE THINGS, SO STOP THINKING ON HIM!

Y'all act like Big Momma and God just died. What's wrong with y'all? God is alive and well. Let me conclude by saying this: YOU ARE IN GOOD HANDS RIGHT NOW---YOUR OWN HANDS AND MOST OF ALL YOU ARE STILL IN THE HANDS OF GOD—SO SHUT UP, STAND UP, PIECE UP (MEANING WORK TOGETHER) AND CHILL. LET'S NOT DISCUSS TRUMP FOR THE NEXT SEVEN DAYS; YOUR IMMUNE SYSTEM WILL BE ENHANCED. I AM JUST SAYING. Holler if you hear me!

THE HARRIETT TUBMAN'S TOWN HALL MEETING WILL BE SCHEDULED VERY SOON—SO GET READY.

WE HAVE BLACK FOLK'S ATTENTION—MAKE IT COUNT FOR SOMETHING!

Now that we have the attention of Black America, let's make a move that can change our destiny forever. A boycott for Black Friday is not enough. As your elder who has stood the test of time and has witnessed the past struggle, and the present struggle, and having lived through these two periods having a conscious mind-set, I have a clear glimpse of the future. I seek to offer advice to the younger generation. I am qualified to do so because I have lived both periods in history—the past and the present. I believe that if Black America will follow my lead of this movement, we will change the dismal plight for our future generation forever. My proposal is outlined below in the last paragraph.

Malcolm X stated the following: "Usually when people are sad, they don't do anything. They just cry over their condition, but when they get angry, they bring about a change." I submit to you that it's time to be angry and it's time for a change now. It's time to bring an end to the killing of our black boys and men. Killing our males coupled with the high rate of incarceration, and new laws for longer sentences and life in prison is a new high technical form of annihilation of the black race. Even animals will fight you if you attempt to bring harm to their young ones. A chicken will attack you if you come close to her nest of eggs where there are baby chicks waiting to be hatched, a dog will not allow you to bother his baby puppies. My point is this: What would make anybody think that black folks are going to sit and do nothing when their children are being murdered and for no good reason or cause.

The boycotting of Black Friday's shopping is not enough to bring about a change that can impact on a large scale. The media has painted a picture of black Americans as the "nothings" of the land. However, because of years of integration, other races have learned that the media speaks lies and that is why other races have joined in the march protesting the injustice against blacks. We must be willing to make a great sacrifice to bring about a change. Remember the Montgomery Bus Boycott? The people refused to ride the city bus; instead, they walked to work, they carpooled, etc. If you follow my lead on the proposal presented it will serve two purposes:

1) It will demonstrate to all ethnic groups how significant we are to their economic survival.

2) It will teach our children the power of making a sacrifice for a necessary cause, and they will learn that postponement of instant gratification is a behavior that will serve them better for the future.

I am asking Black America to not buy the following products from nonblack-owned businesses for the balance of this year—that means the rest of December—less than 30 days of abstaining. Postpone buying the items that you promised your children. The lesson they will learn from this will be very valuable. For those who cannot make this sacrifice—you are satisfied with your condition and you are not concerned about the future of your children, grandchildren, and the black nation as a whole. Furthermore, if black people are not willing to accept this proposal, then Dr. Claud Anderson, others, and I have fought and struggled in vain.

Here is the proposal:

For the rest of December, do not buy the following products or services unless you can get them from a black-owned business: clothing, jewelry, toys, games, cosmetics, haircare products, automobiles, etc. Do not get a manicure or pedicure unless it done by a black person. If you don't know a black person who performs this service, ask someone for a referral or do it yourself—it's time to show everybody and every business and service that we *do* matter. Let's make a powerful economic statement. Let's not allow this period in history—having the attention of the mass—to *not* count. Make it count!—and let Michael Brown's death be remembered as a death that motivated Black America to take a stand for the betterment of their race and the nation. This is a good time to teach our children about the *real* cost of freedom—it's expensive, and somebody must pay for it. *Will you make a down payment on it?* I write because I love.

DON'T LEAVE GOD OUT

Hello, this is Dr. Rosie, "AND I AM JUST SAYING" If you want a successful journey, you must include God in all that you do. I thought that I could make it on my own intellect and experiences; however, I discovered that I could not. Once I decided to say this pray to God, my life changed. I prayed, Dear God, I need you. I am nothing without you, I submit to You, God that I am totally dependent on You. I have worked hard and studied hard all my life. I have done all the things that I have wanted to do. I have gone all the places that I wanted to go. I want you to order my steps from now forward. Every morning, when I rise, I say to God, God what should I do today. After God direct me as to what He wants me to do, then I make out my daily schedule. I used to make out my schedule weeks in advance, and my schedule was 24/7 full. If God had an assignment for me, I would have to try and squeeze it in,

Life is so simple and we make it so hard. I was just thinking, what if I had done this even 40 years ago. It's better late than never. I am approaching 68 years of age and now I know just how simple and easy life's journey can be when you sit in the back seat and do not try to be a back seat driver and just let God drive. It may look like He is going all out of the way to get you where you are trying to go, but sit tight, He will get you there, be patient and take in everything that you see, hear and experience along the way. YOU CAN'T BEAT GOD DRIVING.

I LET GO, AND I LET GOD! It's kind-of –like when you walk up to the market door and the door opens before you get to it, that's how things are happening for me now. I am not trying to "Preach" to you, but my text is, "DON'T MOVE UNTIL YOU HEAR FROM GOD" Allow God to direct you, He will if you ask and step back and allow Him to. I am preaching from experience. More next time!

AN IMAGINARY GOD IS BETTER THAN NO GOD

There is much talk about Jesus not being the son of God, and some scholars say that the whole God thing is a hoax. Some say they believe that there is a higher power, and they refer to that higher power by many names. The fact that one recognizes that there is somebody bigger than you and I, that recognition puts them on a path to search for truth.

Some argue that the white man wrote the Bible to enslave the minds of slaves with the promise of a hereafter called heaven and with hopes that this promise would be so wonderful that their earthly sufferings at the hands of their masters could not compare to the glories that awaited them. Since I bear witness to the fulfilling of end-time scripture as to what would be in the last days and what is to come, I am convinced that the scriptures were written by men who were inspired by God because no man has the intellect on his own to foretell the things to come that have unfolded in chronological order as stated in the Bible. Has the Bible been tampered with? Yes, but those who desire truth and discernment shall find them if they pray and seek God for knowledge and wisdom.

I would rather have an imaginary God than no God at all. My faith in God and my spiritual belief system has worked for my good. Let's look at an example: A doctor can give two people the same diagnosis and prognosis of a death sentence—one will live and the other one will die shortly thereafter. The difference is their faith in God and their belief system.

We take chances every day on one thing or another, such as: Paying into Social Security for a supplemental income, playing the slot machines, a job that offers a great retirement plan. I'd rather take my chances on believing that there is a God who hears me, who can heal me, who can deliver me out of any and all situations, and that there is life after death. It works for me. Without this hope, there would be no hope. Having God in my life works for me.

My mother died when I was five years old. She collapsed while pressing my sister's hair. When the doctor came to our house, I heard him say to my older sister, "God will be your mother and your father." I have never forgotten those words. As years went by, even into my adult life when I was troubled or confused, an angel would appear in the corner of my room that comforted me. Once when I was in the hospital, I heard a knock on the hospital window. When I looked, I saw an angel, the same angel that I always see. When I looked at her, she smiled and disappeared. I knew then that all would be well, as always. Because of my faith and belief system, I am healed from Lupus, and I have faced and conquered many other giants in my life.

Our forefathers changed their dismal plight from slaves to greatness via their faith in God and their spiritual belief system. It was by faith that Dr. Martin Luther King Jr. could see that one day, blacks would be judged by their character versus the color of their skin.

A person without hope is a person who is destined for despair. And if your hope is in this world's system, you are destined for despair. Please know that without hope life becomes meaningless. During my life, there were times when I cried out to everybody reachable—but to no avail. When I cried out to God, my situation changed for the good. This has happened so many times.

I cannot prove to you that there is a God; however, I can tell you this: My faith in God and my spiritual belief system is what has kept me safe and sane for all these 68 years. I would rather believe in God than not to believe at all. Believing in God and having faith in God works for me. I'd rather have an imaginary God than to have no God. **Don't be caught without God.**

I WANT TO ENCOURAGE YOU TO BE MORE THANKFUL

Hello, this is Dr. Rosie, and I want to encourage you to be more thankful.

You will attract more by being thankful for what you have versus complaining about what you don't have. If you want more, then, plant more and your harvest will be greater. A prudent farmer plants seeds versus sitting at the "WISHING WELL" wishing for a great crop. As and ex-farmer, I learned how to get an increase from any and every crop. I am just saying--do your part and watch the crop grow. BE THANKFUL EVERYDAY AND IN EVERY WAY.

Hello, this is Dr. Rosie, "IF NO ONE ENCOURAGES YOU, ENCOURAGE YOURSELF

In spite of what you are going through, God is still good. May I comfort your heart by saying to you that whatever you went through in 2015, you did not go through it alone—God was right there running alone beside you—but you may have been too busy fussing, mumbling, and having your pity party that you could not see Him running alone beside you reaching for your hand which you did not extend toward Him. I get tickle sometimes when I think of what a gentleman God is. He is not pushy; He is not all loud like some folks. People are so used to noise, loudness, fast-talking and over-talking people until they just cannot hear the soft gentle voice of God. God's voice is so sweet and gentle and since He does not come with the routine BLING: therefore, we don't see Him—we miss out on God so many times.

I am saying all of that to say this: Let's drown out some of the noise, fine tune your heart and ears and listen up for what God is saying to you in 2016. And one more thing, stop always begging God and start thanking Him for what He has done and what He is going to do. Show appreciation and thankfulness for the little thing and just maybe you may get more without even asking. A thankful heart touches the heart of others.

Leave all the hurt, pain and disappointment baggage that you collected last year behind, don't be a hoarder. LET GO AND LET GOD! And one more thing, stop staying up all night worrying. If you pray, don't worry. Have faith in the fact that God is capable of doing above what you can think to ask Him to do. I see it like this, since God is a 24/7 watchman, I am going to get me at least 8 hours of sleep no matter what is going on. I am not that smart, but I have gained a little wisdom over these 70 years and I want to share with you—you will be okay—God got your back and your children's back too, so chill because God is real.

BE THANKFUL

Merry Christmas to all and have a Happy New Year. Be thankful for whatever you have and know that you are blessed above many. At least you have your life and whatever you need to change, you have the opportunity to do so. Do not focus on what you do not have but give Praise for what you do have. Enjoy your family, tell them you love them and if you don't love them, talk it out and make amends. It's time to mend relationships; it will be good for them as well as for you. It's really no time to hold on to unforgiveness---God has forgiven you for all your mess and silly mistakes and wrong doing. Realize that most people are doing the best they know how and be thankful that you know better and that is why you are doing better.

While you and your family are all together this year, take a little time to discuss important issues such as: Do you have a Will or Living Trust Do you have a Power of Attorney for Health and Finance, If you have a special need child or adult, have you made plans as to what would happen to them if you made your transition, ask if they have an insurance policy and do someone know where the policy is, ask if they have a beneficiary on their life insurance and on their bank accounts. And last but not least, if they have a Living Trust, ask if the player in the trust are still alive or still mentally okay, if not they need to amend their Trust and Power of Attorney. Ask if they have cemetery property and is everything paid in full such as: the opening and closing and the casket.

If you need help with any of the above, remember, I am Los Angeles's Best Senior Estate Planner, call me at 213-400-6521 or call my office at 323-750-3592.

Much love to you.

DEVELOP A PLAN FOLR SUCCESS

Hello, this is Dr. Rosie and' "I AM JUST SAYING" If you want to have a successful life, you must develop a plan for success. An unwritten plan is impossible to follow. You should spend more time planning your future than planning your vacation. And know that everything becomes an emergency when you do not have an emergency plan. Bottom line is this: Have a Plan.

GET YOUR FINANCIAL HOUSE IN ORDER NOW!

Get your financial house in order now! Here's what you must do: Make sure each of your family members have life insurance. If you own real estate property or if your assets are valued over $150,000, having a Living Trust prepared will avoid the high cost of legal fees and Probate fees—this is money that can go to your loved ones.

If your credit scores are low, restore your credit immediately. (If your credit is not good, and the value of your parents' estate is high, you will not be able to get a bond, therefore, you cannot be the executor/executrix over their estate and whoever is appointed, they will receive the same fee as the attorney.

Make sure there is a beneficiary on all your banks accounts, IRAs and etc., if not, and depend on the value of your accounts, they may have to go through Probate Court.

All adults need to have a Power Of Attorney for Health and Financial matters, if this is not in place when needed, someone will have to go to court and become your conservator—this is very expensive. You must have these document prepared while you are in your right mind. Make sure you and your loved ones have a current Driver's License or California I.D. from the Department of Motor Vehicle, it will be needed when having a document notarized.

These are the services we provide: Revocable Living Trust, Wills, Power of Attorneys, Credit Restoration and Notary service. We can refer you to a trust worthy insurance agents who we work with. Call for FREE A CONSULTATION.

COME ON FAMILY AND DO THE RIGHT THING!!!

DON'T LET PAST HURTS, PAIN AND ABUSE BLOCK GOD'S BLESSINGS FOR YOU

This is Dr. Rosie, "AND I AM JUST SAYING" We have all had our share of hurts, pain, physical or mental abuse, being lied on, taken advantage of, having people borrow money and not back you back. My message to you is this: " It's not what people do to you that blocks God's blessing for you, it's the attitude and behavior you adopt for yourself because of what other have done to you. These undeserving and unwarranted life experiences cause you to develop callous on your soul, a wall around your heart, blinder over your eyes and a spirit of deafness when it comes to hearing what God is saying to you.

When you allow hurt, pains and disappointments put the words, "NEVER AGAIN WILL I" upon your lips and in your spirit; you have closed your ears to God. You have decided you are in charge of your life henceforth and forever. I hear people say, I am always the one giving and helping others and nobody ever gives to me. Let me pause and preach a little bit. You have got it twisted. This should not be a "Complaint" but a "Praise" You ought to be thanking and praising God that you are the blessed one. You are the blessed one because you are able to be the Joseph in the time of famine. You had better hush your mouth from complaining and open your mouth for praising— somebody needs to say AMEN.

If you are the one who is always giving and always helping, can't you see that you are the blessed one? You are blessed when you are the lender and not the borrower. When you are blessed be it with money, time, talent, you are required to share. The Holy Bible tells us that "Whom much is given , much is required" So, shut your month and stop leading the complaint team and join the praise team.

I have had many family members and friends say to me, I know you are not going to help this or that person after all he/she has done to you. Many times I tried to sneak and help him/her hoping my family and friends would not know. But God spoke to me and said these words, who blessed you with the time, talent, money to be able to help other, was it your family and friends or was it Me? You know what I did? I shut my mouth. I rather hear from God than man/woman.

I have been able to melt many stony hearts, remove callous off of many souls and have caused many to rethink putting a coma where they had put a period as a result of me listening to and being obedient to God's words rather than man/woman.. If you are saying the following statements listed below, you have closed your heart and ears to God, and you have allowed your past hurt, pain and disappointments to block the blessings that God has for you because you can no longer hear and obey Him. Below are a list of phrases the can block God's blessings upon your life and cause you to disobey and reject God's gestures and plans for your life.1) I will never ever help anybody else, 2)I will never loan money again to anybody, not even a family member, 3) I will never trust anybody, 4)I will never join another church, 5) I will never get married again, 6) I will never forgive him/her. 7) I will never speak to him/her again, etc. etc. etc.

What I am saying is, the word *never* should only be used in this sentence: I will never turn a deaf ear to the voice of God. Remember, happiness is: Discerning the voice of God and obeying Him. Remember this, you are not perfect and you have caused hurt pain and disappointment in somebody's life knowing or unknowingly—you have. It is of the Lord's mercies that we are not consumed, because His compassions fail not. Move pass your hurt, pain and disappointments, and become the person that God has called you to be. GO AND GET YOUR BLESSINGS!

SECTION 3: ARTICLES AND LETTERS REGARDING FAMILY AFFAIRS

GRANDMOTHERS CAN CHANGE THE DISMAL ILLITERACY PLIGHT FOR BLACK CHILDREN

Helen Carter-Johnson, a grandmother and resident of Long Beach, California, saw a need for grandparents to step up to the plate to inspire Black children to read with the release of her latest literary work, a book of short stories inspired by her grandchildren's journey, *Golden Memories Of Childhood: Fun And Inspirational Reading For Parents And Their Young Children*. Technology and electronic gadgets have put distance between parents and children. However, stories like those told in Carter-Johnson's book can bring back family time and make reading enjoyable, fun and entertaining.

In the United States, 60 to 70% of African-American households are headed by a woman and there are many reasons for such conditions such as: Black men feeling financially inadequate to get married and to take on the responsibility of having a family, the premise of Black families being separated during slavery, the fact that Black men were forced to leave their families in the fifties and sixties so their wives and children could get public assistance. (Remember the movie, *Claudine*, where the mother would be denied public assistance if a man was in the house, which was not the case for a white family who needed financial assistance.) Black men being incarcerated at an alarming rate for minor infractions, and doing longer prison/jail time and being denied jobs upon their release are one of many reasons, and the list goes on…

Women rearing children alone need much help. Many single women are very frustrated having to be mother and father and bread-winner for the family. Many have to work two jobs or are working and going to school in hopes of improving their financial condition. These women are tired when they come home and do not have the time or stamina to help their children learn to read. They feed their children, help them with their homework and send them to bed. This is a time and circumstance when a grandmother is needed to assist. It used to be that way. However, we are witnessing the after effect of the "Babies having babies syndrome," a fallout from the "Free Style" of the 60s, and teens being able to get their own welfare check, moving out from the house of "Wisdom" and creating havoc for their lives and the lives of their children.

Facts according to The Census Bureau: One in 10 American children lived in a home with a grandparent in 2009, a 64% jump from two decades ago. While the vast majority of the 7.8 million children living with grandparents were in "three-generation" families, almost a quarter of those children were being raised by their grandparents alone. Hispanic and Black families have long had higher percentages of homes with grandparents—in 1991, 12% of Hispanic children and 15% of black children lived with a grandparent in the home. Those numbers rose to 14% and 17%, respectively, in 2009.

I have provided you with facts regarding children who live with grandparents. However, I am focusing on Black grandmothers because they too are in most cases head of their household, so I am talking about Black grandmothers—not grandparents. If the truth be told, Black people, in general, are more disenfranchised and have a higher illiteracy rate than foreign students here in America.

There are many Black grandmothers who are rearing their grandchildren. And there are more elderly Blacks who are unemployed than other races. With this being said, Black grandmothers need to step up to the plate and teach their grandchildren to read, write and proper manners, which is what we call behavior today. Manners in the olden days meant saying "Thank you," and "Please," washing your hands before you eat and after using the bathroom, addressing grown folks as Mr. and Mrs., blessing your food, saying your prayers before going to bed, respecting and obeying adults and doing unto others as you want them to do unto you.

Literacy is everybody's business and we must see it as such. It's time to replace some of the electronic gadgets with books. Reading is the basic foundation of education and reading is what's necessary to help one gain entrance into a life of success. Carter-Johnson issues a plea for grandmothers to get involved, now!

I beg of you to get involved and I strongly believe that reading with your children from *Golden Memories Of Childhood: Fun And Inspirational Reading For Parents And Their Young Children* is a great start. I purchased it for my grandchildren and their parents. Come on grandmothers and do what is right—help teach your grandchildren to read. Literacy is everybody's business. The next time your grandchildren are around, assess their reading skills by having them to read to grandma. If they are reluctant, know for sure they have a reading problem; after all children love to show off their skills to grandma.

BLACK FATHERLESS MEN ARE HURTING, TOO

Boys need fathers in their lives. I am making a plea to African-American fathers to be active participants in the lives of their sons; and for African-American women to assist these fathers in the transition of their reentering the lives of their sons.

Most every ill that plagues the Black male child is mostly related to fatherlessness. Having a father as a role model and teacher is critical for a male child. The male who understands this best is the male child whose father was present, and participated, in his life. Unfortunately, for many Black males, they have not had the experience of having a father role model. A male child who did not have his father present cannot relate to the critical differences it makes, for he has no comparison to make. Therefore, it becomes easy for him, as an adult, to abandon his son; especially, when it becomes a challenge to be a part of his life.

In addition, I believe that we must revisit history as we examine the family structure of Blacks in America. An absentee father was the norm for the African-American family. Families were separated by force! Slavery severely impacted the lives of the Black family. Considering the fact that our physical exodus from slavery has only been 140 years, that's not a long time, and we are still experiencing its effects.

Blacks were forced to produce offsprings, not for themselves, but for their master's economic gain. Today, Blacks are not forced to produce babies; however, because of the residual effect of slavery on the Black family, their offsprings continue to be an economic product for the modern-day master called "PRISON." Today, in 2005, Black males in prison are paid less for their labor than they were paid 140 years ago.

Black men were not socialized as other men, that is, to be accountable or responsible for his family. In order to understand why the Black man and Black woman are having such challenges in their relationships, you must understand how their experience and living conditions in America have impacted their lives and the lives of their family.

When a Black family needed assistance from Social Services' programs, the father had to remove himself from the family in order for his wife and children to get assistance. Black men have a long way to go to get back to their African roots of being a provider and protector. Black men have come a long way, and they will get back to their God-Created-Nature, with the help of God, Almighty, and with the understanding of their past.

It is the responsibility of the father to help provide for his child. And providing entails more than financial provisions. I'm pleading with women, to not prevent the father from being a part of his son's life because of the father's inability to support financially. A male child needs his father in his life, and the woman only hurts her son(s) when she tries to prevent them from having a father-son relationship. The many ills of Black men are inevitably traced to their Fatherlessness.

Most Black men really want to be with their families and children. What they need is someone to be a father-like figure for them. A Black man needs guidance. Most of them are trying to be something or somebody that they have never seen or experienced, and must be taught that. The woman's ideal of what a man is supposed to be is distorted because she too has not experience a father in her life.

You see, a father is a role model for his son and a father gives definition to his daughter as to what a man is. A mother is a role model for her daughter and she gives definition to her son as to what a woman is. 70% of Black households are headed and ran by a female with the father most times being totally out of the picture. The sons and daughters are both confused about male/female responsibility.

Many men are not allowed to have relationships with their children. If these men are allowed to participate in their children's lives, it must be on the woman's terms only. When it becomes unbearable, he leaves the woman and the child behind. The real victim is the child.

There are some things that a man needs to teach his son, such as: how to bathe and clean his genital area, how to shop for clothing, how to choose his friends, how to respect himself, how to drive an automobile, how to resolve conflicts, how to fight, how to avoid a fight, how to play sports.

I am not casting blame on the Black woman. I am only pointing out the facts that are hindering the progress of the Black family. I believe that if we could get a perspective of the Black man, as related to who is who he was before coming to America and what America has made him become, then we would have a better understanding of our family dynamics and we can embrace each other and begin to value ourselves and our children again.

Look for the follow-up article, "Why Black Men/Women Suffer Failed and Unhealthy Relationships."

Dr. Rosie Milligan, Counselor/Author: Author of Negroes, Colored People, Black, African-Americans in America—Nigger, Please—Satisfying The Black Man Sexually—Satisfying The Black Woman Sexually and Why Black Men Choose White Women.

BLACK BOYS NEED THE EMOTIONAL SUPPORT OF THEIR FATHER

As a family counselor, I must stress the importance of Black Fatherhood. "Boys need fathers in their lives." I am making a plea to African-American fathers to be active participants in the lives of their sons; and for African-American women to assist these fathers in the transition of their reentering the lives of their sons.

I contend that most every ill that plagues the Black male child is mostly related to fatherlessness. Having a father as a role model and teacher is critical for a male child. The male who understands this best is the male child whose father was present, and participated, in his life. Unfortunately, for many Black males, they have not had the experience of having a father role model. A male child who did not have his father present cannot relate to the critical difference it makes, for he has no comparison to make. Therefore, it becomes easy for him, as an adult, to abandon his son; especially, when it becomes a challenge to be a part of his life.

In addition, I believe that we must revisit history as we examine the family structure of Blacks in America. An absentee father was the norm for the African-American family. Families were separated by force! Slavery severely impacted the lives of the Black family. Considering the impact that our physical exodus from slavery has only been for 138 years, that's not a long time, we are still experiencing its long reach effects.

Blacks were forced to produce offsprings, not for themselves, but for their master's economic gain. Today, Blacks are not forced to produce babies; however, because of the residual effect of slavery on the Black family, their offsprings continue to be an economic product for the modern day master called "PRISON." Today, in 2003, Black males are paid less for their labor than they were paid 138 years ago.

Black men were not socialized as other men, that is, to be accountable or responsible for his family. When a Black family needed assistance from Social Services' programs, the father had to remove himself from the family in order for his wife and children to get assistance. Black men have a long way to go to get back to their African roots of being a provider and protector. Black men have come a long way, and they will get back to their God-Created-Nature, with the help of God, Almighty, and with the understanding of their past.

Keeping a family intact is every person's business. It is the responsibility of the father to help provide for his child. Providing entails more than financial provisions. Again, I am making a plea to women, to not prevent the father from being a part of his son's life because of the father's inability to support financially. A male child needs his father in his life, and the woman only hurts her son(s) when she tries to prevent them from having a father-son relationship. You can trace the many ills of Black men to their *Fatherlessness*.

According to research, 63% of youth suicides are from fatherless homes; 90% of all homeless and runaway children are from fatherless homes; 85% of all children that exhibit behavioral disorders come from fatherless homes; 71% of high school dropouts come from fatherless homes; 75% of all adolescents patients in chemical abuse centers come from fatherless homes; 70% of juveniles in institutions come from fatherless homes; 85% of all youths sitting in prisons grew up in a fatherless home.

A PLEA TO BLACK WOMEN—DO NOT BLOCK YOUR SONS FROM SEEING THEIR FATHERS

Boys need fathers in their lives. I am making a plea to African-American fathers to be active participants in the lives of their sons, and for African-American women to assist these fathers in the transition of their reentrance into the lives of their sons.

Most every ill that plagues the Black male child is mostly related to fatherlessness. Having a father as a role model and teacher is critical for a male child. The male who understands this best is the male child whose father was present and participated in his life. Unfortunately, for many Black males, they have not had the experience of having a father role model. A male child who did not have his father present cannot relate to the critical differences it makes, for he has no comparison to make. Therefore, it becomes easy for him, as an adult, to abandon his son; especially when it becomes a challenge to be a part of his life.

In addition, I believe that we must revisit history as we examine the family structure of Blacks in America. An absentee father was the norm for the African-American family. Families were separated by force! Slavery severely impacted the lives of the Black family. Considering the fact that our physical exodus from slavery has only been 140 years, that's not a long time, and we are still experiencing its effects.

Blacks were forced to produce offspring, not for themselves, but for their master's economic gain. Today, Blacks are not forced to produce babies; however, because of the residual effect of slavery on the Black family, their offspring continue to be an economic product for the modern-day master called "PRISON." Today, in 2005, Black males in prison are paid less for their labor than they were paid 140 years ago.

Black men were not socialized as other men, that is, to be accountable or responsible for their family. In order to understand why the Black man and Black woman are having such challenges in their relationships, you must understand how their experience and living conditions in America have impacted their lives and the lives of their family.

When a Black family needed assistance from Social Services' programs, the father had to remove himself from the family in order for his wife and children to get assistance. Black men have a long way to go to get back to their African roots of being a provider and protector. Black men have come a long way, and they will get back to their God-Created-Nature, with the help of God Almighty and with the understanding of their past.

It is the responsibility of the father to help provide for his child. And providing entails more than financial provisions. I'm pleading with women to not prevent the father from being a part of his son's life because of the father's inability to support financially. A male child needs his father in his life, and the woman only hurts her son(s) when she tries to prevent him from having a father-son relationship. The many ills of Black men are inevitably traced to their fatherlessness.

The Black man, his wife, and his children all had to look to the white man for food, clothing, and shelter. In essence, the wife and children provided for themselves; they worked side by side with the Black man in the field from sun up to sun down. The Black man could not protect his family. The white man impregnated his wife and daughters and there was nothing that the Black man could do about it, if he wanted a place to live and if he wanted to live.

The white man positioned himself as the surrogate parent for Blacks, giving them the illusion that he was their caretaker while he abused them, molested their children, and raped their women. He, the white man, was in charge. If the Black man did something to his wife and she felt he was out of order or she did not consider it was proper treatment, she would tell the white man on her husband and he would talk to, punish, or beat the Black man. As you can see, the Black man could neither provide for nor protect his family.

When Blacks were so-called freed from slavery, there was no economical provisions made for them to provide for their families. Therefore, many of them had to continue to be beholding to their masters under the same harsh conditions. Some families were able to leave the plantations and move up North with family members to start a new life.

Many men left their families behind; they left to secure a job and then sent back for their families. Men who resisted the abusive treatment or who refused to be treated as less than a man had to flee, find work, and send back for his wife and children. The pain, the heartache, and the financial struggle was so much to bear; therefore, some of them never looked back, went back, or sent back for their families.

The Black man had to always pretend about something. He was not free to express his true emotions. He had to grin and pretend that he was happy in the presence of his master, because being unhappy was disturbing to the master. Being unhappy equated to one possibly thinking for himself or just thinking of running away. The Black man could not show his feelings towards a woman for fear that the master would ship him or her to another plantation.

You see, the white man knows the value, power, and strength of being a family or having a sense of family unity; therefore, he did not want to see Blacks socialized to be an intact family unit. After all, being an ideal family for Blacks was not good for the white man's economy. The Black man was not brought here to start a family; he was brought here for economic profit, to work for free, and to produce as many babies by as many women as possible, so that he could deliver more workers for his master.

Feelings and emotions were almost beaten out of the Black man. In fact, it was detrimental for him to express feelings and show emotions. He was safer when he was a man of few words, for he knew the consequences if he was misunderstood when communicating. Black fathers passed their behaviors and experiences down to their sons as a safety precaution. Black men could only show emotions and feelings at church or at a funeral service, and during the time of intimacy with his woman or wife.

During slavery, sex and family was the only enjoyment that was within the economic reach for the Black man. Even today, 2005, sex is the only form of gratification for the average economically challenged Black man. He cannot get on his yacht, or take a cruise on weekends, etc. He cannot buy expensive toys to play with; he does not have a get-away home.

Therefore, sex becomes the only reachable pleasure for him. Sex becomes his pleasure, his tranquilizer, his drug, his everything. As an escape from pain, racism, and injustice, sex is like a safe haven. It's like returning to your mother's womb where there is comfort — where you are free of the cares of the world and no one can hurt you there.

Black men's emotions, feelings, and dialogue are still guarded even in his relationship with his wife, because if either is misinterpreted, he is placed in the "dog house" and the one thing that he cherishes the most — sex — is taken away from him; and he does not function well without it.

Most Black men really want to be with their families and children. What they need is someone to be a father-like figure for them. A Black man needs guidance. Most of them are trying to be something or somebody that they have never seen or experienced, and must be taught that. The woman's ideal of what a man is supposed to be is distorted because she, too, has not experienced a father in her life.

You see, a father is a role model for his son and a father gives definition to his daughter as to what a man is. A mother is a role model for her daughter and she gives definition to her son as to what a woman is. Seventy percent of Black households are headed and run by a female with the father, most times, being totally out of the picture. The sons and daughters are both confused about male/female responsibility.

The son sees the mother as a nurturer and the provider. All of his life he has been provided for by a female — his mother, grandmother — both females. Being cared for all one's life by a female is a familiar comfort, and this familiar comfort is what makes it easy for a male to allow and to feel comfortable having his woman/wife to take care of him, because that has been his experience.

The daughter of the broken home experiences her mother as the sole provider; therefore, she takes on the role of her mother and she will accept a man into her life who does not have the means to provide for himself, and she will have a baby with him. When the responsibility of providing becomes overwhelming, she lashes out at the one who she perceives deserves the blame — her man/husband.

The male is now frustrated, insecure, and unsure of what to do. He now feels that she got what she wanted from him — a baby — and now that is the only person who matters to her. He now begins to feel like the outsider, the insignificant intruder. When he can no longer take the pressure, he leaves or she leaves him, or she puts him out since she has the baby.

The drama is on. He could not provide the help needed when they were together, and now he has to provide shelter for himself and she now expects more monetary support from him than he could give while living with her. Recall that in the first place, she knew of his financial status, and second, she made the decision to have the baby without his consent or permission.

He is no longer allowed to have any relationship with his child. If he is allowed to participate in his child's life, it must be on her terms **only**. When it becomes unbearable, he leaves the woman and the child behind. The real victim is the child.

I am not casting blame on the Black woman. I am only pointing out the facts that are hindering the progress of the Black family. I believe that if we could get a perspective of the Black man, as related to who he was before coming to America and what America has made him become, then we would have a better understanding of our family dynamics and we can embrace each other and begin to value ourselves and our children again.

FAMILIES MUST DISCUSS DEATH, DYING, AND INCAPACITATION

While death, dying, and incapacitation may not be a pleasant topic for discussion—it is necessary. We all agree that we will die. We buy life insurance, make Wills, and prepare Living Trusts because we are cognizant of death as being imminent. We buy disability insurance and long-term insurance to protect us should we become disabled in our old age. However, these topics are not a table-topic family discussion in most homes. Why?

In Chapter Three of my book *Creating a New You in Six Weeks Made Simple*, I discuss the importance of having a family meeting. I provide safe and friendly rules for having a productive, fruitful, and a purpose-driven family meeting. It is a good time to have dialogue about these issues and a time to make plans for such an occurrence.

I was motivated to write this article after witnessing the devastation of a senior in the community. Here is her story: She and her husband were both receiving Social Security allotments, and he also received a retirement check which was not transferable upon his death. Their combined income was $2,400 per month. The wife's allotment for Social Security was $900; her husband's Social Security was $1,100; and his retirement check amounted to $400, a combined income of $1,500 for him. Their rent was $1,450 per month, which did not include utilities, phone bill, etc. The wife and husband both had to pay a portion of their medicine cost, and both were very ill.

Soon, the husband passed away. The household income changed drastically. No longer was it $2,400 per month. Now it was only $1,100 monthly, less than half of what the household income had previously been. The husband's private retirement check stopped upon his death, and the wife was only able to receive one Social Security check, not two. She was given the greater amount of the two Social Security checks. (Remember that a surviving spouse is not permitted to receive both the deceased person's Social Security check as well as her/his own. The smaller one of the two will be terminated.)

I contacted a senior citizen housing facility for the widow, which would cost her $682 per month for rent. Her monthly income is only $1,100 per month now, and she has to pay out of pocket a large portion of her medication costs until her medical benefits kick in. Not only did this woman lose her husband, he was also her caretaker. She lost her husband, caretaker, and she lost his income. She is now facing eviction four months after his death and will have to seek residence in a homeless facility. I asked her, "Did you and your husband ever discuss how either of you would survive if either of you died?" She said, "No, we never had such a discussion, but I thought about it at times. In fact, I thought he would die first because he had been very sick for many years, but during the last six months, I became very ill and he had to take care of me. You just never know."

Is this couple alone in being ill prepared for death, dying, and incapacitation? The answer is a resounding NO. Unfortunately, this is a common scenario for many couples, not just elderly couples, but for couples in general. I must remind you, the reader, that death does not discriminate when it comes to age; therefore, we must all prepare for death, dying, and incapacitation.

When a family member is facing death, it can become a tremendous burden on the family going back and forth to the hospital, knowing that the family member's prognosis is grave. Family members develop great strife among themselves when one sibling has to assume most of the caregiving responsibilities, while others do nothing more than talk, make suggestions, and many times criticize the one who is doing all the labor and making all the sacrifices. This situation sometimes causes family members to be alienated forever. All of this could be avoided if the family would have a meaningful discussion about end-of-life decisions and they let their wishes regarding death/dying and incapacitation be known prior to their health decline.

We cannot continue to avoid planning for and talking about death/dying and incapacitation. We must make our choice about how we want to die as well as making choices about how we want to live. Families should have discussions regarding long-term skilled nursing facilities and their choice to die in a hospital or at home under hospice care.

Dr. Rosie Milligan

As a nurse, I provided hospice care for my best friend who chose to make her transition from her home, being surrounded by her loved ones and friends. She was very ill and eventually died from cancer. But it was so beautiful because the times when she felt well during her sickness, she would share, laugh, and we would all gather around and sing songs. She would often ask me to sing particular songs, and she would sing along with us. And when she made her transition, there were approximately 30 of her family members at her bedside. She left so peacefully—no strain or struggle, no machines or tubes—and she looked so beautiful, so peaceful.

We should make our choices about how we want to live and die. When we make our wishes known to our family members, it takes away all assumptions and the guesswork. It takes away the confusion that family members can cause and makes home going for our loved ones "sweet" versus "bitter." Family, let's talk—it's necessary. There is one thing for sure that you must realize: one day, YOU WILL DIE! AND YOU MAY BECOME SICK OR INCAPACITATED FIRST. In the meantime, how you live and how you die should be your choice! Make your choice today and share it with your family

"IT'S TIME TO GET IN YOUR PARENTS' BUSINESS"

As the Bible tells us, there's a time for all things, and it is definitely a time to get in your parents' business. As a professional estate planner, a woman of God, a Hospice nurse, and an elder, I have witnessed enough—and enough is enough now!

During 2010, I knew of 10 people who died and seven out of 10 had no life insurance, no burial policy, and no money in the bank to cover their funeral expenses. When there is no plan made for departing this life, it poses a great hardship on the loved ones left behind. Today, as we face many economic crises, we must all become more conscientious about the cost involved in making our earthly transition. It's expensive for a birth and so it is with a death, and financial preparation is necessary for both.

It's not out of line to get in your parents' business. In fact, there are circumstances that dictate a need to do so. Death is a promise, and with death comes a price. Many of our elders suffer from dementia and Alzheimer's, and both of these diseases cause memory loss, mental incompetency, and create decision-making challenges. Even though our parents may have made preparations for death expenses during their lifetime, sometimes they simply fail to pay their life insurance policy, causing the policy to lapse. They may have totally paid for a burial plot or crypt but never told anyone, and the paperwork may have been lost.

What I am saying is, sit yourself down and converse eyeball to eyeball with your parents and gather pertinent information that's necessary to assure their well-being—mentally, physically, emotionally, and financially. Remember, when people are challenged with dementia, Alzheimer's, or other forms of senility, they don't come and tell you that they suffer from these challenges. In fact, they are not even aware that they have a problem. When you try to point out their problem to them, they think that you are the problem. Eventually, I will do a follow-up article on what signs to look for regarding dementia and Alzheimer's disease.

This is the type of information that you need to obtain from your parents:
1) Their doctors' names and telephone numbers

2) The location of their will, trust, insurance policies, and cemetery papers.

3) The location of their safe deposit box. (If your loved one should die and you do not have access to their safe deposit box (meaning your name is not on the account) and you cannot locate the safe deposit box key, it could cost you nearly $300 to have the box opened. The banker will only allow you to take out the will, trust, and insurance policies.)

4) Their bank accounts, name and address of their banks, and if they have a named beneficiary on the accounts.

5) Their stocks and bonds, IRAs, etc.

6) Determine if they have an Advanced Healthcare Directive (Power of Attorney for health care) and Durable Power of Attorney (Power of Attorney for financial matters). If they do not have these documents, explain the importance to them. If there are signs of senility and forgetfulness, ask to see their bills, mortgage payments, insurance policies, utility bills, and call to make sure they are being paid.

7) Find out if they have a written description of how they want their burial service to be handled.

8) If they have real property or assets valued over $100,000, talk to them about a living trust; if the property or assets are under $100,000, talk to them about a will. If they cannot pay for a living trust, suggest that the beneficiaries pay for it. After all, the money saved by avoiding attorney, probate, and other fees will be monies for the beneficiaries.

Following is a quote from *Women's' Guide to the Insurance Industry* by Chris Rodgers.

LOST LEGACY

"It is estimated that up to 40 percent of insurance policies and annuities go unclaimed (maturity) each year. This is due to death or incapacity (sickness). Most are 'forgotten' about, plans from old company employer's retirement, bank safe deposit boxes, secret hiding places, new residency, foreign country, and general gifts. Not surprising is the fact that this situation was due to people 'not' informing family, godparents and trustees of prearranged purchases. This is one secret you should not keep."

I heard of a case where a brother had paid for the funeral expenses for his sister. He later discovered while clearing out her house that she had a crypt and funeral arrangements had already been paid in full.

Come on, family, we *are* our brothers' keeper. Let's be family for real. Let's start having more personal conversations. And yes, *it's okay* to get in your parents' business. Be there for them.

"IT'S TIME TO GET IN YOUR CHILDREN'S BUSINESS"

As a professional expert estate planner for more than a decade, I can tell you from an eye witnessed view point that it's time to stick your nose in your children's business. I will address the five areas of concern that you ought to make a part of your business. These areas are: spiritual, mental/emotional, physical, financial, and sexual. Let's start with spiritual business.

SPIRITUAL BUSINESS: It's time to ask your children some questions, such as: If you should die today, where would you spend eternity? Do you understand God's plan of salvation? Read with them Romans 10:9–10. Let them know that no one is perfect and that God extends His salvation and protection to imperfect people. In fact, God gave His only begotten son's life to redeem imperfect people. We often hear people say, I don't *feel* saved. Let your children know that salvation is not a feeling; it's about what the Word of God says. Pray with your children. Let your children see you praying at home and not just in church.

MENTAL/EMOTIONAL BUSINESS: Ask your children how they are doing mentally and emotionally. Observe their behavior and mood changes. It's important to pay close attention since depression and suicide are on the rise due to the recession and the often accompanying depression which causes people to feel insecure, inadequate, uncertain, despair, and hopelessness. Communicate with your children face-to-face as much as possible or talk to them often via telephone. By doing so, you can detect when things are not well with them. You can hear it in their voices—pay attention to your gut feelings and instinct.

If you think they are depressed or using drugs or alcohol, confront them in a concerned, loving, caring manner and tell them your suspicions. They will probably lie, but just continue to observe and lovingly confront them. If they tell you they are depressed, believe them and seek help for them. Be aware of behavioral changes, such as: avoidance, silence, being withdrawn, snappy, and giving only short responses.

PHYSICAL BUSINESS: Do not be afraid to inquire about your children's health. Pay attention to any lack of energy and obesity. Encourage them to have a physical examination annually. Ask if they have health insurance. If they don't, be resourceful and help them to find a free clinic or medical services where payment is based on one's ability to pay. Pay attention to them if they complain of being tired often or sleep too much. This could be a sign of depression, anemia, diabetes, or other health challenges. If they urinate frequently and are excessively thirsty, hungry a lot, and/or losing weight, they could be diabetic. After all, diabetics is rampant among adults and children.

Be an example for your children. Talk openly to them about your own health. Let them see you having annual checkups. Let them see you being physical, like walking and exercising, eating healthy foods, and avoiding fast foods. Remember children imitate their parents. If they see you cooking home meals, they will grow up to do the same; it will become a healthy lifestyle for them. Teach them to include vitamins and mineral supplements in their diets, especially since our foods are mostly nutrient bankrupt and the soil's mineral content has been depleted by 85%. (Be on the lookout for my article "Nine Reasons People Get Sick.") Bodies come only one per customer. And if your body is the temple of God, then treat it as such. Health is a matter of choice—your choice. Help your children to choose a healthy lifestyle and to practice prevention by eating healthy, reading about health issues, and having annual examinations.

FINANCIAL BUSINESS: Ask how your children are doing financially. Be blunt. Find out if they are paying their bills on time. Do they have a savings account? Do they have life insurance? Do they have a beneficiary on their life insurance policy and their bank account? These are important questions because if a person dies having a large amount of money in the bank without a designated beneficiary, it will have to go to probate court incurring court and attorney fees and a long waiting period before the funds will become available to be used by loved ones who may need the funds.

If you pay close attention to what your child is saying, doing, and how he/she is acting, you will pick up clues that something may be wrong. If you see that they are struggling, offer advice or assistance when possible. Many times children will not ask for help, especially if they know you are not doing well financially. Ask if they would like to move back home, pay less rent, and save more money until their financial situation improves. Do not apply pressure by setting definite time limits, like six months to a year. However, make sure that they are saving their money or paying off bills and not buying unnecessary things and wasting their money; otherwise, your helping them will have been in vain.

Teach them how to make a budget. A good budget plan is important. It must include all expenses, and spending includes tithes, vacations, holidays, subscriptions, entertainment, medications, etc. Go to my Web site **www.911forblackamerica.com**. Scroll down to the bottom of the home page and click on join our mailing list. Provide your e-mail address and I will send you a comprehensive sample budget.

If you have made bad financial decisions, point them out to your children. Be honest so they can learn from your mistakes and avoid making the same mistakes. After all, it's harder to recover from financial mistakes during these difficult times.

SEXUAL BUSINESS: Do not shy away from talking about sex. After eating, sex is the next most-sought-after drive—so let's talk about sex! With HIV, herpes, many other sexually transmittable diseases, the high rate of abortions and unwanted babies being born and teenage pregnancies, how can we neglect talking about sex? We must come to grips with double standards for our girls and boys and began to teach sexual accountability and responsibility to both males and females alike. Why is the curfew different for girls than boys? I truly believe that if parents were not concerned about their daughter becoming pregnant by staying out late at night, their daughters would have the same curfew hours as the boys.

Nighttime may be the most conducive time for parents to have sex, but for teens, there is no set time. In fact, many have sex in your house during the day while you are at work if you allow your daughters to have boys over to your home when you or other adults are not at home. They have sex when you are home, if their room is off-limits to you and if it's okay for them to keep their doors closed or locked when they have company. Don't you ever wonder what they do in their rooms, especially when you are not permitted to ever intrude upon their privacy?

Teach your child sex is an expression of love, bonding, and intimacy between mature adults who are committed to each other and who are financially capable of shouldering the responsibility of the results from being sexually involved, mature adults who are aware of the consequences of what could happen. Tell your child sex is not a recreational game and having sex does not make someone love you. Teach your son to have "protection" before "erection." Teach your child about signs and symptoms of sexually transmittable diseases. Encourage your children to talk to you about sex issues, their sexual desires, and feelings about sex. We have been saying, "Just say 'NO'" for years, and that has not worked for many—so let's face the facts: teens, our youth, and unmarried people are having sex.

Encourage your children to come to you if they are pregnant or have contracted a sexually transmitted disease so that you can help them get proper medical treatment. Keep open dialogue. You may have to initiate the dialogue on sexual issues. Parents, continue to seek knowledge. Read books on life issues and attend seminars on these issues as well. Read books on parenting. Unfortunately, there is no manual that comes with instructions of being a parent or on teaching your child about sex. If you teach your child what your parents taught you, you know that will be next to nothing.

Remember, Generation X and Y are off the chain and in another world, so be willing to step into their world screaming like you did when you were forced to learn the computer. Be willing to save your child from sexual ruin. Remember what the Bible says about "train" versus "raise." You raise crops and animals. But train up a child in the way he/she should go and when he/she is old, they will not depart from it. Let's get busy teaching our children about sex.

Expect more articles to follow on getting in family business: It's time to get in your parents' business. It's time to get in your husband's business. It's time to get in your wife's business. It's time to get in your grandchildren's business.

THE DIVORCE RATE EVEN AMONG CHRISTIANS IS TOO HIGH SAVING MARRIAGES IS EVERYBODY'S BUSINESS

My sister, Attorney Clara Hunter King, and I, based on my work as a minister and counselor, have penned our new book, *What To Do Before You Get Hitched*. From the courtroom and from counseling sessions, we have seen the devastation of our community due to marital turmoil among husbands/wives and the impact it has had on young children/teens. Stormy marriages and divorce can prevent adults from developing a healthy and balanced relationship. Yes, it is true that children learn what they live and see, and their value systems/belief systems are predicated on their environment. All that we do or fail to do is based on our socialization to life and our environment from birth to the present.

We are convinced that if both parties had more information about the person they chose to marry, many of these marriages would not have been consummated. Something must be done to curtail the divorce rate. The future of our next generation will be very dismal if the cycle is not broken. Divorce even jeopardizes our economic stability. Can you imagine what it will be like in the future when our children become elderly and try to live on one Social Security check, considering the rate of inflation? Having two Social Security checks together, they may have a chance of not becoming homeless or starve to death, and may even be able to purchase needed medications.

It is a fact that grown children tend to work things out in their marriage if they were reared in a family where their parents hung in there with their marriage. They learn the process of seeing two people compromise and work things out—versus running and starting all over again—and again. If the truth be told, the average man cannot provide for one household without a second/third check coming into the household. When there is a divorce, the children from the first marriage suffer. They are disconnected from their father in most cases, and they are deprived of his love, emotional, and financial support. Children feel hurt when they see their father providing for a new family and leaving them to struggle for basic necessities—and in most cases, the mother reminds the children of how their father is taking care of his new family—and rubs it in good.

What To Do Before You Get Hitched was written to provide both men and women with information that will increase their chances of having a happy, enduring marriage, and decrease the chances of their children becoming dysfunctional in their relationships or ending up in the "system." Many people simply do not obtain enough information before saying, "I Do." Questions that should have been asked *before* marriage are asked *after* the wedding bells have rung. There should be no questions that cannot be asked of your potential husband/wife. It's better to find out sooner than later. Each question asked should be answered truthfully. After all, a marriage should be based on honesty.

We have discovered through professional and legal counseling that most people have no clue about what questions they should ask before marriage. After witnessing too many failed marriages and the impact divorce has had on the family and children of divorced parents, we were compelled to write this book. We believe that this book should be recommended by every clergy member who counsels couples before marriage. In this informative book, we have provided you with some basic questions that you need to have answered by your intended mate and ways to find answers to questions that your beloved may not have or be unwilling to answer.

Questions you need answers to: Are you paying alimony/child support? If so, are you current? Do you want to have children? If so, how many? What are your five-year goals? How much debt do you have? Do you like pornography? Are you into kinky sex?

Things you need to check out: Spending habits—Churchgoing habits—Tithing habits—Health status—Credit history—Criminal history—Tax status with the IRS—Proof of divorce.

What To Do Before You Get Hitched will also teach you why it is important to meet your significant other's family, as well as how to handle his/her mother not liking you, what to expect regarding his bosom buddies, etc. This book will empower you with the information you need to make the right choice when choosing a mate for life. Knowledge is power. Lack of knowledge can cause you and others a lot of grief and pain and doom your marriage to failure right from the beginning. Statistics suggest that over 50 percent of all marriages end in divorce. Don't become a part of those statistics.

THE BEST THING YOU CAN DO FOR YOUR CHILDREN IS...

The best thing you can do for your children is to lead them to God and teach them the Word of God. The second-best thing is to teach them how to read. The third thing is to teach them to think for themselves and to develop self-confidence. These three things are the prescriptions for a healthy life; they will need these to weather the storms of life and to fight life's battles.

It is important for your children to know and to have a relationship with God. God is their protection. He is the one whom they can always lean and depend upon. He is the same 24/7. He does not wake up grumpy in the mornings. He is the same today, yesterday, and tomorrow. His love is unconditional; there is nothing you can do to earn His love.

It's not enough to just take your children to church Sunday. They need to know what the Word of God says about how they should conduct themselves in every aspect and situation, and they will not gain this knowledge from merely listening to Sunday morning preaching and singing in the choir. They must be taught what the Word of God says about how they should conduct themselves. The Word has much to say about parenting, as well. You parents should become a living example of a godly parent, living and conducting yourself according to the Word of God—it's better for your children to *see* what you do, rather than to merely *hear* what you say.

Being able to read with understanding is a must so that your children will know the truth and follow it, and not be misled by those who proclaim to know the Word of God but do not. Self-confidence will come automatically when you know God. Knowing God, you will understand that you are made in His image and you are an expression of Him. He is great, and therefore, you are too. Knowing these facts, no one can ever make you feel less than anyone else, because God made us all.

Writing these thoughts made me realize that I should write a book instead of an article, and I will do that, but in the meantime, chew on this and digest it well for now. These words will provide you with nourishment. I am living proof that what I am telling you works. My mother died when I was five years old. She was pressing my baby sister's hair, and I was standing beside her, holding on to her dress. She just collapsed from a heart attack. The doctor came to our house to pronounce her dead. I heard the doctor say to my older sister, "God will be your mother." Later, I heard my father say these same words. I did not know the meaning of this phrase—but I never forgot those words.

I was an adult and had children of my own when my father died. He did not leave us money, but he did leave us forty acres of land in Como, Mississippi. However, Simon, my father, left me the best things that a parent could leave a child—the knowledge of God and a hunger and thirst for God's Word. He taught me how to read and its importance. My father used to say, "You need to know how to read for yourself because folks will tell you anything; lie with a straight face while telling the lie." He was so correct. I thank you, Dad.

I know God, and I can read with comprehension. My confidence is over-the-roof, and that is what has led to my success. I have taught my children what my father taught me. It was good for me, and it's good for them. Parents, if you did not teach your children these values, it's not too late to do so now, even if they are adults. And if your children don't hear you, teach it to your grandchildren. You may not have money or property to leave your children, but if you leave them with the knowledge of God, the ability to read, and self-confidence, they can become successful and live a happy and fulfilled life, while obtaining money and property.

YOU CAN READ OTHER ARTICLES BY Dr. Rosie, at www.Drrosie.com

FAMILY REUNIONS MUST BE ABOUT MORE THAN MEETING AND EATING

Dear Family,

It was so wonderful being in the company of my family. July 14-15, 2006 is a weekend I will always remember. I am very much concerned about literacy and the economic plight of our people. I've traveled nationwide; and have found similar problems in every city – widespread illiteracy, high incarceration rates and high unemployment rates. Our future is bleak unless we correct these inequalities. We must correct these problems, if we cannot do it with the experience, history and wisdom we have, how can we expect our children to do it with their lack of experience, history and wisdom? We owe our children "Big Time." For some reason, we have relaxed and fell under the illusion that *all* is well – when the reality is that *all* **is not well**.

We must set new priorities. Entrepreneurship is the basis for strengthening our economic base. We must teach our children while in college or trade school that they must consider a business opportunity for themselves so that they can provide employment for themselves and their children. Jobs do not perpetuate jobs… businesses do.

We must support Black-owned business. We must let our children see us going out of the way to support Black-owned businesses. If you encounter a problem with a Black-owned business report it to the owner. Never say, "I will never go to another Black-owned this or that." I am sure that we have all been treated unfairly or poorly by other races while doing business… however, I have never heard a Black person say, "I'll never do business with another white-owned business."

We must support Black-owned businesses so that they can thrive, versus merely survive. This will encourage our children to want to own their own business. After all, why would your children want to inherit a struggling business?

The Harvest Institute, a Black-focused research, policy and educational organization has uncovered the following facts about unemployment rates for Blacks: Dr. Claud Anderson, President of The Harvest Institute, says, "The hidden national unemployment rate of Blacks is 35%. In cities like Baltimore, Detroit and Pittsburgh, Black unemployment is well over 45%. In New York, unemployment for Black men tops 51%. And, the national black youth unemployment figure is nearly 80%."

Black parents admonish their children to get a good education; telling them to work hard and that success will follow. But, according to an article entitled "Will Your Job Survive?" that appeared in the March 22nd, 2006 issue of the *Washington Post*, the direct connection between education and employment has weakened. (A21) In the article, columnist Harold Meyerson warns of the serious threat that globalization poses to the near-term future of the U.S. He notes that all categories of American jobs are rapidly disappearing. And, in 2004, Jeremy Rifkin wrote in his book, entitled *The End of Work*, "…only 25% of the jobs that exist now will continue to exist in the workplace by the year 2015." Hispanics alone filled over 41% of the newly created jobs since May 2005. Is education the key factor in immigrants getting jobs?

Teach your children to become job producers instead of job seekers. Teach them how to identify business opportunities. It is imperative that we create *Family Resource Guides* and *Family Business Directories* in order to network within your own families. After reading this letter, I trust you will see that economic deprivation is at the root of most of the problems African-Americans face.

Why A Family Resource Guide Is Important

A *Family Resource Guide* will serve as a resource center for our family via:
Providing information needed to excel in one's career, business and one's education.

1. Using ones center of influence to help open doors for a family member and their children.

2. Providing support to family members attending colleges or universities in your state.

3. If a family member is entering a profession or business that another family member has had experience, the more experienced person can serve as a resource to the neophyte.

Dr. Rosie Milligan

Why A Family Business Directory Is Important

The focus in the new millennium has been "*Global Economy*". We are doing business with China and other countries more than ever before. It is time that we consider doing business with our family members nationwide. And, we must seek to strengthen the economy of our Motherland – Africa.

All of us know someone in another state that we can refer to our family member businesses. We can purchase products and some services from businesses run by family members located in other states. After all, many businesses offer products and services via the Internet.

BLACK FATHERLESS MEN ARE HURTING ,TOO

Boys need fathers in their lives. I am making a plea to African-American fathers to be active participants in the lives of their sons; and for African-American women to assist these fathers in the transition of their reentering the lives of their sons.

Most every ill that plagues the Black male child is mostly related to fatherlessness. Having a father as a role model and teacher is critical for a male child. The male who understands this best is the male child whose father was present, and participated, in his life. Unfortunately, for many Black males, they have not had the experience of having a father role model. A male child who did not have his father present cannot relate to the critical differences it makes, for he has no comparison to make. Therefore, it becomes easy for him, as an adult, to abandon his son; especially, when it becomes a challenge to be a part of his life.

In addition, I believe that we must revisit history as we examine the family structure of Blacks in America. An absentee father was the norm for the African-American family. Families were separated by force! Slavery severely impacted the lives of the Black family. Considering the fact that our physical exodus from slavery has only been 140 years, that's not a long time, and we are still experiencing its effects.

Blacks were forced to produce offsprings, not for themselves, but for their master's economic gain. Today, Blacks are not forced to produce babies; however, because of the residual effect of slavery on the Black family, their offsprings continue to be an economic product for the modern-day master called "PRISON." Today, in 2005, Black males in prison are paid less for their labor than they were paid 140 years ago.

Black men were not socialized as other men, that is, to be accountable or responsible for his family. In order to understand why the Black man and Black woman are having such challenges in their relationships, you must understand how their experience and living conditions in America have impacted their lives and the lives of their family.

When a Black family needed assistance from Social Services' programs, the father had to remove himself from the family in order for his wife and children to get assistance. Black men have a long way to go to get back to their African roots of being a provider and protector. Black men have come a long way, and they will get back to their God-Created-Nature, with the help of God, Almighty, and with the understanding of their past.

It is the responsibility of the father to help provide for his child. And providing entails more than financial provisions. I'm pleading with women, to not prevent the father from being a part of his son's life because of the father's inability to support financially. A male child needs his father in his life, and the woman only hurts her son(s) when she tries to prevent them from having a father-son relationship. The many ills of Black men are inevitably traced to their Fatherlessness.

Most Black men really want to be with their families and children. What they need is someone to be a father-like figure for them. A Black man needs guidance. Most of them are trying to be something or somebody that they have never seen or experienced, and must be taught that. The woman's ideal of what a man is supposed to be is distorted because she too has not experience a father in her life.

You see, a father is a role model for his son and a father gives definition to his daughter as to what a man is. A mother is a role model for her daughter and she gives definition to her son as to what a woman is. 70% of Black households are headed and ran by a female with the father most times being totally out of the picture. The sons and daughters are both confused about male/female responsibility.

Many men are not allowed to have relationships with their children. If these men are allowed to participate in their children's lives, it must be on the woman's terms only. When it becomes unbearable, he leaves the woman and the child behind. The real victim is the child.

There are some things that a man needs to teach his son, such as: how to bathe and clean his genital area, how to shop for clothing, how to choose his friends, how to respect himself, how to drive an automobile, how to resolve conflicts, how to fight, how to avoid a fight, how to play sports.

I am not casting blame on the Black woman. I am only pointing out the facts that are hindering the progress of the Black family. I believe that if we could get a perspective of the Black man, as related to who is who he was before coming to America and what America has made him become, then we would have a better understanding of our family dynamics and we can embrace each other and begin to value ourselves and our children again.

Look for the follow-up article, "Why Black Men/Women Suffer Failed and Unhealthy Relationships."

Dr. Rosie Milligan, Counselor/Author: Author of Negroes, Colored People, Black, African-Americans in America—Nigger, Please—Satisfying The Black Man Sexually—Satisfying The Black Woman Sexually and Why Black Men Choose White Women.

TAKE FAMILY INVENTORY DURING YOUR HOLIDAY GATHERING

While meeting, greeting, and eating is the order of the day for holiday and family reunion gatherings, I submit to you that it is also a great time to take family inventory. It's a good time to inquire as to where each family member stands in regard to their personal and business affairs.

There is a time for all things and it's time for parents to get into their children's business and for children to get into their parents' business. If either one's business affairs are not in order and they make their transition, then it becomes a family member's business—and somebody will have to step up to the plate.

I hear you. You said this is *not* the time to discuss business—pardon me, please. My niece suffered an aneurism and died at our family reunion. My niece was thirty-five years old. She had her affairs in order and that made it easy for the family to have her body shipped back home—can you imagine the position the family would have been placed in if she had not had an insurance policy?

It's time for all of us to get our personal and business affairs in order. These are the questions you need answered when taking inventory of a family member: 1) Do you have a life insurance policy, and are the beneficiaries still alive? If there is only one beneficiary, an alternate one should be named should the one designated as beneficiary die. 2) Do you have a Living Trust or Will, and if so, where is it kept, and is everyone named in your Living Trust or Will alive and competent (sound mind, able to make proper decisions)? If no one can locate your Will or Living Trust upon your death, it's like not having one. It's a good idea to give your Successor Trustee a notarized copy for keepsake. 3) Do you have an Advanced Health-Care Directive (naming the person who will make health-care decisions on your behalf if you are unable to do so)? If your loved one becomes unable to make medical decisions for himself/herself when a medical decision must be made, someone would have to go to court to become the conservator in order to make a medical decision, and that could cost $4,000 or more. 4) Do you have a General Durable Power Of Attorney (appointing an agent to make financial decisions for you if you are unable to do so)? 5) Do you have a special needs child, and if so, have you made plans about who will be guardian over that child when you die?

Other information you will need to know: Does your family know where your life insurance policy or your burial plot is located? Do you have a beneficiary on your bank account/insurance policy? Has someone died who you had named as a beneficiary on your bank account/insurance policy? Do you need to make changes to your Living Trust, Power of Attorney, or Will?

It's time for all of us to get our personal and business affairs in order. I have discovered that most people, including spouses of business owners, have no clue about their husband's/wife's business structure or business affairs. Come on, Family, let's *be* family and look after each other in every aspect. Do the right thing—take inventory this holiday gathering, and you will be glad that you did.

LET'S CELEBRATE OUR YOUTH WHO ARE DOING THE RIGHT THING!

We spend far too much time focusing on the youth who have taken the wrong path in life, while we spend so little time celebrating our youth who are doing good things. There is something wrong with this picture. Is there somebody out there concerned about the wheels of our youth that are not squawking?

I often wonder how our young people feel who are doing the right thing, when they see how we glorify and give mega attention to those youth who make bad choices or are involved in something negative. I wonder…

We too often talk about the problems of our youth, while we offer no solutions for them. In fact, many are blaming the youth the so-called hip-hop generation for the dismal condition of the Black race. How can we lay the blame on the children? Too many Blacks have a distorted perception of reality.

We talk about the illiteracy problem among our youth, well the fruit does not fall too far from the tree. We have a high rate of illiteracy among the adults of these children. We are witnessing the fall out of the 60's-which ushered in the "do what you feel" syndrome without any consideration of accountability and responsibility. Now we are experiencing the ill effects of the second and the third generation of babies having babies , the consequences of such is functional illiteracy among adults.

In addition to illiteracy among parents, the school system fail to provide these parents' children with text books to bring home, while at the same time, there are school who provide students with a set of books for home and a set for school.

I invested my own money in publishing books for three Black youths: Marquis Cormire, author of "I Am Not A Problem Child: How A Seven Year Old Black Male Child Fought Against Special Education Placement." The school had written this child off. This young boy is indeed a little genius. We printed 1,000 books. This seven year old, respectful, well-trained youth attends Faithful Central Church, which is held at the Forum in Inglewood, California. Marquis mentions in his book of how his pastor has inspired him. He also gave the pastor a copy of his book. Now with a ten thousand plus membership, should it have taken me and his grandmother, who is a working and tithing member of the same church, nearly two years to sell 1,000 books? This is definitely inappropriate pastoral behavior.

The other two authors are sisters, Miya and Meryl McCurry, they were 10 and 12 years old when I met them, respectively. They wrote and illustrated their books. I met these children at the library. They were disgusted because they could not check out more than 10 books. They were unbelievable. Their books are titled "The Foods" and "The Sea Monster's Darkest Night". The sequel to The McCurry's books will be unveiled at the 2005, 10th Annual Conference on April 2, 2005 at the LAX Radisson Hotel, 6225 W. Century Blvd., Los Angeles, California.

Whatever our children are and what ever our children are not, it is the fault of the adults. Our children are our future writers, they are the ones who will tell our story. Therefore, I believe that literacy is everybody's business.

For more information regarding The 2005 Black Writers On Tour Conference, call (323) 7503592.

SECTION 4: HEALTH ISSUES

FAST FOODS AND LACK OF EXERCISE IS DESTROYING OUR CHILDREN'S HEALTH TOO!

Cherry Marie, a Los Angeles Resident and a Healthy Children Advocate pen her new children book, *The President Eats Vegetables*. Cherry states, "Since our children are our future, then Let's change the health status of our children by Any Means Necessary. Our children are a reflection of us, the adults and they model us in every way even our poor food choices and our "Couch Potatoes Syndrome.". Modern-day electronic gadgets are wreaking havoc on children's lives as well as adults.

Medical science has made great strides, now able to perform Robotic Heart Surgery with efficiency. Life expectancy has increased, yet the quality of health in the elderly is atrocious. If there is truth in the adage, that The Wealth Of a Nation is dependent upon the Health of it its People, then promoting health children is everybody's business.

Every child has a role model and a hero and children tend to model their hero.

President Obama, and First Lady, Michelle Obama are a role model and hero to many children. Michelle Obama is committed to changing the health direction of our children. Michelle is traveling and teaching the importance of eating healthy, gardening and exercise, she has raised awareness that we need to do something about the health of our children.-The increase in Diabetes, has the attention of the nation, and there is an increase rate of High Cholesterol and Hypertension in children.

In this beautifully illustrated children's book, Obi does not want to give up his cheese curls and chips and candy. But then one day, his dad takes him on a tour of the Obama White House and vegetables garden, and Obi starts to see things differently. This charming story just might persuade your little one to follow Obi's example, and make a commitment to health and better nutrition.

Keeping our children healthy is everybody's business.

NINE REASONS PEOPLE GET SICK

LACK OF KNOWLEDGE

"We perish due to lack of knowledge."

Some food for thought: We have the best technology in the world. We rank #1 in trauma care among industrialized nations, but when it comes to degenerative diseases, we only rank about 37th in the world. Why?

We must seek knowledge that will empower us to live a healthy life. It's up to each one of us to search for our own cures. As Americans, we spend billions of dollars every year on research, trying to find cures for diseases, yet we have witnessed an increase in cancer, heart disease, and diabetes among children, as well as adults. What's wrong with this picture? I truly believe that when we learn better, we will do better.

I strongly suggest that you have an annual medical checkup. Physicians play an important role in society and some of them are finally realizing that nutrition plays an important role when it comes to maintaining optimum health. Our intended diet—natural foods—did a great job of providing the body exactly what it needed. And we evolved as nature intended. However, today's American standard diet is so far removed from what God had intended for us. Our processed foods are filled with toxins, growth hormones, preservatives, and a host of synthetic compounds, which cause us to be nutritionally bankrupt—that's why we are so sick. It is important that we learn what causes us to get sick in the first place, and then learn how to get well.

LACK OF PROPER NUTRITION

Poor nutrition equals BIG BUSINESS. The large food-producing companies don't want you to think about nutrition. Their products have very little health value. The food giants do not focus on nutrients needed for optimum health, but instead, focus on that which market to "your taste buds." It's up to you to seek out foods that provide nutrients for optimum health for you and your family.

Learning The four food groups is not enough. Different bodies require different nutrition. The one-size-fits-all approach to nutrition is completely ineffective. If you would eat seven meals a day, your body would still be lacking in nutrients necessary for good body function when we are consuming foods that are nutritionally bankrupt. The American standard diet is destroying our bodies.

Our fruits and vegetables have become hollow, void of substantial nutritional value, and even so, many people do not consume even one vegetable or fruit on a daily basis, neither do they take vitamin/mineral supplements. Most people do not drink more than two glasses of water per day. They do not consider water an important nutrient. Instead of water, they drink carbonated drinks which rob their body of Calcium, which is necessary for the body. The average person begins their day with a high acidity diet found in foods like: pancakes, syrup, meat, eggs, and orange juice. What you have here is nothing more than a load of sugar. These are all acid foods, and there is nothing ingested to balance the acid intake. The least one can do is to drink an eight-ounce glass of water with lemon juice one hour before having breakfast. It would serve the body well to start the day off with fruits or vegetables for breakfast.

LACK OF MINERALS

Minerals and vitamins work together. They have a chainlike dependence. One mineral depends on another mineral, which depends on a vitamin and so on. This is called synergy. According to leading scientists, the North American soil's mineral content has been depleted by 85 percent. Minerals are one of the most important nutrients known to man. Therefore, this statistic should cause an alarm. Due to the depletion of minerals from the soil, our fruits and vegetables are hollow and void of any substantial nutritional value causing sickness and disease to sweep our nation.

Most minerals on the market are made from micron-sized particles, which are small, but at a cellular level, they are too large to be readily absorbed by the cells and used as food. This is why most supplements have such low absorption rates. You need minerals the size of what is typically found in nature. Fruits and vegetables absorb minerals that are angstrom in size through their root systems. Angstroms are 10,000 times smaller than microns.

Your small intestine can only absorb an angstrom-sized particle, which is 10,000 times smaller than a micron-sized particle.

LACK OF VITAMINS

Vitamins are necessary for proper body function. They help to extend life, keep you looking younger, help prevent certain diseases, boost your immune system, boost your energy level, and much more. A healthy immune system is important. Your immune system is to you as what the Army, Navy, Air Force and the Marines are to our nation's defense.

It is true that you can get vitamins from food, and more so when you prepare your food at home versus eating out most of the time. Food eaten at most eateries are void of nutrients needed to sustain healthy body function. Many of the foods we eat when eating out are canned/processed foods. And in many cases, the vegetables are overcooked, causing the vitamins to escape from them.

We often hear people say, "Just eat a balanced diet and you will be okay." What a balanced diet is means different things to different people. However, let's face it. If I told you to make sure that you consumed 1,000 mg of vitamin C twice a day and 2,000 mg of Calcium per day, would you know what foods to eat and how much of each food you needed to get the proper amount? Bottom line is that you need a vitamin/mineral supplement. Even if you feel that your diet is sufficient, taking a supplement can be your "nutrient insurance."

Our on-the-go lifestyles make it difficult to provide our body the nutrients that it needs. Standard vitamins and minerals can help, but most pills are expelled from the body before they have had a chance to be absorbed. And in many cases, because of a lack of digestive enzymes, the vitamins/minerals people take are not able to be broken down so that they can be used by the body. Essential nutrient elements should be broken down into small particles so that they are quickly and fully absorbed into our digestive systems

LACK OF DIGESTIVE ENZYMES

Enzymes boost the body's ability to break down nutrients for absorption in the digestive tract. We get enzymes from fruits and vegetables. A poor quality of soil diminishes the quality of minerals and enzymes. Processing food at average cooking temperature will destroy enzymes. Enzymes aid in the digestion of foods. If the foods that we eat cannot be broken down where they can be used by the body, then the foods we eat are passing through our body while leaving the cells starving and craving for nutrients. We tend to keep eating all day, trying to satisfy our bodies' craving, but to no avail. What we are providing the body with is excess calories which yield excess fat and excess body weight—which is a precursor to many diseases.

The fact that antacids are the #1 over-the-counter products sold in the U.S.A. is an indication that millions of people are suffering digestive problems involving enzymes.

LACK OF OXYGEN

Nobody has enough hydrogen or oxygen, not on this planet. Your body cannot use vitamins and minerals without hydrogen, oxygen, and enzymes. We need oxygen in our bodies. The air we breathe formerly contained 50 percent oxygen. But today, we only have about 20 percent in our air. And there is even less in large cities. The medical profession has confirmed that most viruses, parasites, bacteria, funguses, and pathogens are anaerobic and cannot live in oxygen. Since we are not getting enough oxygen, our bodies are becoming fertile breeding grounds for many diseases.

LACK OF WATER

Lack of water causes dehydration in the body. When the body is dehydrated, the cells just do not have enough fluid. Water is important for good body function. Water helps to get toxins and waste materials out of the body and out of the cells. Dehydration causes all types of medical problems, such as: pain, stiffness, arthritis, asthma, allergies, and numerous other medical problems.

Many people substitute carbonated drinks for water, but it is not a substitute. You need water. Carbonated drinks block Calcium absorption. Calcium is one of the most important building blocks of nutrition. (Too much caffeine and too much protein rob the body of Calcium that is needed for many body functions.)

LOW pH LEVEL

pH is a measure of the acidity or alkalinity of a solution. The lower the pH number, the more acidic the solution is. The higher a pH number, the more alkaline the solution is. The body has an acid-alkaline ratio called pH (potential of Hydrogen), which is a balance between positively charged ions (acid forming) and negatively charged ions (alkaline forming).

Scientists have discovered that the body fluids of healthy people are alkaline (high pH), whereas the body fluids of sick people are acidic (low pH). Most people who suffer from unbalanced pH are acidic. This condition forces the body to borrow minerals, including Calcium, Sodium, Potassium, and Magnesium, from vital organs and bones to buffer the acid and safely remove it from the body. This strain on the body can cause the body to suffer severe and prolonged damage due to high acidity. This condition can go unnoticed for many years.

The pH measures the status of the body's fluids as they relate to the amounts of acid/alkaline that is formed within the body. Almost everything we ingest, infuse, or inhale is either acid or alkaline-forming once it comes in contact with our bodily fluids. A special scale, called a logarithmic scale with numbers ranging from 0-14, is used to measure the body's pH at given times. The midpoint of the scale is 7. When the pH measures below 7, the concentration of acid is higher than the concentration of alkaline. When the blood pH reaches a range above 7.3-7.5, symptoms of disease begin to form.

Research has proven that total healing from any chronic illness can take place only if and when the blood has been restored to a normal (slightly alkaline) pH. Oxygen delivery to cells is directly related to the body's pH balance.

Diseases do not grow well in slightly alkaline environments. To gain and maintain a healthy pH balance, it is necessary to eat 80 percent alkaline-forming foods and 20 percent acid-forming foods. Alkaline-forming foods include, but are not limited to: fresh fruit juices, melons, and vegetables (raw is better). Acid-forming foods include, but are not limited to: all animal products, sugar, liquor, coffee, and caffeine.

Anything green is alkaline. Citrus fruits like limes and lemons have a very strong acid pH right off the tree. However, inside the body, after digestion, they have a mild alkalizing affect. A typical breakfast for many is: a meat product, toast with jelly or pancakes with syrup, and a glass of juice. Look what is happening here: everything consumed is acid forming. What do you think your pH balance looks like?

LACK OF BOWEL ELIMINATION (CONSTIPATION)

If you do not have two bowel movements per day, you are constipated. Colon health is very important. It has been stated by leading health experts that 90 percent of all diseases begin in the colon. Most diseases take hold where basic toxic conditions give them a breeding ground. The body poisons itself by maintaining a cesspool of decaying matter in the colon. This cesspool contains a high concentration of harmful bacteria just like a cesspool under the house.

The toxins released by the decay process gets into the blood stream and travel to all parts of the body, weakening the entire system. Now the immune system is broken down. The amount of putrefaction and decay in the body depend upon how long the food stays in the body. When putrefaction sets in, within this cesspool you now get worms and parasites. Signs of worms and parasites are: craving and the inability to lose weight no matter what you do.

Nine out of ten Americans are said to have parasites living inside them. Some people have parasites in the brain. Parasites eat us, and then expel their waste in us. This waste is called toxic sludge. Signs of toxins and decay in the colon are: foul odors when urinating or defecating, bad breath (halitosis) when there is an absence of tooth cavities, or body odor and foot odor. You may experience bad breath odor due to not brushing the tongue and rinsing the mouth well.

LACK OF EXERCISE

There is a myriad of exercises that you can choose from. However, the most importance thing is that you choose to exercise. The Surgeon General recommends at least thirty minutes of activities seven day a week. Walking is still considered one of the best exercises that you can do, and it is free, no equipment needed, therefore, there is no excuse for any of us to not exercise. There are numerous books on the market about the different types of exercises and how they improve certain body functions. So stand up and get your body moving. For better health and better energy, get up and work that body! Your lymphatic system cannot function at its optimum level without some form of exercise.

SECTION 4: ARTICLES AND THOUGHTS ON SEX AND SEXUALITY

SEX—THE WEAPON OF MASS DESTRUCTION

SEX—from the pulpit to the White House! Sex—men have lost their jobs for it. Men have lost their lives for it. Men have left their wives for it. Men have left their children for it. Men have dropped out of school for it. Men have gone AWOL from the military for it—SEX!

During every presidential election, a candidate has had to bow out due to sexual encounters, alleged or true. Sexual encounters have been the downfall of pastors of mega ministries throughout the United States of America. Don't take my word for it. And if you think that I am just blowing off smoke, Google the subject and see for yourself. The names are too numerous to mention. Google "political sex scandals" and "church sex scandals" to see what has gone down.

In 1990, I warned the churches and the nation about what would happen to our society if we failed to address the topic of sex. The church didn't want to address sex. And parents couldn't teach what was never taught to them.

There has never been an answer to the question: "At what age do you teach a child about sex?" My question is: "Why not teach children about sex?" Since after eating, sex is the most sought after drive, why do we continue to not want to make it a family discussion? Sex is in almost every movie, magazine, and commercial—it's okay to see it, but not to discuss it in a healthy manner. What's up with that?

When the schools introduced the idea of teaching sex education, many parents went into an uproar thinking that the schools had gone too far. Many felt that a child should learn about sex from their parents. There is an old adage, "When the horse is stolen, the fool locks the door." This old adage reminds me of the following. The dos and don'ts about sex for many parents become a topic of discussion *after* their child has been raped, molested, or is pregnant. *Anytime sex is taught to a child/youth is good.* The sooner the better.

Television talk shows raised the consciousness of this nation regarding the hundreds of young boys who have been molested by their priests, pastors, and family members. Many asked why they didn't they tell their parent(s). The answer is this: They didn't know how to address a topic that had never been a topic of discussion in their home—sex. They had never been told about inappropriate sexual gestures and touching of body parts that should not be touched. Molestation for many continued for years, leaving emotional scars forever.

In 1990, I wrote two books, *Satisfying the Black Woman Sexually Made Simple* and *Satisfying the Black Man Sexually Made Simple*. These books raised eyebrows across the country. When it comes to sex, all races share commonalities. However, it is a known fact that many Black girls/women experienced a history of rape as slaves which therefore impacted their sexuality, how they feel about sex, and how they teach their offspring about sex and men.

I was ridiculed by ministers across the country when I talked about sex over the airways and on television. My response to the ministers was this: "Every time I hear of a church breaking up, somebody had sex with somebody or somebody ran off with the money, so get with the program and let's talk about sex."

Except for money, sex is the only factor in our civilized society that people permit themselves to indulge in at the risk of losing their jobs or causing harm to themselves and their families—all for a few, brief orgasmic thrills. It is the only factor that can cause a communitywide, citywide, national, or international calamity. And just think, all it entails is two people having sex by their own consent. However, if you do it in a manner in which people say is wrong, they will destroy you! Sex is a dominating factor in our lives. It is a moving force that keeps us going, and most of us will admit that. Sex, that obscure and yet paradoxically, mundane biological necessity, dominates us all in one way or another.

The emergence of rape, pornography, and incest is related to psychosexual problems. The most sought after experience by humans, after eating, is SEX, and to continuously keep it in the closet will undoubtedly cause serious problems for future generations.

I am launching a blog and new Web sites, Drrosiesextalk.com and Drrosiesextalkforteens.com. While our nation has revolutionized the medical industry and has made great technological advancements, we fail to make talking about sex a family discussion. In short, we fail to see that "Sex" is a *Weapon of Mass Destruction*.

IMPOTENCY ON THE RISE

Impotence used to be considered the lot that awaited the middle aged and elderly; however, today, we know that age is not as much a factor as you might think. We are seeing more of it today in younger men as well as older ones.

Impotence is the failure to achieve erection, ejaculation, or both. Men who experience sexual dysfunction express the following complaints: loss of sexual desire, not being able to obtain or maintain an erection, ejaculation failure, premature ejaculation, and the inability to achieve orgasm.

In the past, impotence was considered to be 90 percent in a man's head. Because of ignorance, many men today do not seek medical help for impotency. It is now believed that the majority of impotent men have a component of underlying organic disease. Some common causes of erectile impotency and lack of sexual desire in men are boredom, resentment, anger, grief, anxiety, depression, diabetes, and prescription drugs, such as antihypertensives (used for treating high blood pressure), antidepressants (used for treating ulcers), and drugs of habituation or addiction, such as alcohol, methadone, heroin, and marijuana.

An erection for a man is equivalent to lubrication for a woman. The male erection and female lubrication both signify readiness for intercourse. A man cannot have intercourse if he does not have an erection, but a woman does not have to be lubricated in order to have intercourse. It can be uncomfortable if she does not lubricate, but there are ways around that. Salvia or a lubricator may be used.

Some experts believe that we are seeing more impotence in men today because the modern-day woman is demanding equal joy in sex. Women are educated consumers regarding sex. More is being written about sex, and women are speaking out on national television talk shows, etc. discussing the topic. Women are now more sexually aggressive and feel entitled to sexual satisfaction and demand it. This assertiveness of the modern-day female has created performance anxiety among men. Many men entering into a sexual experience are afraid that they may not meet the woman's expectations. Those anxieties can cause problems such as impotence. The big "O" (orgasm) is the talk of the time; therefore, men are feeling pressured to guarantee women an orgasmic experience every time during sexual intercourse.

It is important for a male to have a thorough physical examination if he has demonstrated little or no interest in sex for a long period of time. A man's impotence is said to be psychological if he can get an erection by masturbating or looking at pornography, or if he has early morning erections or an erection with another woman.

Intermittent impotence has been found to be caused by an endocrine imbalance. Endocrine problems are very sneaky. Their only symptom may be that of impotence. A man experiencing impotence should ask his doctor to check his testosterone level. Testosterone is a male hormone. A man has an erection when blood floods through the penile arteries into the blood vessels in the penis. This rush of blood is triggered by the nervous system, which gets its signal from the sex hormones. Impotence can be a symptom of a number of life-threatening diseases. It is one of the symptoms of diabetes. Diabetes can cause impaired circulation. Remember, a good erection is a healthy blood flow to the penis. Diabetes may damage or destroy the nerves that trigger the rush of blood to the penis.

SEXUALLY ABUSED CHILDREN—THEIR STRUGGLES AS ADULTS

Cherry Marie, a Los Angeles-based health advocate and author, pens memoir, *A Child's Journey Through Sexual Abuse: A Journey of Healing Through Confronting and Exposing Sexual Abuse from Childhood to Adulthood.* Today, living in the United States, there are 39 million adults who have survived child sexual abuse, and 3 million American children are victims. Most of them are children, struggling alone, believing there is no adult who can help them. Can you imagine the pain and shame a child feels when his or her innocence is taken, and the perpetrator, in many cases, is someone the child loves, trusts, and expects to protect them?

Television talk shows stimulated national discussion on sexual abuse as they interviewed adult males and females who were struggling mentally and emotionally as adults due to being a victim of child molestation. The question becomes, why didn't the child tell somebody? The fact is, until society fully embraces being comfortable talking and teaching about sex issues in the same manner that they teach about keeping the doors locked, not talking to strangers, washing your hands before you eat and after using the toilet, etc., then children will continue to be victims of child sexual abuse.

There is an old adage, "When the horse is stolen from the barn the fool locks the barn's door." In today's society, when the child's innocence has been taken, their parents tell them things such as: no one should touch your body in certain places, and if someone does do that, do not be afraid to tell a parent. If most adults are afraid to report rape because of the fear of disbelief, just think what a molestation experience must be like for a child!

Cherry Marie's life is a testament that healing as an adult from incest is possible. Cherry makes herself transparent so that she may help others to heal from sexual abuse too. She states, "I have no right not to forgive, and neither do you." You will learn that as difficult as it may be to forgive the perpetrator, forgiveness is the key ingredient in the healing process. Remember, it's not your fault. You did not invite someone in to sexually abuse you.

Sex is a weapon of mass destruction. Sex abuse has destroyed the lives of many adults and children. The perpetrator, as well as the sexually abused victim, is in need of healing. In many cases, the perpetrator has experienced sexual abuse him/herself. Therefore, sex education and sex talks for our children are very important. Our children deserve to be protected; they are our most valuable assets. Sex education is everybody's business and reading and sharing *A Child's Journey Through Sexual Abuse* can help to stimulate a healthy family discussion around sexual lessons and issues. Let's teach and protect our children from this dreadful, devastating experience—incest, molestation, and rape.

WHAT YOU NEED TO KNOW ABOUT SEX AND SEX METHODOLOGY

Sex is not everything in a nutshell; however, sex has an effect on everything we do. A couple needs much more than sex to bridge and sustain a well-balanced, healthy relationship. Sexual activities have a strong influence on the way one thinks, behaves, and performs in all areas of activity.

Sex is a dominating factor in our lives, a moving force that keeps us going, an obscure paradoxical and biological necessity that dominates and impacts our lives in every way. Except for money, sex is the only activity in our civilized societies that people will engage in, sometimes at the risk of causing harm to themselves, their families, or to the loss of their jobs, the loss of their children, the loss of their prestigious position—all for a few seconds of orgasmic thrills. It is the only factor that can cause a community-wide, citywide, or national or international calamity. And just think, all it entails is a minimum of two people having sex with each other by consent. But if you do it in a manner in which people say is wrong, it may destroy you.

Male and female sexuality has been suppressed by Christian thought. Sexual pleasure in the past has been condemned as a sin, and its suppression has been an inducement in men and women in developing new forms of perversion and neurosis. The emergence of rape, pornography, and incest is closely related to psychosexual problems. Sexual confusion, bedroom turmoil, lack of conversation about likes and dislikes when it comes to sex are among the leading causes of divorce. Therefore, knowing what I know, and seeing what I have seen in dysfunctional marital relationships, I am compelled to discuss sex issues and sex methodology.

I hear you saying, "When are you going to get to the sex methodology?" Just hold on, I will get to it. However, there is much to be learned about sex, sexuality, about yourself and your partner before you engage in sex. So just chill out . . .

There are some health issues that can impact sexual appetite and performance. High blood pressure and diabetes are very prevalent in today's society. And medications taken by men for hypertension sometimes cause impotence. Diabetes is a condition that causes circulation impairment, which leads to poor circulation. Poor circulation can have an effect on the ability of the male having and sustaining an erection. When men do not have an understanding of what is taking place when facing these challenges, they erroneously believe that it has something to do with their partner's ability to arouse them sexually.

Some men when dealing with sexual challenges will seek sex outside the marriage or relationship, hoping to restore their ability to be sexually aroused, but only to find themselves more frustrated by the increased risk of disrupting their family unit. Men have a greater challenge than women when it comes to physical sex. The man has to focus on getting an erection and keeping the erection until his partner is satisfied. This can become a big challenge, especially when the woman takes no responsibility for her own desired results. A man becomes embarrassed when he cannot get an erection, and he is embarrassed when he cannot maintain his erection.

There are women who are impotent also. Since there is no physical evidence of her readiness, impotency in women goes unnoticed. Impotency is when a person is unable to perform sex physically or when a person has no desire to have sex, and there are many women who have no desire to have sex due to health conditions, medications, or past history of molestation/rape. These are women who have sex with their partner only as a duty or obligation.

Here are a few questions that one should ask his or her partner before getting married:

1. Do you have any sexual challenges?

2. Do you have any medical conditions that impact your sexuality and sexual performance?

3. Do you have high blood pressure or diabetes?

4. Are you taking medications for high blood pressure or diabetes?

5. Do you have any medical problems that we need to discuss?

6. Do you get regular/annual physical checkups?

This may seem a little bit much to ask, but it is not. You should be comfortable with each other to have such conversations, especially if you are entertaining the thought of getting married.

Even though I am writing for couples who are anticipating getting married, I would be remiss not to give a word of caution for the couple about sex after being married. Listen, and listen good. If you are having sexual issues with your husband/wife, please, please, please, do not discuss your sexual problem with your friends/employees of the opposite sex. The best person to discuss these problems with is your spouse. If you cannot resolve the challenges, seek a counselor/sex therapist. People tend to want to help you when you bring them a problem, and help in this area when dealing with sex issues can cause you more problems than you need or can deal with, so talk to your spouse.

Now, let's talk about sex methodology. It is not my intention to provide a judgment call regarding sexual methodology and sexual preference. However, it is of utmost importance to discuss sex methodology/preference before getting married. That is the time to honestly discuss your sexual appetite. Intimacy and sex play a very important role in a healthy marriage. The most sought-after experience by humans, after eating, is sex. Therefore, it is my belief that we need more conversations about sex and how it impacts our relationships. I would suggest you read these two books, *Satisfying The Black Man Sexually Made Simple* and *Satisfying The Black Woman Sexually Made Simple*. These books have implications and applications for men and women of all ethnicities. After all, men and women have much in common, and there is no getting around it. But because of various social, psychological, and economic factors that have greatly impacted the lives of Blacks, their sexuality has been impacted on a different level.

There are experiences in one's life that can impact how one feels about sex in general and sex methodology that one may feel comfortable engaging in. If a male/female has suffered molestation/rape, they are less likely to feel comfortable being placed in a helpless position, being slapped on the buttocks during sex, being tied up, or hearing dirty talking during sex. These are things that you will never know unless sex methodology is discussed. There are many way in which people choose to have sex. I will mention just a few:

1) Missionary Style (Woman/man lying on his/her back when having sex)

2) Doggie Style (Woman on her knees and hands, male entering the vagina from the rear)

3) Oral Sex (Male uses his mouth to bring sexual pleasure to the woman; female inserts the penis in her mouth to bring sexual pleasure to her husband)

4) Anal Sex (Male inserts his penis in his partner's rectum)

5) Finger Sex (Male uses fingers to stimulate the clitoris or thrusts a finger into the vagina to give sexual pleasure; the female places her hands on the man's penis to cause ejaculation)

Now that you have knowledge about sex methodology, it's time to ask a few questions about intimacy such as:

Do you like to be kissed?

1) Do you like lots of hugging? (There are people who do not like being kissed or lots of hugging. They will kiss during courtship but will cease after the marriage has been consummated.)

2) Do you like a little or a lot of foreplay?

3) How often do you like to have sex? This is an important question because the person whom you are about to marry may have a sexual addiction problem, like nymphomania or hyper sexuality. This condition is more common in men. Having an overwhelming sex desire becomes a problem when it is repeated often enough to interfere with normal daily living and when long periods of time are given over to sex-related activities.

4) Do you have sexual fantasies, and if so, what are they? Your partner may have some way out fantasies. For example, your partner may want to tie you up when having sex, whip you with a belt or towel, etc. He/she may want to engage in sex with you and other partners of both genders or want to watch while you have sex with someone of the same sex.

5) Do you have sexual hang-ups; if so, what are they?

6) Do you have sexual fears; if so, what are they?

7) Have you ever been molested/raped? If so, did you receive counseling afterward?

8) Do you like sex? There are people who do not like sex and do not want to have sex. They want to be married so they will have sex as a duty/obligation.

9) Do you like watching pornography movies?

7. Now that you are comfortable talking about sex, let's talk on a more serious note.
    1) What position do you enjoy most when having sex?
    2) What position do you dislike the most when having sex?
    3) Are you comfortable performing oral sex?
    4) Do you like having oral sex performed on you? Some people like to have oral sex performed on them but do not like to perform oral sex on their partner.
    5) Do you like having anal sex? If you have never done such, are you open to it?

As a counselor, I have witnessed the bedroom turmoil in married couples' lives. Therefore, I admonish every person before getting married to ask questions that are important to you when it comes to sex and sex methodology. If you are unsure of your and your partner's sexual compatibility, it's best and more cost-effective to bow out now rather than later. As stated earlier, sexual gratification is vital in a marriage.

When married couples enter the divorce court for a divorce decree, the divorce is granted most often based on "irreconcilable differences." It would be interesting if the judge required couples to name those irreconcilable differences. If sex were not a taboo subject, I can guarantee you that many would say, "I am sexually frustrated, and those frustrations have spilled out into other areas of our marriage. "Remember, if you want answers ask questions. Marriage is a big step for anyone to take. Please note that *if you don't ask, they won't tell*.

LACK OF KNOWLEDGE ABOUT SEX IS DESTROYING OUR CHILDREN

Sex is the weapon of mass destruction for our nation, religious leaders, political leaders, married couples, singles—the churched and unchurched alike. And for all you Holy Ghost-filled, speaking-in-tongue-sanctified dancers out there who are always turning your nose up at what I write, you need to start thinking outside the box when it comes to sex. Check this out ... Many of our Sunday school children are having babies, having abortions, and getting sexually transmitted diseases just like non-churched children. How do I know? I know because they talk to me; they feel comfortable talking to me because I made it easy for them to come to me—they don't go to their parents because they have not opened the door to have conversations about sex. Some have told me that they feel that if they bring up sex to their parents, they are afraid that their parents will think that they are having sex or want to have sex; therefore, they feel that their parents will think badly of them. Well, true or not true, that's what they are telling me.

Our children are being destroyed for lack of knowledge about sex and sexuality; yet, we refuse to have an honest conversation in our homes and in our churches about this issue. After eating, sex is the next most sought drive in humans. SEX—from the pulpit to the White House! Sex—men have lost their jobs for it. Men have even lost their lives for it. Men have left their wives for it. Men have left their children for it. Men have dropped out of school for it. Men have gone AWOL from the military for it—SEX!

Parents should have discussions with their teenagers about sex, sexuality, and a healthy, balanced relationship between males/females. One of the leading causes of divorces is sexuality confusion and bedroom turmoil. Below are four CDs that I have produced in an attempt to empower you and your family with information needed to have a healthy and balanced relationship as well as to arm you with information to provide to your children for their well-being. You can order these CDs from my Web site: www.Drrosie.com. You can listen to these CDs by going to www.youtube.com/drrosie11 and click on videos

- ***Romance And Finance In Teenage Relationships* CD**

- ***Church, Let's Talk About Sex!* CD**

- ***Romance And Finance In Adult Relationships* CD**

- ***What The Black Man/Woman Must Know And Do To Have A Healthy And Balanced Relationship In These Financially Challenging Times* CD**

You can also read great articles written by me regarding sex and sexuality on my Web site: **Drrosiesextalk.com**.

IS SEX REALLY ALL THAT?

The most sought after experience by humans, after eating, is sex, and to continuously keep it in the closet will undoubtedly cause serious problems for future generations. Sex is not everything in a nutshell, however, sex has an effect on everything we do. A couple needs much more than sex to bridge and sustain a well-balanced healthy relationship. Sexual activities have a strong influence on the way one thinks and performs in all areas of activity.

Except for money, sex is the only factor in our civilized societies that people contemplate at the risk of causing harm to themselves, their families, or to the loss of their jobs, and all for a few short hours of pleasure and a few seconds of orgasmic thrills. It is the only factor that can cause a community wide, a city wide, or a national or international calamity. And just think, all it entails is two people having sex by their own consent. But if you do it in a manner in which people say is wrong, they will destroy you! sex, a dominating factor in our lives—that moving force that keeps us going, and most of us even admit to it. Sex, that obscure and yet paradoxically, mundane, biological necessity dominates us all in one way or another—if the truth be told.

Sexual double standards have placed the full responsibility for the failure or success of sexual intercourse upon the man. Good sex is when a man and a woman take the time to explore each other fully and learn to work together for mutual gratification. However, often time the Black man finds himself in a position that makes him feel like he is a sexual performer, because society has stigmatized him with myths regarding his sexuality. He has been labeled as "Mandingo," "Long John," and a sexual robot full of energy with everlasting endurance.

The Black man takes those myths into the bedroom with him. He needs constant validation that he is living up to his script. If he does not receive this validation, he will continue to seek it from his woman or another woman.

Women tend to expect men to provide foreplay. However, men also enjoy the luxury of foreplay. Foreplay provides an opportunity for a man/woman to discover and to explore their mate's erogenous zones. Women think that an erection for a man signifies his readiness for sexual intercourse, this is not a fact. The erected penis is only a physical readiness and women need to get past what they see and try to tap more into their man's emotional status.

Sexual chaos and bedroom turmoil are among the leading forces contributing to the high divorce rate in our society. Sex is not a cure, but it can soothe the pain. Sex has a profound effect on our lives and influences almost everything we do. It impacts how we rear our children, relate to the significant mate in our lives, and how we interact with our colleagues in the work place. Therefore, it is time that we address it head on with honesty and open mindedness.

When married couples enter the court for a divorce decree, the divorce is granted based on irreconcilable differences. It would be interesting to hear the responses if the judge required couples to explain their irreconcilable differences. If sex was not a taboo subject, I guarantee you that many would say, " I am sexually frustrated." One of my clients shares her sexual frustrations in the following manner. "I would feel so angry and deprived but I would not admit that it had anything to do with the lack of sex. I would explode at him for any little thing. I could not control my temper with him; I had a kind of contempt for him because he had not figured out that I wanted him sexually without me having to tell him. I was so angry; I did not want to cook for him. In fact, I did not want to do anything that would give him joy."

Sex and lovemaking do not start in the bedroom. They start early in the morning when you pat your mate on the buttocks or just touch their nipples (men like their nipples touched too) when they are stepping out of bed or when they are leaving the house. (This is like sautéing and flavoring a dish you want to cook when you get home.)

Is sex really all that? If the truth be told—it is. For men who are economically challenged, sexual gratification is the only thing within reach for them. They cannot go and hang out in their yacht or take that weekend cruise. So what is it that they can afford and enjoy—a good sexual treat! It is all that and more.

SECTION 6: LETTERS AND ARTICLES TO AND ABOUT MINISTERS, POLITICAL LEADERS AND NAACP

AN OPENED LETTER TO THE NAACP

The NAACP's plan for marching to the Capitol on August 1, 2015, is a "BUNCH OF BULL SHIT." This is a bunch of BULLSHIT and a waste of time, money, and energy. The jobs are not at the Capitol. If you want to march, then march downtown to your city, county, state, and federal building and ask why blacks are not working there. Shut down the construction sites until blacks are working. March to the hotels in your city and inquire why blacks are not working in the hotels, and especially when black churches and black organizations are hosting their events at these hotels. March to your city, county, and state representative's office and take a look at who is working—not many blacks, if any at all.

It's time to stop the "NONE SENSE' and start doing something that makes sense. STOP WASTING PEOPLE'S TIME AND MONEY. When one does not know what to do, do nothing until you figure out what makes common sense.

Why would the NAACP march to Washington on August 1, 2015, when they know that Minister Farrakhan has planned his march in October 2015? This act shows stupidity and adds to the fact that we continue to move in a singular movement. With the status of the hate climate in America, why would one place people in harm's way? This is stupidity at its highest.

Why doesn't the NAACP march to the homeless section of town where thousands of black folk and their children are sleeping in cardboard boxes and are waiting in line for a chance to sleep in a shelter during the night where first come, first served? As an elder, I have been many places, and I have seen many faces. I have seen a lot, heard a lot, and witnessed a lot, and through my many years of experience, I have gained some knowledge, and I know foolishness when I see it—and this is "F O O L I S H N E S S" that must be aborted.

We have more pressing issues at hand that need immediate attention. Folks continue to lose their homes due to the banks not working with them with loan modifications, especially since the Obama administration bailed them out. More blacks are added to the homeless roll every day—women, men, and children. Last, but not least, we should focus on having our own businesses so we can hire some of the many unemployed black folk. We must create a code of conduct for black business establishments, and we must ask questions about why black-owned businesses are hiring everybody *but* blacks in their own establishments. We must find out why this is happening, and if there is a problem, we must attack the problem and find the solution. And for all the black people out there raising hell about the condition of black people, I have a few questions for you: Do you own a business? Can you name five black businesses that you frequent? Can you provide employment for just one black person? How are your children doing economically? Can you provide a job for your children? Are you and your children hanging on the white man's economic "Life Support" machine? Let's stop wasting time, energy, and money and get serious about changing our economy. When our economic status changes for the better, all the problems/issues we face will change in proportion to our assets.

Much Love to My People—And, Yes, I *am* tired of the BS!

JULY 16, 2010

Subject: For lack of knowledge, God's people are too sick and too broke

Dear Pastor:

For lack of knowledge, God's people are too sick and too broke. I greet you in the name of our Lord and Savior Jesus Christ. I hail from the South, like many of you whose roots stem from the great plantations. Yesteryear's church was the pillar of the community. The church house was our school for Blacks. Let me get to the point, or as the old folk would say, "Let me make a long story short." Our people are perishing for lack of knowledge; they suffer abandonment from their own government and from politicians whom they help to put in office.

Pastoral leadership is all the people have at this time. If you fail to provide proper guidance, the people will greatly suffer spiritually, physically, socially, and financially. Time is of the essence as Blacks have already become an underclass. We must prevent the permanent underclass position. The church must return to being the "pillar" of the community. Black pastors have power and influence; politicians and others recognize that power and influence—we witness that during election times and when there is community turmoil. It is time for all Blacks having power and influence to use it as a means to help Black people get out of the ditch—help them to escape their dismal plight. It is not God's will that we perish or suffer at the hand of any oppressor. You have the power to help save the people from social and financial devastation. God may have placed you in position for such a time as this. Reread the book of Esther; you just might get a new revelation. You may ask who am I that I might send you such a message. I am a servant of God, a woman of God, an elder who has paid close attention along this journey called life. I have been in the church all of my life, and I have paid attention. The insight that I have comes from the wisdom of God, and I offer it to you in love.

God wants us to enjoy health and prosperity. Lack of knowledge is what stands between what God wants for us and what we have. We have faith but are lacking in works. An example of what God can do should be witnessed throughout the lives of God's people—physically and financially. Our prosperity speaks nonverbally about our God, communicating that He provides. How can we convince the world that we are sons/heirs of God, who owns the cattle on a thousand hills, and we can't get a hamburger for our table? The pastors and their families are not the only people who are supposed to live well. It is high time that pastors take the front lead when it comes to presenting a healthy body.

Here is what I would like to see the Church involved in: Financial literacy, such as: how to get out of debt; entrepreneurship; planning for retirement in general and as a widow/widower should one's spouse die; estate planning: wills, living trusts, healthcare power of attorney, and financial power of attorney. I would like to see every church have a church business directory with Christian business owners listed to help support the community. The more we empower Christian businesses, the more financially empowered the church will be. If the church can promote politicians who contribute nothing to the church for support, certainly they can promote their members' businesses. After all, if they are tithe-paying members, the church will benefit from helping to increase their income, and thus, it becomes a win-win situation.

It is evident that Blacks have become an underclass. They lead in unemployment, underinsured, health disparity, incarceration, sickness, the list is endless. The Black communities are economically suffering greatly, and Black businesses are closing at an alarming rate. When the money dries up in the Black communities, you will witness the impact of it through your church finance department. Many churches are already suffering financially. I saw in the news where a church was being evicted from its building. It can happen to any church. Look around and you will see how many Black churches are sharing their church building with Latino churches for added income—just to keep afloat. As the demography shifts and younger members have to buy homes away from the city for affordable housing, you will eventually see a decline in church membership. It is important to plan for the future for your church; otherwise, many of you will be building a church, only to have it taken over by other ethnic groups, the same as many of the Black businesses that were once Black-owned but no longer—just look around Los

Angeles. You may have a multicultural congregation; however, it was Black dollars that helped you to get to the top. Do not be afraid to address Black issues because you have a mixed congregation, for we as Christians should consider that all of us are all of our brothers' keepers. Poverty in any race impacts us all.

Churches are going to have to take a serious look at their budget. All businesses and major corporations are scaling back on their expenditures and downsizing; churches will have to do the same; pastors may also have to take a cut. It does not take a rocket scientist to see what's happening. Church folk are hit by this recession too. Christians are losing their jobs, businesses, and their homes. Many of your members have to help their children or a family member who is suffering losses, so now they are having less finances to contribute to the support of the church. We must all be sensitive to the economic conditions and the hard times of others. Help to empower the members so that they can continue to empower the church economically. Have someone come in to teach on money matters, budgeting, getting out of debt, estate planning, eating healthy, meal planning, diet and nutrition, parenting, caring for the elderly, elderly abuse, entrepreneurship, peer pressure involving the youth, what to look for when buying insurance, computer literacy and literacy in general. You would be quite surprised by the number of your members who are literacy challenged.

Time is running out. Let's get involved helping to save God's people. In spite of all that's said and done, when the rubber meets the road, as the old folk used to say, "All We Have Is Each Other. And God."

I have enclosed a copy of my newsletter on Estate Planning. If you are interested in having a copy of future newsletters, request them by e-mailing me at Drrosie@aol.com, and in the subject section, type "*newsletter request.*"

Visit my Web site: www.Drrosie.com. Call me to schedule a Living Trust Seminar for your church.

Thank for your time,

Dr. Rosie Milligan

THE CHURCH NEEDS TO '*DO* CHURCH VS. *HAVING* CHURCH'

Yesteryear, the church was the pillar of the community. The church was there for the community, not just for its members. The church was concerned about the whole man, not only his spiritual self. The *Black Church* also served as a schoolhouse for the community. Many of our parents were educated in a church school. In times when Black folks did not have access to televisions and newspapers or other means of media, the church was where people assembled for information that was necessary for their total needs.

In times past, the *Black Church* served and met the needs of the people of the community. Today's pastors need to step away from the pulpit for a little while and get involved with the communities' needs.

When Rosa Parks said, "Enough is enough!" the Reverend Dr. Martin Luther King Jr. came from his pulpit and took to the street with the community at large. A church that is contained inside of four walls serves its pastor and members only and is only concerned about church work — and not God's work. You see, God's work is ministering to the needs of the *whole* man, like feeding the hungry, clothing the naked, visiting the sick, visiting those in prison, and caring for the widows and orphans.

The *Black Church* of yesteryear did church work so well that we did not need convalescent homes, foster homes, or adoption agencies. We did not need home care providers because the church folk cooked, cleaned, and cared for the sick.

The church, the pillar of the community in times past, could galvanize the community to disseminate information by just toning the church bell. The church needs to tone the bell today for literacy, self-determination via business ownership, and valuing the family.

The church needs to step up to the plate and assess the needs of the community. If you are serving a community that has a large population of children in foster care, high unemployment rates, single mothers, health care system disparity, illiteracy issues, and high crime rates, your message needs to address those needs.

You cannot use an "out of the can" message. It is easier to talk spirituality to people when their physical needs are met.

The church can change the dismal path of the urban communities. We only have a few media outlets that have a positive agenda for African-American people. However, if we had no radio, television, or newspapers, the pastors could outdistance all media combined when it comes to spreading the right message to its people during Sunday morning service alone. Many churches hold 2–3 services per day. Can you imagine what would happen if the appropriate and empowering message went forth? Imagine what would happen if the pastor encouraged each member to give $5.00 per month to a fund to build Black-owned businesses like supermarkets, hotels, motels, etc. This would create jobs, jobs, and more jobs in the community.

How can Black pastors ignore the young, Black, fatherless boys in their community who need a role model and mentor? Bishop Edward R. Turner, raised in a home with a mother and father, understands the difference it makes to have a father figure in a male child's life. He organized *The Sons of Hope*, under the leadership of Marco Ware. The group is made up of 65 young men from the ages of 7 to 21. I watched them train and as they said in unison, "We have hope. We don't carry guns. We carry fountain pens with which we sign contracts and checks." I have never seen such discipline and respect. These young men are a part of a Financial Literacy Program. I also heard Bishop Turner say to his congregation, "If you want a pastor who is confined to these four walls, I am not the one!" Bishop Turner is an unorthodox and "out of the box" preacher.

I heard so much about what Black pastors are not doing, so I began my journey of trying to catch one doing "good for the hood." I found Bishop Turner to be one who looks out for the community, sometimes at the expense of his members. I heard him say once, "Building and empowering men and women can do more for the community than building churches." Allow me to introduce a preacher who is trying to give people on earth a taste of heaven.

Approximately 15 years ago, while driving by the Power of Love World Ministries at 1430 W. Manchester Avenue, in Los Angeles, I observed a crowd of young people on the church parking lot. I decided to check it out. I was impressed at what I heard from the bishop — Bishop Edward R. Turner.

He was awakening his flock to the cold realities of life. He admonished them, saying, "You are the head and not the tail! You are more than a conqueror. You will not stay on welfare! You will be homeowners! You will go back to college and get your degree, and you will own your own businesses!" The young flock all nodded their heads in agreement.

I thought to myself, other preachers are telling people what Heaven is going to be like, preparing the people to live there, but this preacher is preparing the people to live productive and meaningful lives here on earth. I said, "Wow!" I then began monitoring his work. Most of his members bought homes; they went back to school and obtained degrees; many of them started their own businesses.

Bishop Turner believes the concept that "I am my brother's keeper." He started the Community Day 15 years ago with activities that included a Job Fair, Business Expo, Homebuyer's Expo, Clothing Distribution, and a Massive Food Give-away. People of the community looked forward to Community Day. They would leave with empowering information, plenty of clothing, and lots of food.

Turner is a man of faith and a man with hope. He possesses what our people at large are in need of — FAITH and HOPE. Bishop would hang the food give-away banner a month before Community Day. Six years ago, he had no commitment for the food to feed the thousands of people they always fed, still he hung the banner. The food commitment came two days prior to the event. Bishop was also elated that they were able to give away ten bikes that year.

"Walk like you got it 'til you get it," is synonymous with Bishop's faith. When you walk in destiny, help will come to you. Help did come, and now Bishop is the director of the Multi-Faith Clergy Council, under the leadership of Sheriff Leroy D. Baca, of the Los Angeles County Sheriff's Department. With the help of Sheriff Baca, the Multi-Faith Clergymen, and the Community Workers, Community Day took a quantum leap in 2003. It was held at Southwest Community College, with over 20,000 attendees. Ten cars were given away. It was a great success!

Ask and it shall be given. During Community Day 2004, 20 cars were given away. Hope comes to South Central and faith is manifested in the "hood." For more information, please call 323-753-HOPE (4673) or visit www.communityday.net

SHOULD BLACK MINISTERS BE ENGAGED IN THE FIGHT FOR GAY MARRIAGE?

Hello. This is Dr. Rosie, "AND I AM JUST SAYING." Listen Up! Black ministers/pastors need to focus their attentions on the *economic divide* between blacks and other races. This issue is causing more harm to blacks than who blacks are sleeping with and who they are marrying. We need to fight our own battles versus always joining in with somebody else's struggle. (What is the number of black men who are fighting to get married?) Forget about gays getting married and, instead, try to figure out how black ministers can keep their own marriages together—many of them are divorced, and for many who are not divorced, their wives are suffering from abuse and neglect. Probably many of them are afraid to get out because they are not in a financial position to do so.

Black ministers need to take their attention away from gays getting married and focus on trying to get more black men and women in their congregation "out of the financial ditch," and then to get married. Ministers need to focus on being a good role model for marriage that would motivate others to say "I Do." My final words are: *Blacks are not an economic underclass because of who they are sleeping with or who they are marrying, but because of their economic conditions.*

Blacks drop out of college for lack of finances—some cannot keep up because they cannot purchase their books early enough, and then fall behind in their grades. Drug use and drug selling is motivated by poverty. Black women are straying from their moral values and biblical teachings and are shacking up with a man who refuses to marry them, and this is motivated by poverty. Black men fear marriage because they fear the financial responsibilities associated with it. A man does not feel as bad getting evicted being a boyfriend as he would being a husband. The list is endless. I have much more to say, however, I will save it for later. Somebody better hear me up in here!

RESPONSE TO BLACK MINISTERS WHO DON'T LIKE WHAT I WRITE

Dr. Milligan,

With your permission, I would like to use your e-mail in my article that circulates among pastors and ministers around Los Angeles. I have read conflicting and controversial messages that you've issued regarding ministers, and, of course, it makes me feel edgy to push hot buttons, but I think there are some, like Jerome Fisher, Pastor Emeritus of Citizens of Zion, Compton; or Solomon Drake, Pastor of Greater Ebenezer, LA, who have stories that need to be told. Please permit me to run with this story. I promise to keep your links attached in the electronic version.

Dear Sir:
Feel free to do so. And you are right; many of our black ministers should leave a written legacy if no more than to clear the air about lies that have been told on them. I am a minister too, and I have an obligation to speak truth and, hopefully, the truth I speak will move all ministers to a new consciousness to look closely at themselves and their behavior. That's the problem now—everybody turning their head and saying, "Let God handle it." Remember, there is a sin of omission as well as sin of commission.

The behavior of some of our ministers is causing many to become unchurched, and when adults stray away from the church, their children are not introduced to the church. I am just doing my job as a Christian, minister, and as an elder. I speak truth to all issues, so why should I skip around the issues of the church when I have witnessed the devastating effects on the community and families as a result of unspiritual behavior of ministers? I know some of them don't like me, but I love them. I love them enough to tell them the truth. I love them more than they love their members because some of them are afraid to tell their members the truth—especially those who pay big tithes—that is the truth. Well, I am not bound by man's ideology but by God's truth instead.

In fact, one of my workers said to me the other day when we were putting packages together to mail to churches about Black Writers On Tour Conference, "I can hear the pastors saying, 'That's the lady who writes to/and about ministers/preachers.'" I said to her, "If they forfeit an opportunity to encourage their members to be literate because of what they think about me, then I have not written enough about them—because they are *not* getting it." Their job involves more than just standing in the pulpit and preaching their favorite segment of the Gospel. How can your members understand the Word of God and do what the Word says to do when they cannot read with understanding? Of course, maybe that's what many of them want—a congregation of members who cannot think for themselves—maybe that works for them.

It's a shame about the number of children and adults in church who cannot read, and their writing is pitiful. In fact, that's true for many of the ministers. How can this be when there are educators in their congregation? We need to care about the whole man. Members die every day, and the church has to help bury them because the family has made no preparation and they have not been admonished to get life insurance. Why? Is it because the minister thinks it will take away from their tithes?

I am not the beehive that you should get stirred up because I will sting you with truth from head to toe. I was speaking to a pastor one day about doing an estate-planning seminar for his members, explaining the importance of having a Living Trust and Power of Attorney—the importance of not having one's property going to probate, whereas the attorney's and probate's fees eat up most of their estate. This pastor looked at me and said, "Sister, the Bible says take no thought for tomorrow." I ended that conversation and started talking about the weather. I was thinking out loud, *Didn't the Bible say that we should leave an inheritance for our children's children?* Oh, well, what do I know?

Bottom line: If I never get an opportunity to stand in anybody's pulpit ever again, it's all right with me because I can preach the gospel anywhere and everywhere I land my feet, and foremost, it should start in your own home. I have said enough—for now.

WARNING TO BLACK POLITICAL LEADERS, RELIGIOUS LEADERS, AND CIVIL RIGHTS LEADERS—
COME OUT OF HIDING!

Blacks suffer continued injustices from their own government. Blacks have been fighting for years to get their financial due from the 1865 Treaty but to no avail. Dr. Claud Anderson and the Harvest Institute Freedmen Federation, LLC, have fought all the way to the Supreme Court. The powers that be are counting on us running out of money, and we may just do that after spending thousands of dollars fighting in the courts. This administration provides 3.8 billion dollars for redress to descendants of the Five Civilized Tribes (Seminole, Cherokee, Choctaw, Creek, and Chickasaw) because the United States Department of Interior did not make payments as required by the 1866 Treaty, nor did it properly enforce other aspects of the treaty. However, the 1866 Treaty was written primarily to force the Five Civilized Tribes and other Indians to release the slaves they owned and mandated that freedmen have the same rights and benefits as Indians.

Every group that has requested reparation for the wrong done to them by our government has been paid—except Blacks, and none of them have had to spend millions fighting in courts. The United States Department of Agriculture admitted that they discriminated against Black farmers; however, they continue to fight to NOT pay Black farmers what they owe. The Black Farmers lawsuit is one of the largest civil rights suits for Blacks in America . . . so where are the civil rights organizations? Since the Black Farmers claims were filed, a few got paid, but others are still fighting to get paid. The USDA has been taking claims from Hispanics and women farmers, ranchers and Indians, and the Indians have started receiving checks . . . while Black farmers are still fighting in the courts.

We have three money issues on the table: the 1865 Treaty lawsuit, Reparation, and the Black Farmers lawsuit. Our political leaders would not even respond to our cry for help after receiving thousands of letters. Why is everyone afraid to address Black issues? If there were ever a time that we needed to hear from our political leaders, religious leaders, and civil rights leaders, it is *now,* in these dark economic hours. Please come out of hiding. We need you. We have supported you. Why can't you help now in our time of need?

As an elder, a mother, a grandmother, a voter, and one who loves Black people and cares about their plight, I frequently recall the predictions Dr. Claud Anderson made more than a decade ago when he said that the Black race would become a *permanent underclass by 2013.* As I watch the accelerating decline of the race and see Black people abandoned, I am saddened and disappointed in the way our political leaders, our civil rights leaders, and our spiritual leaders have sat as quietly as "church mice" and remained silent on issues that are driving Blacks into a permanent underclass position.

To all politicians and leaders—as you sit in your comfortable spaces and in high places—let me remind you to read a few scriptures from the book of Esther from the Bible. While reading, pay close attention to Mordecai and Esther's relationship during racial turmoil and the annihilation attempt. Mordecai helped Esther to become queen in the royal palace of King Ahasuerus. Look at the comparison between then and now. We helped you to get into your position as well. In case you do not keep a Bible near at all times, permit me to quote these scriptures that will refresh your memory of the story.

> (Chapter 3:13) *And the letters were sent by couriers into all the king's provinces, to destroy, to kill, and to annihilate all the Jews, both young and old, little children and women, in one day, on the thirteenth day of the twelfth month, which is the month of Adar, and to plunder their possessions.* I will also quote Chapter 4:13–14 which reads: *And Mordecai told them to answer Esther:* **"Do not think in your heart that you will escape in the king's palace any more than all the other Jews. For if you remain completely silent at this time, relief and deliverance will arise for the Jews from another place, but your father's house will perish. Yet who knows whether you have come to the kingdom for such a time as this?"**

I pray that you will read the entire book of Esther and substitute the words "Black people" where it reads "Jews." May I remind you that as Blacks vanish and become an underclass, so will you, your children, and your children's children. We are beginning to see it now. As the demography changes, Black politicians are becoming a disappearing act—Blacks have lost many elected political positions. And Black churches are feeling the effects of the demography shift and the economic decline of its members and have to rent their churches to Latinos for church services in order to meet their financial obligations. As of today, there are over 50 Black churches in the Los Angeles and surrounding areas *in bankruptcy*. I warned you that when the Black community suffers financially so would the Black church, but nobody listen to me.

TIME IS OF THE ESSENCE FOR YOU TO GET INVOLVED AND "TIME IS THE ONE THING THAT YOU CANNOT CALL BACK!"

BLACK PASTORS STUCK ON STUPID

Allow me to say, I am not talking about all Black pastors—just many of them. I, myself, am a minister, and I am in no way attempting to tarnish Black pastors. However, being a woman of God, I am spiritually obligated to seek truth. We are losing too many of the young generation because they sense that there is something wrong or something missing with Black religion.

Our youth are confused about the God who owns everything, like the cattle on a thousand hills, yet they can't even purchase a ham hock for their family. Black youth must feel like unwanted stepchildren to God because they are on the back burners and at the end of the line in most situations.

I realize that I will get few invites to speak at churches after writing this—so be it—but I am compelled and mandated to speak truth. Somebody has got to speak the truth. The hour has come for the real men and real women to please stand up. Can't you see that in every city, we have more megachurches than any other race? It's a shame and a disgrace that Blacks do not own *one* supermarket in any city. We know that we eat, and we eat a lot. The proof is in the pudding. Just look at our obese pastors and their members.

Here is what caused me to write these words. I read an article in the *Raise The Praise Church* newspaper dated February 17, 2013, page 5, titled, *The Greater Zion Church Valiant Effort To Purchase Compton Landmark*. You have to read this. Here is a quote from the article: "The Greater Zion Church family is attempting to honor this awesome request to preserve the legacy of our spiritual pioneers and forefathers. It's all about legacy. Our culture has a right to preserve our inheritance for generations to come."

My question is this: Was there an attempt made to recover the alleged $800,000 that the former pastor stole from the church? I heard that he is out of jail and has started a new church. If this is true, what has the Black Minister's Organization attempted to do about this? Is there a code of silence among pastors? It would be nice if some of the pastors stop stealing the inheritance. Can we leave more than merely churches as an inheritance for Black folk?

I would like to suggest the pastor of The Greater Zion Church proceed with the purchase of Double Rock Baptist Church, but rather than taking people's tithe money to purchase it, allow the members and the community to invest in the building and make it a culture center and a place where events and conferences can be held, or a supermarket, etc. Such would better serve the community, provide jobs, a sense of pride, and then it would be a real legacy.

To the older pastors, you need to teach the younger pastors to seek a path that will help their members become balanced in every aspect of their lives, not just spiritually only. We are at the bottom of the bottom in every area. Carest thou not that we perish?

The Black church used to be the pillar of the Black community; it was the schoolhouse for our forefathers. Black churches started schools, colleges, etc. We have more than enough Black churches. In fact, some of the churches we have should merge. Tithes were never meant just for us to build big churches. We should be helping to provide for the orphans, the widows, the needy, the hungry, the homeless, etc. Stop taking the people's money to build more churches; instead, invest in something that can yield a return for our children's children.

There are many churches that are doing a good job. I will just mention a few: Dr. Fred Price and The Crenshaw Christian Center have many employees, and they are paid well. They have schools and many venues that help the community at large. Consider Dr. Scuffie Shigg and The Love Lifted Me Missionary Baptist Church. Pastor Shigg's legacy is that of building up and restoring Black men who have fallen by the wayside. He helps them to get back on track via feeding, housing, training, and helping them gain skills needed for a job—that's a legacy.

In my book *Black America Faces Economic Crisis*, you will find solutions, and you will find out how Black churches can help solve Black America's problems. Come on, Black pastors, let's do better and make better decisions. Didn't the Bible tell us to leave an inheritance for our children's children? If we are going to eat from the biblical plate, let's eat it all. PASTORS, STOP BEING STUCK ON STUPID, TRYING TO IMPRESS AND OUTDO OTHERS. AND CHURCH MEMBERS, YOU HAVE A JOB TO DO ALSO—HOLD PASTORS ACCOUNTABLE. AFTER ALL, GOD GAVE YOU SOME SENSE TOO, AND YOU ARE GOING TO HAVE TO ANSWER FOR YOUR SIN OF OMISSION.

URGENT CALL TO HELP BLACKS WHO SUFFER DUE TO POLITICAL ABANDONMENTS

Blacks suffer continued injustices from their own government. In a few weeks Congress will vote on the Cobell settlement agreement, HR4213, Section 607, which is currently before the Senate Committee on Finance. I want to make you aware that this is a very, very important issue for African-Americans. This legislation provides 3.8 billion dollars for redress to descendants of the Five Civilized Tribes (Seminole, Cherokee, Choctaw, Creek and Chickasaw) because the United States Department of Interior did not make payments as required by the 1866 Treaty nor did it properly enforce other aspects of the Treaty. However, the 1866 treaty was written primarily to force the Five Civilized Tribes and other Indians to release the slaves they owned and mandated that freedmen have the same rights and benefits as Indians.

The Cobell settlement however, as written, continues to reward the Five Civilized Tribes who were disloyal to the United States and fought for the Confederacy and continues to ignore and exclude Black freedmen and mixed Black Indians for whom the 1866 Treaty was written. The disparity of the Cobell settlement continues an historical wrong and is a priori racial discrimination which is against federal law. We therefore beseech you, as the representative for whom we voted, to use your power and influence to cause Congress to make an attachment to the Senate's version of HR 4213, Section 607 that, in accord with the Harvest Institute Freedmen Federation, LLC's request, adds $600 million to the Cobell settlement to include the freedmen of the Five Civilized Tribes and mixed Black Indians.

This attachment also has important implications for Congress as a body. During America's Civil War, which ended in 1865, the Five Civilized Tribes entered into agreements with the Confederate States of America and fought with the South to maintain slavery. After the Civil War ended in 1865, those tribes, as sovereign nations, refused to release the slaves they owned. They refused to acknowledge the Emancipation Proclamation, the 13th Amendment, and the conclusion of the Civil War --- that slavery could no longer exist in the United States. Therefore, in 1866, a year after the Civil War ended, the United States government required that the Five Civilized Tribes sign a new treaty.

The new Treaty redefinded the relationship of those Five Civilized Tribes with the United States. The 1866 treaty: 1) Forced Indian tribes to release the slaves they owned. 2) Provided all freedmen (former slaves) and their descendants within the Five Civilized Tribes protected status, which included equal civil status with other tribe members. 3) Made freedmen equal tribal members. 4) Granted freedmen the same rights to land, government benefits and resources which other tribal members were granted. The Cobell Settlement is based on the 1866 Treaty which is still in force, but as written, Cobell ignores major portions of the 1866 Treaty, specifically those portions written for the freed slaves and mixed Black Indians and excludes them from the remedy. Does Congress want to participate in a blatant act of racial discrimination?

As an elder, a mother, a grandmother, a voter, and one who loves Black people and cares about their plight, I frequently recall the predictions of Dr. Claud Anderson, the author of *PowerNomics: The Plan to Empower Black America. More than a* decade ago, he said that the black race would become a permanent underclass by 2013. As I watch the accelerating decline of the race and see Black people abandoned, I am saddened and disappointed in the way our political leaders, our civil rights leaders and our spiritual leaders have sat as quietly as 'church mice' and remained silent on issues that are driving blacks into a permanent underclass position.

As you sit in your comfortable spaces and in high places, let me remind you to read a few Biblical scriptures from the book of Esther. While reading, pay close attention to Mordecai and Esther's relationship during racial turmoil and annihilation attempt. Mordecai helped Esther to become queen in the Royal Palace of King Ahasuerus. Look at the comparison; we helped you to get into your position as well. In case you do not keep a Bible near at all times, let me quote a few scriptures that will refresh your memory of the story. Chapter 3:13, *And the letters were sent by couriers into all the king's provinces, to destroy, to kill, and to annihilate all the Jews, both young and old, little children and women, in one day, on the thirteenth day of the twelfth month, which is the month of Adar, and to plunder their possessions.* I will also quote Chapter 4:13-14 and it reads: *And Mordecai told them to answer Esther: "Do not think in your heart that you will escape in the king's palace any more than all the other Jews. For if you remain completely silent at this time, relief and deliverance will arise for the Jews from another place, but your father's house will perish. Yet who knows whether you have come to the kingdom for such a time as this?"* I pray that you will read the entire book of Esther and replace the word Black people where it reads Jews. May I remind you that as Blacks vanish and become an underclass, so will you, your children and your children's children. We are beginning to see it now. As the demography changes, Black politicians are becoming a disappearing act—Blacks have lost many elected political positions.

Attaching freedmen and Black Indians to Senate Bill HR4213 is critical. If this door of economic justice is slammed in our face, especially in today's economic crisis—we will consider it to be an economic funeral for Black America. Any and all black people must use any power and influence that they have to compel Congress to abide by the 1866 Treaty. If the law that was written for freeman and mixed black Indians is ignored and they are excluded from the Cobell settlement, then we are truly back to the conclusion of the Dred Scott's decision – that a black man has no rights that the white man is bound to uphold. Dred Scott would echo loudly if our government selectively chooses to acknowledge and enforce only those portions of the 1866 Treaty that provide benefits to Indians but knowingly excludes black freedmen and black Indians.

I truly believe that with clear understanding of the facts regarding the Cobell settlement agreement, HR4213, Section 607, you will conclude that the attachment requested is the politically correct thing to do.

Thank you for taking the time to become acquainted with this issue.

SECTION 7: MEDIA PROFILE MEDIA SAGAS

THE REAL KILLERS OF THE FIVE COPS IN DALLAS TEXAS

The persons responsible for the loss of lives of the five policemen in Dallas, Texas are as follows: Those who continue to perpetuate institutionalized racism throughout America—in its schools, universities, legal and criminal justice system. This also includes every law enforcement officer—black, white and others—who stood by and said nothing, and did nothing, while white officers beat or killed black men unjustly. The racist defense and prosecuting attorney, every juror who stood up for the policemen who were guilty in taking the lives of black men—yes, you are the guilty ones. And if you have any conscience today, you should be haunted by the trigger pulled by the gunman on that dreadful evening July 7, 2016.

I have lived seventy years in America, and I am a third generation removed from slavery. I experience the past, the present and the future all in one. I have a glimpse of the future, which is based on the facts that the more things change, the more they stay the same. The black man/woman is just as enslaved today legally as in the past. The criminal justice system upholds the law when it comes to disregarding the black person as a human being—which appears to be legal.

My question to all non-blacks is: what if your men were being brutally and unjustly murdered at the rate black men are being murdered, how would you feel and what would you do? When I saw those cops on top of a black man—who was in a helpless position, then shot, I had a flashback. Pain gripped my abdomen. I thought about when I was young, living in Mississippi when white men would roll up on horses to a black person's house and call for a father or a father's son to come out the house so they could either beat him in the presence of his family, or kill him. Nothing was done to the killer then, and nothing is done, in most cases, now. After witnessing the black man, Alton Sterling, who was killed just recently, I cried, I cried and I cried.

We must all stand up, and speak up when injustice is done. Here is a good quote I read online. "*The only thing necessary for the Triumph of evil is for good men to do nothing.*" Remember, the crop we plant today, our children will be the reapers of it tomorrow. Is it the masses who want a race war, or is it just a few evil ones who are trying to ignite a race war? You may not witness a race war in your time, however, if things do not change, there will be one. Is this what you want your children to inherit from your wrong doings? Think. If you have any doubt about what I am saying to you, you had better ask your young people how they feel about what's going on. You will be quite surprised.

Here is another quote I read online,

"Young whites do not ascribe to the notion 'We want our country back.' It's the old evil power thirsty white folks. Young whites know that you evil ones have lied to them. Their association with blacks in school, in sports, etc., they know truth. And they want to be like blacks, they want to sing like us, dance like us, dress like us, preach and praise like us—don't you get it? They want to live in peace as God would have it to be—can't you see how many of them are marching in the Black Life Matters Movement? Does that tell you something?"

America, you have pushed blacks against the wall, and they have two choices: give in to the ills of society, or stand up and fight for themselves and for their children. You have created a monster in your own back yard. Many black men are in prison unjustly. They pled guilty to a felony because they did not have the money to hire an attorney to represent them. Upon their release, due to a felony, they cannot obtain federal/state assistance such as: low-income housing, food stamps, federal grants for education and cannot be caught in the presence of another felon—Oh, America, America the beautiful, what are you doing to black people? Where there is no justice, there will be no peace. Young blacks will not continue to take, and to put up with, the injustice and do nothing; they have been placed in a positon whereby they don't have much to lose. The new culture, the new crop, would rather go down fighting than to stand still, do nothing and be killed.

Let me leave you with these words of wisdom: A house divided, cannot stand. An enemy inside of a house can destroy you quicker and faster than the enemy on the outside. America, we have enemies all around the world. If we are to survive, we must come together as one race. We can do better, and we must do better, starting today and henceforth.

A DOG'S LIFE IS WORTH MORE IN AMERICA THAN A BLACK MAN'S LIFE

I am an elder, and I long to see America live out its creed that all men are created equal. However, America falls far from the mark of justice for all. In America, it is justice for some. For this reason, I do not pledge allegiance to the flag for its wording does not hold true for African-Americans. This Zimmerman/Martin's verdict is a disgrace to America. And you say it's not about race, and the jurors are color blind. You are right; they were color blind because they saw white and they did not see black. They were blind to color and that is why they only saw and took the side of a murderer—George Zimmerman.

I can guarantee you that in America, there would have never been six black women as jurors when a white man's life was on the line. Never. Never. Never. If you want to know why there were all women and all white women, let me tell you why. They knew that if they had just one black woman, she would have seen both sides and voted for justice. Why women? They needed a not guilty verdict and they counted on the emotional side of a woman who could not stand to see her white son in prison, especially for taking the life of a black person. After all, history bears record that it's okay for a white man to kill a black man and walk free—the more things change, the more they stay the same.

Revisit the movie, "A Time To Kill," where a white man was on trial for raping a black girl. When the lawyer asked the jurors to close their eyes, he said imagine that this little girl who was raped was a white girl, and then give your verdict. They all quickly agreed that the perpetrator was guilty.

Consider the facts. Michael Vick was given two years in prison for dogfighting and George Zimmerman gets zero time for killing a black boy. What's up with that, America the beautiful? Every American who believes in freedom and justice should be outraged about this verdict because injustice hurts us all. How do you think the world sees America? No wonder they hate us. They see us trying to control how they treat their people and we treat some people in our country worse than we treat animals.

Don't be surprised if non-black business owners start burning down their businesses like they did in Los Angeles after the Rodney King's verdict. They saw it as an opportunity to collect insurance and FEMA money and get from under the debt they owed. Blacks did a small share of the burning, but very few black business owners were given insurance money to rebuild their businesses.

America, the beautiful, you won't be beautiful long if you don't stop your wicked ways. God is watching. To the rich and mighty, you have more money, more power, more gun power, and more influence in the legal system. However, you are no match for God. God is still in charge of the elements such as: the wind, rain, storm, tornados, hurricane, floods, and fires. And haven't you notice how God's elements are destroying those who oppress the lesser ones and those who stand by and allow it to happen and turn their heads, you are being judged, too. You don't get it?

The blood of the ancestors is crying from the grave for God to avenge for the wrong doings and God is hearing their cry. If America does not turn from her wicked ways, the worse is yet to come. Just wait and see. Every believer and God-fearing person had better speak up where injustice is being done because when the wrath comes, the good will have to suffer for the bad. Justice for all and not just for some is everybody's business.

Dr. Rosie Milligan, minister, author, publisher, talk-show host, estate planner, and owner of Professional Business Management/Consulting Services, 1425 W. Manchester Avenue, Ste B, Los Angeles, CA 90047, 323-750-3592, e-mail www.Drrosie@aol.com, www.Drrosie.com

WHO IS TO BLAME FOR THE IMMORAL ACCUSATION OF KOBE BRYANT?

They Will Destroy You!

Except for money, sex is the only factor in our civilized societies that people contemplate at the risk of causing harm to themselves, or their families, or losing their jobs, and all for a few short hours of pleasure and a few seconds of orgasmic thrills. It is the only factor that can cause a community wide, a city wide, or a national or international calamity. And just think, all it entails is a minimum of two people having sex with each other by their own consent. But if you do it in a manner in which people say is wrong, they will destroy you!

Unfortunately, men—from the pulpit to the White House—have been given a silent and invisible license to have sex with whomever they please, regardless of their marital status. "Get all you can" is like a rite of passage for a man—especially when he has money and power.

Every person who says "A man is going to be a man," or "He is only a man," when a married man has sex with another woman, and especially if he has money, fame or power, that person is the blame for the predicament that young Kobe is in today. In fact, women have become so accustomed to their men cheating on them, or either have witnessed it so frequently, that women have now consigned themselves to the idea that "A man is going to be a man." What does all this mean? Could it be that it is an innate right or a male hereditary trait to have more than one woman?

Should we make polygamy legal so that we can ease the suffering and pain for women? It's time for some answers. As Marvin Gaye said in one of his releases prior to his death, "We need a sexual healing." I contend that we also need a "sex education and awareness revival."

America must revisit her spiritual womb and rethink her acceptance of immoral sexual behavior. We must know that the things that we accept are the things that we will never change.

For parents who hold double standards for young boys and girls, you are responsible for the predicament that young Kobe is in also. Sexual double standards have taken a toll on our society. The only reason parents insist that their girl's curfew is earlier, is because they feel that if she stays out late she may have sex and may get pregnant and bring home a baby. The boys have no curfew—why? There are no limitations or restraints placed upon boys and when they become men they continue to sow their oats when and wherever they please.

I am requesting that American people not watch the T.V. drama of the courtroom trial of Kobe. Let's send a message to the media that we are sick of their drama.

The media is making money and the viewers are losing precious time. Rape allegations are tried daily, what make Kobe's case one for T.V.? The public must say enough is enough. Our children do not need to watch anymore T.V. about married men who had extramarital sex.

For all the people who are angry with Kobe, I am asking you to pray for him and his family and to have compassion for him. After all, Kobe is a victim of a society that has sexually licensed "men to be men."

JUSTICE FOR ALL and NOT JUST FOR SOME IS EVERYBODYS' BUSINESS
GEORGE ZIMMERMAN SAGA

I am an elder, and I long to see America live out its creed that all men are created equal. However, America is far from the mark of justice for all. In America it is justice for some. For this reason, I do not pledge allegiance to the flag of the United States of America, for its wording does not hold true for African-Americans. The Zimmerman/Martin verdict is a disgrace to America. I believe the jurors sided with white America and displayed a blatant disregard for African Americans, by siding with George Zimmerman.

I can guarantee you that in America, there would have never been six black women as jurors if a white man's life were on the line. I believe the jury selection of five White women and one-half Hispanic and African American woman was meticulous in order to assure a decision of "Not Guilty." Defense was dependent on this jury protecting the "Stand Your Ground Law" in light of the discovery of ill will or predisposed homicidal intent on behalf of George Zimmerman. Perhaps too, defense in many respects painted a clear picture to the jury that this could have been their son facing life in prison for killing an African American male child. God forbid, they will not have that. Historically White men have walked away free from accountability after killing a black man. This is the travesty and so I contend, the more things change, the more they stay the same.

In the movie, "A Time to Kill," a white man was on trial for raping a black girl. The prosecutor asked the jurors to close their eyes before making their decision and imagine this little girl was a white girl raped, then give your verdict. The jurors' quickly returned a verdict of guilty. Injustice hurts all of us. Every American who believes in freedom and justice should be outraged about this verdict. The trial of George Zimmerman brings into question the reason why the world views America with disdain. America the beautiful is always trying to control how other countries treat their people, while they show more regard for animals than they do the black man. Michael Vick spent two years in prison for dogfighting, yet George Zimmerman gets zero time for slaying an unarmed, young black boy, 21 days of his 17th birthday, while walking home, in the rain from 7/11 with an Arizona Watermelon soft drink and a bag of skittles.

Hello, this Dr. Rosie, "AND I AM JUST SAYING" *Justice for All and Not Just for Some Is Everybody's Business."* Romans 12:19 reads in the Kings James Version, Dearly beloved, avenge not yourselves, but rather give place unto wrath: for it is written, Vengeance is mine; I will repay, Saith the Lord. God is watching America the beautiful and the blood of our ancestors cry out from the grave for God to avenge wrong doings and God hears their cry. If America does not turn from her wicked ways, the worse is yet to come. Every believer and God-fearing person must speak up where injustice prevails, because when wrath comes, the good will suffer along with the bad.

WARNINGS REGARDING THE CHRISTOPHER DORNER AND THE LOS ANGELES POLICE SAGA

Let's keep Christopher Dorner's mother, Nancy Dorner, in prayer. My heart hurts for her. Her son was not born a killer. Chris may have pulled the trigger, but who is the real murderer in this case? Just put your thinking cap on. Who is really responsible for the precious lives that were lost? Who triggered the rage? I am sure that there will be a lot of sleepless nights for those whose actions of hatred and racism triggered this saga. There is a God, and He sees, hears, and knows all. I pray that a lesson was learned from this saga so that the lives lost will not be in vain. I pray that a thing such as this will never occur again. However, if we do not learn the lesson of the impact of hatred, prejudice, racism, and standing by saying nothing when injustice is being done to others—then history can repeat itself.

It's important to the citizens of Los Angeles to witness a pure, transparent investigation of the allegations alleged by Chris Dorner because far too many citizens and their families have experienced maltreatment at the hands of the Los Angeles Police and the Los Angeles Sheriff's Department from the streets and from the jail cells. If we are to survive the insanity of this nation, the madness in the streets, the chaos induced by those in power, throwing a rock and hiding their hands, if we are to feel safe, we must see law enforcement as our friend and not a friend to some and an enemy to others.

Let me bring to your mind a good example: When the media demonizes Black men, non-Blacks will cross to the other side of the street and clutch their purses when approaching a Black man for fear of the unknown. When citizens, including women, have this same fear of those who are supposed to serve and protect them—the police and the sheriff—this is a bad situation. There are times that the law enforcement will need help from the citizens. In fact, recently, a policeman was in a struggle with a man who had overpowered him, and a Black man looking on, jumped in and saved the policeman. Now *that's* how it ought to be. Our law enforcement is not to be public enemy #1 but our rescuers, instead.

It's time for a real cultural sensitivity training program for the Los Angeles Police Department and the Los Angeles County Sheriff's Department. We are not an island unto oneself; we all need each other. We must begin a healing process. It's hard for a wound to heal when every time you think it's healing, someone comes along and digs into the scab, thus, reopening the wound that's trying to heal. That's what happens when law enforcement continues to mess up.

The good should not have to continue to suffer for the bad guys/gals. That's exactly what happened in the recent Chris Dorner and the Los Angeles police saga. That young couple and the other police officer killed had nothing to do with the pain suffered by Dorner at the hands of the police department. My case and point is this: this is a situation where the good had to suffer for the bad. A note from me, the elder: let us not remain silent when injustice is being done. May we always be reminded of this SAGA!

THE CHRISTOPHER DORNER, AND—THE LOS ANGELES POLICE SAGA, WHAT CAN WE BELIEVE?

"AND I AM JUST SAYING..." We've heard time and time again over the news about the cleaning ladies that were bound by Christopher Dorner, and how one of them broke loose and called the police. So... where are these ladies now? And should the $1,000,000-plus reward not go to them (if the charred remains are really those of Christopher Dorner)? Instead, a white couple surfaces (out of nowhere) to claim it was they and not the cleaning women, who were bound by Mr. Dorner, and they are the ones who called the police. From where did they come? Why are we just now hearing about them? Want to bet who will get the reward? This is a statement made by a friend of mine, Dr. Dumas.

These were my sentiments exactly. And I have a few questions also. Was there ever any intent to really give the reward, or was it just a trick? Was there any intent to truly capture Dorner and bring him in alive before a court of law? Could more truth have been exposed about this case? In every situation people must read the small print in any offer. Simon, my daddy, always said, "If you tell one lie, you will have to tell two; the second lie is to cover up the first lie, and the beat goes on." How many lies have we heard this past week from the mouth of the media and the police department? We cannot see all or hear all, but there is one who can, and that one is God Almighty, and one day, He is going to read the VERDICT and hand down a sentence that no man can appeal. No man is a match with God, no power is a match with God, and no guns are a match with God. God controls the elements, He can speak and the lightning will flash, the thunder will roll, the rain will fall, the floods will come, the tornadoes will rip up a town, the earthquake will swallow up a city, and a fire will burn down a whole community. You evil people, you wicked ones, and the oppressors—don't mess around and make God angry! If you make God mad, neither your money nor your powerful weapons will be able to protect you.

And for those who just watch injustice, sit quietly and don't say anything, those who turn their face from evil and fail to speak out, I have a word for you too. The Bible tells us in Proverbs 31:8, "Open your mouth for the speechless, in the cause of all who are appointed to die, open your mouth, judge righteously and plead the cause of the poor and needy." And somebody needs to say AMEN. We need to preach this truth today. My text for today is: GOD'S EYES ARE WATCHING YOU AND YOU CANNOT HIDE, SO COME OUT WITH YOUR HANDS UP!

SECTION 8: OTHER ARTICLES BY DR. ROSIE MILLIGAN

BLACKS HANGING ON LIFE SUPPORT

Blacks must fund their own economic liberation. How long will Blacks depend on others for economic oxygen? We must learn economic CPR and resuscitate ourselves. Almost every major event held by Blacks in Los Angeles, California, was cancelled last year due to a lack of funding/sponsorship from non-Blacks. If it were not for White folks' money, the NAACP and other groups would not be able to hold their events.

I had to cancel Black Writers On Tour last year for lack of financial help. I have funded a large amount of this event's cost from my personal funds. I am at retirement age, and I cannot continue to do so. Via these writing conferences, I have helped authors from age 7 to age 95 tell their stories, because Literacy Is Everybody's Business. I have helped 275 Black authors see their books in print and have helped more than 30 authors start their own publishing companies. I helped launch a major literary agent's career on the West Coast, Thompson's Literary Agency. Our forefathers took their stories to their grave because they had no one to help them tell it. History will repeat itself if we do not learn from their experience. When we fail to record what we did, others will come along and claim those honors; and if we are not mindful, we will be written out of history. Instead, we will be remembered by the pages written by a one-sided player-hating and insensitive media.

I hope and pray that even after my transition there will be someone whom I have touched who will carry on the legacy of assuring that our stories will be told. Mary McLeod Bethune stated in her will, "I leave you hope, I leave you love, I leave you a thirst for knowledge." I want to leave you a thirst for knowledge, and I challenge you to continue to make literacy everybody's business and to see to it that *our* stories, not *his-story*, is passed on to the next generation. I challenge you to leave no Black child behind when it comes to reading and writing. Our stories may not be televised, but they can be written in the pages of history.

Haven't you noticed that it is our Black children and adults who lag behind in reading and writing skills? So, then, who should be concerned? As a publisher, I see poorly written manuscripts with three hundred pages containing no paragraphs, without proper nouns capitalized, and many more major mistakes. If you don't believe me, ask your child, even your adult child, to write a one-page topic on any subject and you be the judge for yourself.

The days are gone when one could just call a meeting to discuss, face-to-face, a grievance, complaint, etc. Instead, you are asked to "put it in writing," and a poorly written communiqué will get no response in most cases. Be it politically correct or not, people tend to judge one by the way they write and speak—so we must do better.

I need you to financially help me to keep this venue alive and well. I am reaching out to you so that you will not be able to say what people often say when things go south, "What happened to that business/organization?" I need your help. It's not for me; it's for those that I am concerned about. You can go to www.Blackwritersontour.com and make a donation via PayPal, or you can send your donations to Black Writers On Tour, 1425 W. Manchester Avenue, Los Angeles, CA 90047. 323-750-3592

THE IMPACT OF THE INCREASE OF BLACK WOMEN GOING TO PRISON IS DEVASTATING THE BLACK FAMILY

Donna Ann Smith-Marshall, Carson, California, is a mother, wife, and a prison reform activist. In her new book, ***"TIME ON THE INSIDE: Behind the Walls in a Maximum Security Women's Prison from an Insider's View,"*** Donna Ann helps the reader to understand the need for compassion for those who are incarcerated. She vividly takes you behind the walls of Central California Women's Facility, the United States' largest women's penitentiary, and Sybil Brand Institute, formerly the largest women's jail in California.

Psychologists, scholars, and politicians, when trying to make a score for election, will paint a picture of the criminals of today being hardcore and violent, but the masses aren't. It is important for society to understand that the people behind bars are not always what the media has portrayed them to be. Yes, there are some who have committed horrific crimes against adults and children, but please understand that these are not the individuals who continuously go in and out of the prison system.

If you cannot find compassion in your heart for Mrs. Smith after reading her story, you will not be able to have compassion on your child, your sister, or your mother, any of whom could easily be staring at the steps of a prison door. It takes just *one* slip-up. It's easy—not hard—to get there.

Donna states, "I had high hopes of going to college and becoming a journalist. Instead, I became a teen mother and had to quit school and go to work. In spite of my situation, I landed a job with the Internal Revenue Services and General Services Administration. However, providing for my children became an overwhelming burden. I needed to prove that I could make it, despite being a teenage mom. I tried to remain independent and not ask anyone for help. That's how I began my journey of falsifying financial statements and forgery. It didn't take long to land 2½ years in a maximum security women's prison. Am I worthy of an opportunity for a new chance? Do I deserve compassion? I think so, and so do many others who committed a non-violent crime."

The book points out that the penal system does not actively pursue rehabilitation. With a current capacity of over 165,000 inmates in the state of California and an operating budget of $5.7 billion, the average annual cost per inmate is almost $31,000. According to the CDC's projection report, women currently make up 14 percent of this population, with over 12,000 women in prison today as opposed to 8,000 ten years ago. An inmate doing a sentence of 2½ years, earning a mere $0.15 an hour, will never earn more than $780 within a year. Sounds like a new form of slavery to me. The question that should be raised is—how come inmates can work for the federal government and large corporations while in prison, but cannot get employed by them when they are discharged from prison after serving their time and making restitution?

When inmates are released from prison, they are given only $200 to begin their new life on the outside again. Donna Ann was lucky. She had help from her family. But she was saddened to think about those women who had no one to help them. Her sister and mother kept her children while she was in prison, but for many incarcerated women, their children are caught up in the foster care system and their mothers are never able to get custody of them again.

An employer's survey revealed that 80 percent of employers said that they would not hire an ex-convict. And the punishment does not stop even after serving time, because if you were convicted of a felony, you would not be able to receive general relief, you could not receive food stamps, you could not receive a Section 8 certificate for housing, nor could you receive a school grant to further your education. Therefore, without the aid of a good support system, many are forced to return to what they were doing before they went to prison—non-violent crimes.

The author states, "There are those who would like you to believe that everyone in the state prison has done some hideous crime and they aren't worthy of being a part of society. This is not the case. I am worthy, and so are many others. I was in prison from 1993 to 1995, but I was determined to start my life over again, so I lied on my job applications. I was hired as a program director in the pediatric department at King Drew Medical Center in April 1996. In 1998, I was employed by Molina Healthcare. I managed a $6 million dollar budget, was responsible for

12 employees, and managed three departments. I am no exception to the rule. I am just one who penned my story in hopes that it would educate the public to the truth about what really goes on behind bars.

Black women are the pillars of the Black community—by necessity, not by choice. Black men were forced out of the home in order for their families to receive welfare assistance when they were not able to provide their loved ones with shelter, food, and clothing. In the past, many Black men had to leave their families behind to avoid lynching. Today, when Black men cannot provide the basic necessities for their loved ones, they sometimes just disappear. I realize that the media portrays these men as trifling, lazy, and irresponsible, however, that is *not* the case in most instances—ask Black men. They can speak for themselves. My point is that 60 percent of Black households are headed by Black women. Therefore, when Black women are incarcerated, the Black family is highly impacted in a devastating manner. Black children are displaced and are cared for most often by someone other than a family member due to financial hardships, resulting in the children being placed in homes outside of their culture and familiar environment.

An entire generation of Blacks is being destroyed—adults and children—because of an unjust penal system and media propaganda about those who are at risk. I am grateful to Mrs. Donna Ann Smith-Marshall for bringing this issue to the forefront while making her life transparent. But why is it that our political leaders and high-profile ministers are so silent on this critical issue? Why? Or do they truly understand the cancer associated with the prison industrial complex which eats away and destroys Black families? What will happen to the remnant? What will happen to these children who are scattered? Will they grow up to be loving or hateful adults? Will they learn to be forgiving or resentful? Will they become an asset or a liability to themselves, their loved ones, and society? The children of these Black women who are being incarcerated will grow up to be our neighbors, our children's spouses. Will they value life or will they take lives? This may seem like a Black problem today, but I promise you the effects of incarceration on Blacks and denying them the opportunity to reenter society whole again WILL impact *every* race, creed, and color.

Blacks are impacted the most by incarceration because there are fewer Black employers who have the ability to hire their own people. So when you couple this with racism and the current economic climate, the picture looks gloomy for

Blacks and their offspring.

After reading *"**TIME ON THE INSIDE: Behind the Walls in a Maximum Women's Prison from an Insider's View**,"* I cried. I became depressed for a quick moment, then I decided to do something constructive about it and bring it to the public's attention, and that is when I began to write. And so I did my part. Now it's up to the media, especially the Black media. The media needs to raise public awareness of this cancer that is slowly destroying the Black family when Black women go to jail and leave their offspring behind. *This is a cry for help! Help, somebody—anybody—everybody—help!* Prison may be closer to your house and your family than you think.

For additional information about the book, contact the author at 310-438-3483 or e-mail her at Fmapublishing.com

YOUNG BLACK MALES ENTERING THE CRIMINAL JUSTICE SYSTEM IS AT A STATE OF EMERGENCY!

Clara Hunter King, ESQ, an Atlanta based attorney, has joined forces with two female criminal defense attorneys who says, " The number of African-American youth entering the Criminal Justice System has reached a state of 'Emergency.'" These attorneys are tired of seeing young lives—and they tend to be young Black males lives—wasted through ignorance. It has been said that what you don't know can't hurt you, but in fact, what you don't know can get you locked up in prison for a lifetime. The legal system is not about what you don't know but whether your behavior constitutes a crime and "what you should have known

Clara is founder of the organization "Watchdogs For Justice." Clara, and fellow attorneys Yvonne Hawks and Lawanda Jean O'Bannon, have written a series of short stories that brings the reader face –to-face with bad decisions and common and most frequent mistakes made by young people. These attorneys have written a series of short stories that tell, clearly and directly, how one wrong decision can have lifetime tragic consequences. "This Is Not Cool" brings the reader into the lives of Shontez, David, Dana, and Bill, and demonstrates how urgent the need is to educate our young people about the consequences of their actions.

These are excerpts of mistakes demonstrated in their new book, " This is Not Cool": Legal Lessons For Youth & Their Parents.

Shontez was out riding with his friends when one of them suggested they rob an old man they saw in a phone booth. Dana was a hard-working young lady who was nice enough to cash a check for a colleague she didn't know very well. David let his friend talk him into robbing people so they could buy pizzas and play video games. Bill was in the car with his friend Johnny when a cop car pulled up behind them, and Johnny decided to try to outrun it.

None of these young people realized the very serious consequences of their actions until it was too late. Even decisions that seem very innocent—like cashing a check for a friend—can impact a young person's life forever. Every young person should read "This Is Not Cool" over the age of ten. Parents, foster-parents, all children caretakers and any organization that works with youth. Religious organizations should provide this book to their youth.

Why Blacks contribute about half of all the prison inmates when they are only 13 percent of the U.S. population is subject to much speculation. Some believe that it is due to poverty, lack of job opportunities, inferior education and single parent households. Some believe the residents in urban areas demand more police visibility for protection because of the high rate of street crimes such as: drug dealing, armed robbery and gang related problems. We believe that education in "prison prevention" will curtail the rate of incarceration of our youth.

According to the Bureau of Justice Statistics Criminal Offenders Statistics: Based on current rates of first incarceration, an estimated 32% of Black males will enter State or Federal prison during their life time, compared to 17% of Hispanics males and 5.9% of White males. The report further stated that an estimated 57% of inmates were under the age of 35—this being males who are in their most productive and prime years of life. What this means is that we are looking at incarcerating almost an entire generation of people.

According to Dr. Claud Anderson, the hidden national unemployment rate of Blacks is 35%. In cities like Baltimore, Detroit and Pittsburg, Black unemployment is well over 45%. In New York, unemployment for Black men tops 51%. The national Black youth unemployment figure is nearly 80%.

On March 29, 2006, Clara King spoke with students at King/Drew Magnet High School in Watts California. Their teacher, Ms. Pamela Woodlief, had her students read the short stories from "This Is Not Cool" prior to attorney King's visit. The students wrote letters expressing their appreciation for King's visit and for the legal lessons they had learned. The following are excerpts from their letters to attorney King:

"I want to say thank you for coming to my school. In your book "This Is Not Cool," the story with Shontez, my brother is in a similar situation. I wish he could have read that story before he got locked up. I just want to thank you for that."

"My brother was one of those who had problems. As of now, he is in jail for the rest of his life. I believe that this is because he didn't have that one person that told him that his life could be better."

"I learned so much from the things that you shared with our class. Before you shared those things with our class, I never knew that you could get in trouble with the law when

you didn't even know that your behavior was a crime but you should have known. So I have to be careful and watch out for certain things."

"Thank you for visiting our 6th period class. I really was able to relate to the stories in your book. I understood the stories and how someone can easily fall into the life of tragedy just by meeting the wrong friend. Thank you very much for your time. I hope that you can come back again."

"Many of the things that you talked about I was relating to them because have been through a situation like one of the scenarios in your book. It really made me think. And today, I made a list of all of the people that I know and I realize how little I know about those people. Thank you so much for making us think about the people we call our friends"

"Thank you for coming to share your knowledge with us. I found your stories and facts very interesting. I learned much about my rights. I liked it a lot when you gave us scenarios and asked us questions because it made us think and we learned a lot from you."

Watchdogs For Justice holds interactive seminars at schools, churches, group homes and any place where there are young people in attendance. .I believe that every young person and their parents or caretaker should read "This Is Not Cool" together and should have a discussion about the stories. Our youth are getting erroneous information from peers on the streets. And many of their parents are not discussing issues that are causing our youth to become locked behind bars, because they do not anticipate their children being caught up in these legal situations that can cause them to go to jail or prison. These are unsuspecting parents. Therefore, jail and prison prevention is not a topic that seems necessary as a topic for family discussion.

Most parent have no clue about some of the things that young people are involving themselves in today which can cost them years and even life in prison. On many occasions the youth who initiate the trouble that your child finds himself involved in, is not really known by your --- they don't even know their legal name, just his/her nick name. In most cases your child doesn't even know their hangout friend's parents name or their addresses. So when trouble comes your child is left along paying the consequences for something he had not even thought about doing, he only went along, because he had not been taught to stand alone when things do not feel right.

For information regarding interactive seminars for youth, how to obtain the book "This Is Not Cool" Call Dr. Rosie Milligan 323-750-3592 or visit www.professionalpublishinghouse.com or visit Express Yourself Bookstore, 1425 W. Manchester Ave. Ste. C, L.A. Calif.

BLACK FARMERS CLASS-ACTION LAWSUIT ATTRACTS THOUSANDS

The Black Farmers and Agriculturalists Association, Incorporated **(BFAA, Inc.)** filed a recent **Motion To Intervene** on May 19, 2010, in the class action lawsuit, otherwise known as The Black Farmers Lawsuit. This organization seeks intervention on the behalf of African American farmers, their heirs, assigns and administrators (PIGFORD et al. Plaintiff) who are both currently in the lawsuit, as well those who believe that they have a meritorious claim of discrimination against the government but were not notified of the legal proceeding in the lawsuit. The United States Department of Agriculture (Defendant,) discriminated against African Americans for decades when it, "denied, delayed or otherwise frustrated the applications of those farmers for farm loans and other credit and benefit programs," according to the Judge Paul L. Friedman in his opinion regarding the case.

After several years of mediation, the parties negotiated a settlement and entered into a Consent Decree to resolve the Pigford litigation. The Consent Decree established a process enabling farmers who had been discriminated against as applicants for farm loans or credit and benefit programs to obtain an adjudication of their discrimination claims through a two-track dispute resolution mechanism. Under Track A, class members with minimal, or even no, documentary evidence was entitled to receive a "virtually automatic cash payment of $50,000.00 and forgiveness of debt owed to the USDA. Track B option required a higher burden of proof—preponderance of the evidence—but allowed for uncapped damages.

HOW SHAMEFUL: In 1920, according to USDA and U.S. Census data, 55 % (over half) of all farmers in the U.S. were Black. However, today these same agencies state that Blacks account for about 1.5 percent of all farm operators. More disturbingly, of the estimated 96,000 claims filed in the lawsuit, only about 13,000 got paid the $50,000.00 settlement. Mr. Thomas Burrell, president of the Black Farmers Agriculturalists Association, Incorporated **(BFAA, Inc.)** has been traveling do different states trying to understand why so few African American farmers and the heirs got paid. He soon discovered that, most African Americans had no knowledge of the lawsuit. When he made an appearance in Los Angeles to a meeting being sponsored by the Council of the Elder, he drew hundreds from as far as San Diego and Stockton, California who were unaware of the Black Farmers Class-Action Lawsuit.

THIS YOU WILL NOT BELIEVE! We discovered that there were many Blacks who filed for the settlement in 1999 and got paid but never told their siblings about the opportunity for them to get paid. What is wrong with that picture? One man told us at the meeting that his brothers and sisters got paid but they told him that he was not eligible because he had, "left the south."

THIS HAS BEEN A JOURNEY AND AN EYE OPENER FOR MANY. As people began to searching their lineage to farming, they were quite surprise to discover that their parent and grandparents "farming occupation" was certified by the states in which they were born by affixing and certifying this "farming occupation" on their **Certificates of Live Birth.** Farming is something that Blacks knew so well, in fact, we taught the others. It has been reported that the first Africans were brought here as consultants, as it were, in agriculture and not as slaves. We farmed when it was tough; without the modern equipment and technology; while others made it a profitable business upon the sweat of our backs. I remember, when my father and other black farmers took their cotton to the gin, they had to wait in long lines until the white farmers finished doing their business first, before they could have their cotton weigh and processed. As a little girl, I knew then that something was wrong with that picture.

IT IS TIME TO GET PAID. The Obama administration announced a $1.25 billion dollar settlement for decades of agricultural discrimination against Blacks and Congress (The House of Representatives) gave its approval last week. We have come to get paid for real this time. Why are there insufficient funds when it is time for Blacks to cash their checks? This 1.25 billion is simply not enough to pay the number of claims in the lawsuit the agreed upon amount of $50,000.00 per claim. We did not get our 40 acres and a mule: we have been pleading for "Reparations" and have only gotten an apology. Thank you, but we cannot take that to the bank. This is the time for all Black folks and all folks who believe in justice to stand together with us until we get paid. All roads should lead towards Blacks farmers and their descendants getting paid—because it is the right thing to do. How long shall we wait while others get paid?

Mr. Thomas Burrell will continue to tour the United States of America until all are aware of the Black Farmers Class-Action Lawsuit and as victims of discrimination by this government, we should have been notified also. A meeting will be held in Los Angeles on Saturday June 12, 2010 at the Carson Community Center, 801 E. Carson Street, Carson, California 90059. He will be in Bakersfield on Friday, June 17th & June 18th, Location for Bakersfield to be announced. For further information, contact Kenyaka at 626-363-4495

BLACK WRITERS ON TOUR UNITES AUTHORS—TO SAVE THEIR INDUSTRY
By Dr. Maxine Thompson

"If we collectively come together—we can accomplish anything!" Dr. Rosie Milligan, Executive Director of **Black Writers On Tour**, is an accomplished woman who is uniting Black writers for positive change.

Dr. Rosie Milligan, this Mississippi native and economic empowerment activist is often referred to in the community as "our modern-day Harriet Tubman" and the "Motown" of the Black publishing industry. She has authored eleven books and co-authored two; since 1997, she has helped to launch ten Black publishing companies and has published more than 150 new African-American authors ranging from ages 7 to 90 years.

Milligan Books is the fastest growing female owned African-American publishing company in the nation. As a literary agent, she has sold works to some of the most prestigious publishing houses in New York and one of her authors has a movie option contract for his novel.

Dr. Milligan was also motivated to start the Black Writers On Tour because, she states, "I was simply tired of Black folks taking their stories and ideals to the grave because of mainstream rejection letters. I was also tired of New York publishers making the decisions on what literacy work get published and what doesn't not get published. I realized that what we Blacks) write and read can shape and change the image that we want for ourselves and for others."

"I believe that *Literacy Is Everybody's Business*!" We want our children to create a love for reading and writing at an early age. Our children will preserve our history and culture, as well shape our images through their writings."

If Blacks collectively come together, we can accomplish *anything*! It is time that we—African-Americans set the rules to game for the publishing industry. Our images are etched into the minds of the world by what people see on television news and by what they see on B.E.T. Unfortunately, for us Blacks we are not the decision makers for any of these businesses. The music industry also has a great impact on how the world views us.

Black author and Black newspapers are the only hope for correcting the negative images that have been depicted about African-Americans. Dr. Milligan states, "I am determined to make sure that mainstream publishers will no longer be the gatekeepers for what for what Blacks read or write. I have helped many Blacks to start their own publishing companies. Black Writers On Tour has created a new revolutionary movement in the literary industry."

"We have inspired Black authors who are published by New York publishers to demand that their publicist arrange a book signing at a Black bookstore when sending them on book tours.

Dr. Milligan explains what motivated her to launch the publishing business and Black Writers On Tour. "Well, as an ex-cotton picker and ex-farmer, I would like to answer you in farm language. I want to see Black writers get the rightful economic share from their work. For example, I am tired of seeing Blacks pick cotton, take it to the White man's cotton gin, get paid minimally, and yet leave happy. Meanwhile, the cotton gin owner sells the cotton at a high cost (perpetuating continual wealth for his next generation), while the weary Black farmer dies prematurely—leaving his/her family to struggle. Yet, the cotton gin owner's children and their children's children continue to profit from the business. It's time for Black writers to profit from their intellectual properties and labor in a fashion that will create an economic legacy for themselves, their families and their communities.

What Dr. Milligan expects to see or have happen as a result of Black Writers On Tour is for Black writers to understand that writing can be more than just a fun hobby. Writing is a business, in fact a large business. Every class thought from preschool through college requires a book. There are preparation books for every licensing examination in all profession/vocations.

Also, I she wants African-Americans to reevaluate the writing industry and to participate on a larger scale. She wants to see Blacks start thinking about owning their own publishing houses, their own book presses and our book distribution companies. I want to see us translate our books into other languages and market them globally. We must take a serious look at this industry. Who is printing the growing number of Black magazines and Black community newspapers? It's about time that we come together not just to meet-and-eat, but to make definitive gains in our economic future which includes the "business of writing."

Black book sales are to the point where there is a lucrative market for Black-owned publishing houses, book presses and distribution companies. We have researched that question and found some interesting facts. According to the Target Report, "…between 1990 and 1993, Africa-American book expenditures increased 48% between 1988 and 1993, Black purchases of books at retail outlets increased 100 percent." Interest in books and articles by African-American writers is at an all-time high. Many of them are on the bestsellers lists and have remained a part of mainstream's most popular books for month after month. "In 2003, more than $326 million was spent on books about and by African-American writers." These figures more than merely suggest a demand for our own publishing houses, book presses and distributing companies.

Black Writers On Tour can help the local and unknown authors jump start their careers in the following ways. The publishing industry is vast and filled with career possibilities that the students might not consider while reading their favorite writer's latest or cracking open a textbook. She also wants give exposure to African-American authors and writers, increase their book sales, motivate, and develop aspiring new writers and authors.

Thus event will not only bring the authors face-to-face with readers, but also their peers, which will unite them for the purpose of becoming more invisible in the marketplace. Visibility is key for an author. Authors have joined together as book tour traveling partners. They share hotels and their homes in different cities which help to give authors more exposure.

The conference has been designed to provide writers with the practical information they need to work in the literary industry. Publishers, as well as agent will attend. 14 writer's workshops will be held throughout the day and will cover a variety of topics from **How To Publishing, How To Write A Bestselling novel, Legal Aspects of Writing and Publishing, a Free Writing Class for children 10-15** and much more

General Admission is free. There is a free writing class for children. Chat with fiction, non-fiction, poetry, children, and Christian writers. Attend the Poetry Jam Competition—**WIN CASH!** There will be open exhibits and authors signing throughout the day.

This year's highlight: Mothers of Celebrities Who Write, Beverly Green—Snoop Dogg's Mother, author of *"Real Love"* and Verna Griffin—Dr. Dre's Mother, author of *"Privileged To Live."* African-American writers age 65 and older in a forum called **"Let The Elders Speak."** We encourage your youth to come and listen at the feet of these elders as they share wisdom and life lessons.

We are presenting the 2006 Literary Award to Dr. Frederick K.C. Price, author of *"Race, Religion & Racism,"* and Bishop George D. McKinney, author of *"The New Slave Masters".* These are pastors whose literary work is "outside the box." The renowned **Andre Eggelletion**, Syndicated Talk Show Host and author of *"Thieves In The Temple,"* will be the keynote luncheon speaker. Participants—**Maxine Thompson, Attorney Joe C. Hopkins, Kola Boof, and Rita Hall**. Out-of-state participants—**Erick Henderson, Contessa Walls, Don Spears, and Professor Walter Williams, Andre Eggelletion, and Jeremiah Camara** and others.

THE DEMISE OF THE BLACK BOOKSTORE IN AMERICA

We CANNOT lose another industry that belongs to us. We MUST save the Black bookstores! If we collectively come together, we can accomplish *anything!* Black authors and Black newspapers are the means to correct the negative images that have been depicted about African Americans and supply hope for fostering new images. Images are etched into the mind of world by what people read in the newspapers, books, and magazines; hear on radio stations (of which there are very few Black-owned ones) or in the music industry; and see on television, the news, and BET (Black Entertainment Television). Unfortunately, Blacks are NOT the decision makers for any of these venues.

I was speaking with a Black educator one day about the struggle of Black bookstores and how quickly they were closing. She stated, "I buy Black authors' books all the time from Barnes & Noble." She had no clue how her behavior impacts the survival of Black bookstores. Now you know I told her, don't you?

One of my church members was visiting the nail shop next door to me and decided to stop in to say hello. I told her to take a look at our children's section and make sure to start the little ones reading early so that they will develop a love for literature. She replied, "We always spend time in Barnes & Noble bookstores." You know what I did, now, don't you?

We have lost most of our Black radio stations, and we have lost many Black newspapers. When all the Black bookstores close their doors, our voices will be silenced. Visit any major bookstore and you will not see more than 50–100 books written by African Americans, and these titles are mostly street fiction and books by high-profile celebrities and ministers. Many authors will not be inspired to write, knowing that they do not have an outlet for their books. We must change this paradigm.

Black bookstores are closing rapidly—too rapidly. Between 2006 and 2007, fifty percent (50%) of the Black bookstores closed their doors. Some of the owners had operated their bookstores for twenty-five-plus years. Let's look at the history of Black bookstores. They were ushered in as a necessity, because there was a void and a demand. White-owned bookstores had no interest in carrying books authored by Blacks. In fact, many of them thought that we did not read. They coined the phrase, "If you want to hide something from Blacks, put it in a book." White-owned bookstores had no interest in having black-authored books on their shelves, and mainstream publishers (i.e., New York) had no interest in publishing Black books. When Blacks were rejected by New York, they took their manuscripts home and buried them in a trunk or under the bed mattress. Many literary works of our forefathers were discovered after their deaths—their knowledge and their wisdom lie buried in the cemetery. We never heard what they had to say.

Today, I cringe when I think of the lives and knowledge that were lost in the Middle Passage to the sharks in the ocean and the silt that covers their discarded bones at the bottom of the Mississippi River. This knowledge also died inside of Black men, women, and children who hung from trees in the South. Many of our stories were never told because we were stripped of our language and were beaten and forbidden to learn how to read when we reached the shores of the home of the brave—America.

At last, after much bloodshed and tears, we are able to read, write, and publish our books. Black bookstores grew and harvested their niche in the country and became home for many books written by self-published authors. Black bookstores were soon filled with Black books. Most were self-published authors, men and women who refused to beg white folks to validate their works and who refused to take their knowledge to the graveyard. It was "Heyday" for the Black bookstores. They were having Black authors signing books and lecturing. Blacks finally had books to read by people who looked like them. Even children's books were found on shelves with Black characters. At long last, materials were published that were relevant to the Black Experience. The cash registers were ringing off the hook, and bookstores were popping up everywhere—it was on and crackin'!

In 1989, Queen Shahrazad Ali published her book, *The Blackman's Guide to Understanding the Blackwoman*. Her book was the talk of the town, and it was being sold out of the trunk of her car, in beauty parlors, at barbershops, etc. She was truly the Queen and Mother of taking self-publishing to the next level. Black bookstores were making money. It was likened unto the gold rush. Men and women were buying this book. Blacks had caught the reading fever. Then, Terry McMillan came along with *Waiting to Exhale*. She rode the spirit/fever that Shahrazad had created, and her book went to the top. The fever hit me, and I started my publishing company. Since 1997, it has become the fastest growing and largest female black-owned publishing company in the nation. I have helped 12 authors start their own publishing companies and have published over 200 Black-authored books, as well as 4 white-authored books. These authors are spread across the U.S., and are as far away as Hawaii.

Mainstream took notice. They hired Black editors and went scouting for Black authors. They went to Black bookstores to see which authors had high sales. They came after Black authors with large advances, like $50,000–100,000. When these authors were sent on city tours, they went to the big chain bookstores, making no stops at Black bookstores. Blacks started flocking to the chain bookstores and many of them never returned to the Black-owned stores, which were built on the backs of self-published authors. Even though mainstream publishers took on Black authors and sent them on tours to chain bookstores, the Black bookstores were the ones that sold more of their books. Suddenly, Black authors seemed to have their heads in the air. They had been validated by the white man, and many of them didn't care whether, or not they went to a Black bookstore any longer. Then some Black bookstores started shunning self-published authors and started pushing authors who had been validated by mainstream!

Blacks tend to never win when non-Blacks become their competition. Blacks, again, abandoned the Black community bookstores and flocked to the major chain bookstores. *Moreover, here we are in the year 2008, having lost over **400** Black bookstores and many others are barely holding on.* What will happen if these stores close? It will be a disgrace to you and your offspring! Believe me; you have not seen ignorance and unconsciousness as compared to what it will be like when Black folk put down the pen! Economically speaking, we CANNOT afford to lose ANOTHER industry.

One way to combat this is through participation in the **Black Writers on Tour**. It is a powerful, one-day writers' conference event to examine strategies to empower Black authors, Black bookstores, and Black distributors. *You can't afford to miss this!!* Plan to be there Saturday, April 26, from 9 A.M. until 9 P.M., at the LAX Crown Plaza Hotel, 5985 W. Century Blvd., L.A., Calif. 90045. For more information, contact **Express Yourself Bookstore: 323-750-3592**.

HAVE THE BLACK ELITES LOST THEIR DAMN MIND?

When I read the article, "State of the Black World Conference Aims to Set Post-Election Black Agenda," in the *Pasadena/San Gabriel Valley Journal*, I said aloud, "Black folks, especially many of the so-called informed, need psychological therapy—*NOW!* Have they lost their damn mind?" I used to hear my daddy say, while praying, "Lord, I thank you for being clothed in my right mind." I use to laugh at the saying. Today, however, I understand the blessing and gratitude of having your right-mind.

Many Blacks have lost their mind, and they *"Make Me Want to Holla'—Throw Up Both My Hands."* When Marvin Gaye observed the state and conditions of Blacks, he sat down and penned the lyrics asking, *"What's Going On?"* —while prophetically noting issues of his day that have ultimately carried themselves forward to today.

It does not take a rocket scientist to see that something is psychologically wrong with many Blacks, in particular, the so-called elite and self-proclaimed leaders.

The article reads—*"Unemployment for Black people has crept back into double digits for the first time in three years; currently 10.6 percent (10.6%) in comparison to 5.4 percent (5.4%) unemployment rate of Whites, and the 8 percent (8%) rate of Hispanics."*

And? So? What exactly should one expect, and what is the correlation when it comes to employment and wealth—it's clearly business ownership. Approximately 97 percent (97%) of other ethnic groups work for businesses owned by their own ethnic group, while 97 percent (97%) of Blacks work for businesses owned by others *outside* of their own ethnic group.

As I write, Black-owned bookstores, radio stations, newspapers, and other types of businesses are closing at an alarming rate. Fifty percent (50%) of Black-owned bookstores in this country closed their doors within the last two years—count the job loss for Blacks.

People are coming to America from all parts of the world to carve out of a piece of America's wealth for *"them"* and *"theirs,"* and not for *"you"* and *"yours."* Please get this into your heads. Blacks are so set on someone owing them something and giving them something that it never occurs to most that when everybody is drowning, they had better have their own lifejacket.

Furthermore, I am tired of the fire-spitting rhetoric. The article quotes, *"The adage still holds that when America gets a cold, African-Americans get pneumonia!"* I wonder why? Could it be that when America sees rain coming, she puts on a raincoat or grabs an umbrella and then pulls out her lifeboats while African-Americans sit idly at the *'wishing well'*? After all, aren't we Americans too? Then why don't we learn to do what works for other Americans? Find out what it is that keeps them from getting pneumonia and do the same thing.

"Aims to set post-election Black agenda," as stated in the article. The word *"aims"* bothers me. Why not *"set"* versus *"aims"* post-election agenda? What does that mean? And, by the way, what have Blacks asked for from either presidential candidate in exchange for their votes?

If the conference is about symptoms only, as most of them are, symptoms such as: police brutality; driving while Black; flying while Black; racism; disparity in education and health care; discrimination in housing; etc., then you are wasting people's time and money. However, you are helping the economy for non-Blacks such as airlines, hotels, and restaurants, etc.

If the conference fails to produce means to change the economic plight for Black America, then all is in vain. Changing our economic status will bring about change in the dilemmas we now face. The one factor that can help get Blacks out of the economic ditch is to win the largest lawsuit ever for Black America filed by The Harvest Institute, founded by the renowned Dr. Claud Anderson.

This lawsuit is demanding government enforcement of the 1865 and 1866 Indian Treaty Rights for descendants of Black Freedmen and Black Indians. The suit seeks the economic benefits provided in those treaties such as land, tax-exempt status, free college education, rights to own and build casinos, annual income allotments, medical health, and housing services. The issue is enforcement of the treaties for economic benefits for Black Freedmen and Black Indians. This suit is based on constitutional enforcement of a law. For information regarding this lawsuit, visit www.harvestinstitute.org.

Am I angry? *Yes, I am!* I am angry because I am sick and tired of those who should know better, yet they continue to do dumb stuff. I am angry and hurt because I see what is going to be the future of our youth if we do not build a bridge for them to cross over as our forefathers did for us. Come on, people,—get your minds back!

WILL THE REAL MEN PLEASE STAND UP—PUT AN END TO VAGINA POWER

Many women do not want me to give advice to men for fear that the men will become empowered to put an end to women's devices and inappropriate behavior that have ruined the lives of many good men, and which have caused men to be unable to form healthy, wholesome relationships, even with non-conniving women. But it's time for a no-holds-barred dialogue on romance and finance.

Women have accused me of going for the jugular vein, but I say it's time for a frank conversation that's far overdue between the battle of the sexes about romance and finance. I am presenting this information as an author, counselor, and minister.

What Women Are Saying About My CD on *Romance and Finance*—

- "She is giving men ammunition to treat us worse than they are already treating us."

- "She must not read the whole Bible, because it says that a man is less than an infidel if he does not take care of his family."

My response is: "The side I am on is called the right side. I am giving men the ammunition and the authority to take their rightful place; and to teach their sons by their actions how to be a real man, not a wimp who yields to women's every demand out of fear that she will not have sex with him. I am calling for real men to stand up and put an end to this vagina power. When men learn how to be real men, women will be treated better, not worse. Moreover, women are taking biblical scriptures way out of context. This scripture is pertaining to 'husbands and wives,' not people merely dating or shacking up."

It's apparent that it was God's intent for us to have strong families. Families are the foundation of our great society. Furthermore, the scriptures give us a road map about what to do to maintain a healthy and balanced relationship amongst husbands, wives, and their children.

My intent and purpose is to help heal and mend broken relationships that have already been consummated, as well as those seeking a solid and meaningful relationship. My goal is to arm concerned people with the right information to build a solid foundation for their relationship—a foundation made of stone versus sand—that can and will be blown down by even the smallest waves and/or windstorms of life,

Far too may relationships are built on trickery, false pretenses, economic status, and social clout, and when they have dwindled away, does the excitement of the relationship still hold?

I am tired of the double standard for males and females—from the pulpit to the White House. God is calling for holiness for all. We hold conferences teaching women how to be empowered in every aspect of their lives, such as: getting tested for AIDS, knowing how to check your partner's credit rating, etc.

Well, I am saying to the men you are expected to hold up the finances in a marriage. Your wife may decide to quit her job now that she is married, or she may be forced to quit due to sickness, pregnancy, etc. There are some things that you, as a man, must be able to do before you have sexual intercourse with a woman: Get an AIDS test; and before marriage, check your partner's credit rating.

There are important questions that need to be answered, such as: Does your woman owe back taxes? School loans? How many babies' daddies does she have, and how does she relate to those men? How long has she been on the job? How stable is the job market for her vocation?

In addition to these questions, men should know if the woman he wants to marry desires to have children with him; if so, when and how many? Honest answers to these questions will help a man determine whether he wants to, or should, marry that woman, now or later—or if he should just move on.

I contend that the family is important, and a healthy, balanced relationship is what a healthy family needs most. When men and women are playing to win, versus playing to not lose, we will have stronger, healthier relationships and families.

I pray that men and women stop the "us" versus "them" game, and those men and women will give high-fives to more respectful, considerate, appropriate behavior toward the opposite sex.

911 CALL FOR BLACK AMERICA ATTRACTS HUNDREDS

The West Coast Supporters Of The Harvest Institute, under the leadership of Dr. Claud Anderson, launched a national economic plan where hundreds gathered on Sat. January 27, 2007. Those gathered put their "money" where their "mouth" is. People came with checks in hand to purchase preferred stock for the Maroon Business District in Detroit Michigan and for another venture that we will not publicly disclose.

The West Coast Supporters are following the PowerNomics Principles in order to improve the economic status of Black America via owning a portion of the wealth. As we celebrate Black History month, we must not forget that our ancestors paid too great a price with 400 years of free labor and the shedding of their blood for us to be complacent in such disenfranchised status in 2007.

It is not often that we get the opportunity to purchase preferred stock in a company. We are elated! Los Angeles grass root soldiers responded to the 911 call to help get Black folk out of the ditch. We owe it to our ancestors, our children, and our children's children.

We have invested with others on Wall Street for years, it is now time that we invest in Black owned companies. It's time that we reap more than the crumbs that fall from the table. We must give our people hope here on Earth. Black people across the county are participating in this project. Grandparents are investing for their grandchildren. One elderly woman stated, "I want my grandchildren to know that they hold a stake in something of value

It's time for African Americans to seek to do business with Black owned businesses across the country. If we are doing business globally, certainly, we can do business outside of the state in which we live. The West Coast Supporters Of The Harvest Institute is a model group that will change the behavior of African Americans in a positive manner. We will foster changes in leading Black folk back to trusting each other and to invest in Black owned businesses. The West Coast Supporters Of The Harvest Institute is leading by example. They formed an investment club and have invested in Milligan Books, Inc., and most recently invested in--------a Black owned company that produces positive Afrocentric videos, CDs, and DVDs for children—with positive images. We will invest in Dr. Claud Anderson's project as well.

If we want conditions to change for our people, we must change our behavior towards our people. We must understand and committee ourselves to the belief that "Together, we stand and divided we fall." Dr. Claud Anderson will be the keynote speaker for the Black Writers On Tour luncheon slated for March 17, 2007.

For information regarding the West Coast Supporters Of The Harvest Institute and the Preferred stock investments, contact call 323-750-3592

AMERICA FACES ECONOMIC CRISIS AND BLACK AMERICA SUFFERS THE WORST

Blacks have lagged in business ownership and employment prior to the recession. Therefore, it is truly a state of emergency from an economical stand point for Blacks. Black businesses are closing at an alarming rate; mostly due to high cost of business rent, coupled with the decrease of spendable income for Blacks after rent, car note, gasoline, food, utilities, insurance, clothing, etc.

Remember, most of the income for Black businesses comes from Black folk who live in that community. There has been a paradigm shift in demographics; where many Blacks moved to the suburban areas and most recently, low-income-project housing residents have been forced to relocate to suburban areas such as Lancaster, California, etc.

This involuntary flight from the Black community has taken a toll on small neighborhood businesses. Businesses previously owned by Blacks are now owned by other ethnic groups and much of their income comes from Black consumers.

What can Black folk do? Are we a day too late and a dollar short? The answer is no. However, we must become creative and technologically savvy. If America can do business with China, Europe, Africa, etc., then Blacks can do business with other Blacks in every state within the United States of America. We must think outside the "*box.*"

Here is one solution. There is an internet business whereby customers can buy airline tickets, rent hotels, shop at every major department store, office supply stores (*Office Depot, Staples, Best Buy, etc.*), bookstores (*Barnes & Nobles, etc.*) for those in small towns where there are no Black owned bookstore. They can also buy discount coupons from major restaurants and fast-food chains, shop at their favorite stores, earn points, save money up to 30% in rebates and 60% in discounts, and put money in a Black persons hand even though you are buying from non-Black businesses. WOW!

Maybe you cannot afford to rent a building nor purchase merchandise to sell, and even if you had a business location and merchandise; would it be feasible for your family, friends, and Blacks across America to buy from you? No. What if you had an airline business and your relatives, friends, church members, sorority groups, social groups, etc. shopped with you online versus going to the shopping malls, etc. what if these same people bought airline tickets and rented hotel from your online travel site.

I know things look bleak, but God has not gone bankrupt. We must exercise our faith by the works we endeavor in. Faith without works is dead. What I have laid out before you may seem too simple. Well, just try it. You must not become physically, mentally, and emotionally paralyzed during these hard times.

Don't sit there at the wishing well, hoping things will change for you and your family—move from "*fear*" to "*faith*" to "*works*." Don't let the economic Tsunami, floods, and hurricane cause you and your family to drown. Grab hold to the lifejacket, that power jacket that God has given you. Don't sit here and die; do something that makes sense like pilot your own economic plane and pack your own parachute.

To see how the online business works go to drrosie.travelfhtm.com. For shopping in every category click fhtmus.com/drrosie, put in Rep. Number 5693117; then click on FHTM Rewards Mall, and then click on click here to sign up to enter the shopping mall—it's **FREE**. From the comfort of your home you can purchase any and everything that you could purchase in a mall, including cell phones.

Save yourself, there is no rescue coming for you. There was no one to rescue your forefathers, and there will be no one for you, nor your children, and your children's children.

Think outside the box. The new generation of consumers will be shopping online. Don't lag behind trying to hold on to the conventional business way of selling merchandise. After all, you can do both. Just do it.!

BUSINESS OWNERSHIP IS THE ONLY HOPE FOR SAVING BLACK AMERICA

Business ownership and multiple streams of income are the only hope for saving Black America. Daily, many Black leaders, preachers, and politicians spit rhetoric about how many times the dollar bounces in the Black community versus how many times it bounces for other races. When we discuss the times a Black dollar bounces in the Black community in a negative way, we must understand these facts. We must recognize that Black business ownership yields more jobs for Blacks, and that if Blacks do not own the businesses in their communities where they spend a majority of their spendable income, then Black dollars will continue to leave the Black community. Being cognizant of these facts, we must focus on changing the attitude of Blacks about business ownership and supporting Black businesses. We must support Black-owned businesses. We must let our children see us going out of the way to support Black-owned businesses. If you encounter a problem with a Black-owned business, report it to the owner. Never say, "I will never go to another Black-owned this or that." I am sure that we have all been treated unfairly or poorly by other races while doing business; however, I have never heard a Black person say, "I'll never do business with another white-owned business."

We must support Black-owned businesses so that they can thrive, versus merely survive. This will encourage our children to want to own their own business. After all, why would your children want to inherit a struggling business?

Thirty-five years ago, I began preaching to Black folk about the importance of business ownership and multiple streams of income. I knew then that entrepreneurship was the basis for economic empowerment.

It was very clear to me that jobs come from business—and that all races employ their own race first—and all other races hire Blacks last. Blacks were then—and continue to be—the last hired and the first fired. They are also the first to suffer from downsizing. The Harvest Institute, a Black-focused research, policy, and educational organization, has uncovered the following facts about unemployment rates for Blacks: Dr. Claud Anderson, president of The Harvest Institute, says, "The hidden national unemployment rate of Blacks is 35%. In cities like Baltimore, Detroit, and Pittsburgh, Black unemployment is well over 45%. In New York, unemployment for Black men tops 51%. And, the national black youth unemployment figure is nearly 80%."

While many Black politicians were shouting, "Blacks need jobs," I was shouting, "Blacks need to *own* businesses—jobs do not perpetuate jobs for your children and other Blacks, but *businesses* do." It is important for Blacks to start their own businesses, and it is equally important for Blacks to support Black-owned businesses. Blacks must follow the business principle of "find a need and fill it." Even Black business owners must have multiple streams of income. New technology, new types of services and new products can create new needs that can make your products or services obsolete. If you have income from other sources, you will have the opportunity to regroup. Many Black-owned businesses are not passed down generationally, the reason being that most Black businesses are *struggling* versus *flourishing*. Our children need incentive or motivation to want to inherit a struggling business.

They do not want to start their own business because they see too many businesses struggling, and have seen too many businesses fail.

Blacks starting their own businesses and Blacks supporting Black-owned businesses are the only hope we have for survival. Our schools—our educational systems—will have failed to do their job if they do not make entrepreneurship a vocational option with as much emphasis placed on business ownership as is placed on getting an education in preparation for a job—**and that's real!**

I contend that it is the responsibility of every parent, child care provider, legal guardian, school, politician, and Black preacher to encourage business ownership and keep it in the forefront at all times. Every Black church should have a business directory, and the pastor should—from his mouth—encourage his members to support the business owners in his congregation and to seek out Black-owned business services in general.

After all, they should be aware of the fact that Blacks are in an economic crisis and that our survival is dependent upon Blacks doing for self. People are coming to the United States to find a safe haven and to get a piece of the American pie for "them" and "theirs" and not for "us" and "ours." If others help us, that should be the gravy; however, we must bring our own meat to the table.

Marcus Garvey, W.E.B. Dubois, Elijah Muhammad, Malcolm X, Muhammad Nassardeen (of Recycling Black Dollars), Attorney Joe Hopkins, James Clingman, Dr. Claud Anderson, and the Honorable Minister Louis Farrakhan told us that we must do for self. *When will we listen, and who will we obey?*

CALLING BLACK WRITERS TO ACCOUNTABILITY—
IN HELPING TO CHANGE THE IMAGE OF BLACKS

If Blacks collectively come together, they can accomplish **anything**! Blacks images are etched into the minds of the world by what people see on television, the news, the music industry, and what they see on BET (Black Entertainment Television). Unfortunately, Blacks are not the decision makers for any of these businesses. Therefore, it is my belief that Black writers and Black newspapers hold the key to reversing the negative images that have been etched in the minds of many about who we are, what we will and will not do.

Rev. Al Sharpton, made the following statement in his eulogy at Mr. James Brown, the "godfather of soul" funeral. " Brown asked me, what happen to the love that Black folk use to have for each other? I song to uplift Black folk, in songs like I 'm Black and I'm proud. Tell my people to stop singing about bitches, ho's and niggers and sing songs that will uplift Black people and make them feel proud and good about themselves

How we see ourselves will determine our destiny. All we will or will not do is derived from that picture we see of self. And that picture was sketched and depicted by folk who have no clue about who we are and who God created us to be. When we recognize who we are, then, Black people and the world at large will never be the same. Let me repeat, when we, not when they, but when we recognize who we are, then and only then will Black people take their rightful position in this world where God created us as the original people. Malcolm X, once said, " We must not change the image of the Black man in the white man's mind, we must change the image of the Black man in the Black man's mind.

As an author/publisher and founder of Black Writers On Tour. I am more committed to be a catalyst for fostering changes in the literary works of Black people. We must be ready to fund our own projects, if we are ready for the new "literary revolution." We must 'pen' that true picture of us and remember, our truth will not be televised unless we televise it. Black writers must be held accountable what we write. We must united in our publishing endeavors and Blacks must be willing to invest in Black publishing companies so that they will have the financial strength to give Black writers a book advance to publish those literary works that helps to depict and to define who we were and who we are now, how we got where we are and how we can get back to where we were before being brought to American and I said brought not 'coming' to America. Also books that helps in our true liberation.

I am not opposed to the Hip-Hop, and Urban fiction writer. I am happy to see young people creating an entrepreneurial spirit. They started out selling book from the trunk of their cars and now mainstream publishers area snatching them up, giving large advances. I am happy to see young Blacks writing and young Black reading. However, I do think that our young reader need to have a variety of reading choices. Now, if we want to see a change in the industry, we cannot be just spectators, we must participate in helping to bring about a change. After all, what the Hip-Hops write will be what your children and grandchildren will be reading for the future.

Black Writers On Tour objectives are to help African Americans preserve their culture via telling their stories, Helping writers to write and to publish their works, assist published authors to get their work in the marketplace, promote literary via encouraging the youth and the senior to read and to write. If children fall in love with reading at early age, their vocabulary will be enlarged and their reading speed will increase which will prevent them from feeling overwhelmed by reading assignments when they enter college. We need to buy books for our children as well as for our senior family members. Reading and writing can prevent the feeling of isolation and loneliness so often felt by senior, and reading can help in stimulating the mind of seniors.

We can change the rule to the game in the publishing industry via boycotting literary works that are damaging to the image of Blacks, prohibit our children from buying such books. And as a good solution is to teach Hip-Hop writers how to clean up their writing by depicting some of their character as having intellectual abilities and redeeming traits. If that fail, then write books that counter those books with poor taste. You could also invest in good writer in helping them to get their work published.

One thing for sure is, one can make a lot of money writing the wrong things, but you cannot take it with you. And just think the children you hurt by what you write just might be your own or even your grandchildren. Think before you write.

For information regarding Black Writers On Tour 2007

SINGLE PARENT—DON'T LEAVE YOUR CHILD OUT IN THE COLD, MAKE A WILL

Most of us have heard horror stories of parents who died and left money to the other parent, only to have the child left out in the cold when the other parent failed to provide for the child. In my experience with probate issues, I find that the parents who are irresponsible after the death of the other parent, was almost always irresponsible during that parent's lifetime. Don't expect your spouse and baby's mama/daddy to suddenly become a responsible parent just because you depart this life. If a man/woman did not pay child support, or was forced to pay child support for his/her children during your lifetime, he won't use the money you leave for the children when you die.

So, how can you be sure that your children benefits from the funds you leave for them? Your first step is to make a Will and name the person you want to manage the finances left for your children. You do not want your children to end up in the situation as those of Reggie and Linda. Reggie was a junkie who would disappear for two and three weeks at a time. They had three children. Reggie was the beneficiary on all Linda's life insurance policies as well as the life insurance from her job. When Linda died suddenly of a heart attack on his way home from work, Reggie was the dutiful widower and father. He wept continuously before, during, and after the funeral. He was home with the kids every night. He wept for Linda and promised her as he stood over her coffin that he would take care of the children. He begged her lifeless body to forgive him for his shameful conduct. He hugged the kids and wept with and for them every day. When everything settled down and all the money from the insurance policies was in the bank, Reggie went to Linda's mother's house and explained to her and the kids how he would manage with the money. Reggie also stated that he would get a job. He told them he had an interview at Home Depot and that his friend said he was sure to get the job. Reggie left the kids with Linda's mother while he went for the job interview. It was seven months before they saw him again. Reggie called Linda's mother and asked her to bring the kids to visit him in a drug rehab center. He had been sent there by drug court after a conviction for possession of cocaine. Although Linda's mother knew the money was all gone, she couldn't help but ask. Reggie just stared at her and didn't even try to offer an explanation. What could he say?

If you have insurance or any benefits for your children, make sure you name a responsible person, and an alternate, as financial guardian of your child's assets. The other parent will usually not seek custody of the children if they know they won't have access to the money. That's especially true if they really don't have any interest in raising the children. Don't leave it if to the court. Do the right thing by your child yourself. Do it now.

Clara Hunter King, ESQ, Estate Planner, and co-author with her sister, Dr. Rosie Milligan, senior estate planner, and Clara Hunter King, ESQ, Estate Planner co-author of *Departing This Life Preparations: What You Need To Know To Get Your Personal And Business Affairs In Order.* Drrosie@aol.com, website: www.Drrosie.com, 323-750-3592. Get your copy of the book at Classic One Books, 1425 W. Manchester Ave. Ste B, Los Angeles, Calif. 90047, 323-750-4114

FAREWELL AND WELL DONE— MUHAMMAD NASSARDEEN

The African-American community revisits a moment that's too familiar—the demise of a great leader—Muhammad Nassardeen. Muhammad was the founder of the organization *Recycling Black Dollars*. He was a visionary and a business guru. His concern for the dismal economic plight of the African-American family and community led him to leave a six-figure income corporate job to try and change the economic direction of Black folk.

Nassardeen, in my opinion, understood what fuels the engine that turns the economic key. Daily, many Black leaders, preachers, and politicians spit rhetoric about how many times the dollar bounces in the Black community versus how many times it bounces for other races. Nassardeen understood that entrepreneurship was the bases for economic empowerment. He recognized that Black business ownership would yield more jobs for Blacks, and that if Blacks did not own the businesses in their communities, where Black people spend a majority of their spendable income, then the Black dollars would continue to leave the Black community. Being cognitive of those facts, he was driven to focus on changing the attitude of Blacks about business ownership and supporting Black businesses.

I will mention a few of the tasks Muhammad spearheaded, although to adequately cover all of this great man's accomplishments, I would need to write a whole book. His works encompass picking up the baton from Marcus Garvey, W.E.B. Dubois, Dr. Martin Luther King Jr., and Malcolm X. He possessed all their spirits—he *loved* Black people. He was not one with diarrhea of the mouth and paralysis of the hands and feet; nor was he a man with faith and no works. He was about what he believed in—and he believed that Blacks could do for themselves.

When Black-owned gas stations were struggling, Nassardeen brought the issue before the Black community. He kept the spotlight on the whereabouts of Black businessmen. For years he facilitated weekly meetings. He had each business owner to give a sixty-second commercial about their businesses and to tell what Black business they had supported that week, then how to "speak up" and "shut up." Each non-business owner would introduce themselves and tell what businesses they supported.

Muhammad puts the "B" in the words "Black business." He started the *Recycling Black Dollars Black Business Directory* so that Blacks could find Black-owned businesses. He led the *Change Bank Crusade*, which drove millions of dollars into Black banks (Founders and Broadway Federal). He was the catalyst behind the *Annual Business Competition*, which awarded $20,000 for the best business plan. He rented office space that was large enough to share with other entrepreneurs. He was never about the spotlight for himself; he wanted the spotlight focused on Black businesses and the needs of Blacks.

He recognized that the image depicted of Blacks in the media had caused many Blacks to see themselves from the lens of the media. The image we have of a person or race dictates the attitudes and behaviors that we hold towards them. He understood the impact of media and image. He wanted to right all wrongs and to fix every dilemma the Black man faced. He started his own newspaper to highlight the good things about Black folks. He hosted a radio talk show, *On the Positive Side*. He held an annual recognition luncheon, spotlighting Black achievements.

Muhammad was likened unto biblical characters, such as John the Baptist, who was crying, "Repent." Nassardeen cried out to Blacks to change their ways. He would tell us to "put a dollar in the Black man's hand every time you get a chance." He forced his legs to carry him in spite of the pain. He would not give in or give up. Like Jeremiah, he could not quit. Like David when everyone else was afraid of the giant, Goliath, David merely took what little he had and went for it. Nassardeen didn't have much, but he took what he had and went for it with all his might. Like Nehemiah, who could have been comfortable in the king's palace, his countenance was sad because his "homeland lieth in waste and the gates burned down." Nassardeen could have been comfortable with his six-figure income in corporate America. But instead, he, like Nehemiah, left a place of comfort to help rebuild the walls of the Black community that lieth in waste since the 1965 Riot and from the Rodney King Uprising. I still call it the Rodney King Riot.

What would Muhammad want us to do—cry, mourn, or give long, elegant speeches? The answer is none of these things! He would want us to continue to do for ourselves—starting businesses, supporting Black-owned businesses, putting our money in Black banks, and educating our children. He would want Black men to take care of their families and to "put a dollar in a Black hand whenever you can."

Muhammad Nassardeen—his story and his journey must be told! We talked about it last week. He would always say to me, "Doc, I know, and I'm going to finish my book. In fact, I will have it for your next Black Writers on Tour."

I'm gon' mis' u, Nassardeen.

GET ON THE BUS: SAVING BLACK BUSINESSES BY ANY MEANS NECESSARY

On Saturday April 3, 2004, Get On The Bus Black Business Tour will board in the parking lot of Power of Love World Ministries at 1426 W. Manchester, west of Normandie at 9:00 a.m. We will take back our community by any means necessary. Owning businesses in our community isn't anything new. We used to own many of the businesses on Central Ave., and Vermont Manchester corridor and many other locations. We will not leave, we will rededicate, recommit and revitalize. We cannot wait on anyone to help us.

As chairperson of the West Coast Harvest Institute, under the leadership of Dr. Claud Anderson, we are determined to teach our people (Black people) how to demonstrate appropriate behavior towards each other. We are launching an economic empowerment movement. In addition to starting new businesses, we are determined to help existing businesses transition from merely surviving to thriving businesses by any means necessary.

We want our children to experience the true meaning of a community. A community should be a reflection of its residents in every aspects, not just political positions. This reflection should be in business ownership as well as in the police and Sheriff department.

It is something spiritually wrong with a people who are willing to feed other folk children and starve their own. That's not just a fool, that's a damn fool. For those of you who complain about the high crime in our community and at the same time spending your money with people who do not look like you, you need to know that you are helping to perpetuate crime. How so? you may ask. Well, if you support Black owned businesses they would be able to employ many of those who are forced into a life of crime. Frederick Douglas said in a speech "hungry men will eat." If we believe that we are our brother's keeper than why aren't we acting on that belief?

Let's look at this picture and see if you see something wrong here. Every ethnic community except the Black community is a reflection of its residents. Their children grow up seeing a variety of business owners who look like them. This gives them a sense of what they can aspire to become. What do children in the Black community see as related to business ownership? Can't you see the correlation of the unemployment rate and business ownership among ethnic groups?

Your child goes to college to get a job because that is mostly what he sees growing up, Black folk working for other folk. When he completes college and gets a job, he spends his money with people who are non-Black because that is what he saw you, his parents, do. The cycle is repeated.

I do not want to hear another Black person quote the ethnic spending pattern again, as to how many times the dollar recycle in communities. What is your point and what is your comparison, huh? So think next time before you speak or quote stats.

All ethnic groups own most of the businesses in their communities and they own most of the business in the Black communities. Why don't Blacks own business in non-Black communities like nail shops, mini markets, cleaners, beauty supplies, wig shops, dress shops, etc., etc.? Why? Yes, why? Answer me! I hear you. Yes, right.

We owe it to our children to leave them the kind of community that others are able to experience. How do we reclaim our community? Inch by inch. It does not take a rocket scientist's strategic planning to do it. I have a 5 year plan that can drive the majority of non-Black businesses from our community and replace them with Black owned businesses. I will disclose it at our Black Business summit. I am not against anybody, I am for including my people and myself.

In conclusion, we must come to grips with truth. The truth is, we must become economically self-sufficient and competitive. Another truth is we must improve the employment rate for Blacks in order to reduce crime. When I say we, I mean that Blacks must be in position to employ more Blacks. If we do not do it for ourselves, no one else will do it for us. We can do it. Revisit history, and revisit Black Wall Street in Tulsa Oklahoma in 1923. Do the right thing and Get On The Bus!

IS SOBRIETY POSSIBLE AFTER 25 YEARS OF DRUG AND ALCOHOL ADDICTION?

It's every parent's prayer and hope for their child/children to be free from their drug and alcohol addiction. The last word a dying mother wishes to hear is my child has conquered his/her addiction. Many people who are addicted and their loved ones lose hope. They think that it's impossible to obtain sobriety. They feel this way because there are not enough faces put on the drug/alcoholic conquerors due to the fear of embarrassing their family and the stigma placed upon them by society.

I was compelled to write this article after meeting and publishing Geraldine Thomas's book, *Street Life And Prayer: One Woman's Journey From 25 Years Of Alcohol & Drug Addiction To Freedom.* In her book, *Street Life And Prayer*, Geraldine Thomas takes you on a twenty-five-year journey of drug and alcohol addiction. She makes herself transparent so that others may see how easy it is to get hooked on alcohol and drugs. She says, "It's easy to get started, but it's very hard to quit, and for many they will not stop until they hit rock bottom. For some, rock bottom is losing their children, their spouse, their home and their job, becoming homeless; and for others, rock bottom is death."

Geraldine states, "I do not wish drug/alcohol addiction on anyone, and if I can help others by being transparent and telling my story, and my story will prevent a parent or their child from traveling the path of addiction, I am willing to suffer the consequences. God healed me. I am grateful, and I am no longer ashamed of who I was, because I am so happy celebrating who I am today in Christ Jesus."

There are many unsuspecting drug and alcohol addicts among children and spouses. The downside of this is that these addicts do not get help soon enough because their family members have no clue about the signs and symptoms of addiction. Many are doing well in school, going to work every day as usual. You will recognize some of the symptoms if you read Geraldine's new book. You will learn that the one thing all addicts have in common is becoming an expert liar.

They start scheming and will manipulate everyone within their circle. In this book you are given clear, easily recognizable signs and symptoms of addiction—and when you see the symptoms, don't be in denial—confront your loved one and help them to get help. You are not alone.

Drug and alcohol addiction has reached epidemic proportions, and it does not discriminate by gender, race, age, or economic status. As an educational and cautionary action, I feel that everybody should make *Street Life And Prayer* a must-read book. Many of our loved one could have gotten help sooner if we had only known the symptoms of drug/alcohol addiction.

You will come to understand that God is truly a "Life Jacket" for those sinking to rise no more because of their inability to stop using drugs and alcohol through their own attempts.

WHAT BLACK AMERICA MUST KNOW AND DO NOW!

Our problem is not that we do not have enough religion, churches, and political leaders. We have more than enough. Our problem is that we have left our first love—God, and we are neither cold nor hot. Our other main problem is that we have not pursued economics in the way we should have. We are suffering from economic anemia, economic hemorrhage, and economic paralysis. We display a failure to do for self and failure to support Black-owned business. We still suffer from the White man's ice is colder than the Black man's ice. Here is what others who came before us have said about economics and self-determination:

Booker T. Washington said to us, *"Now is the time, not in some far-off future, but now is the time for us as a race to prove to the world that we have the ability and the inclination to do our part in owning, developing, manufacturing, and trading in the natural resources of our country. And if we let these golden opportunities slip from us in this generation, I fear they will never come to us in like degree again. Let us act ... before it's too late, before others come from foreign lands and rob us of our birthright."*

Let's see what Mr. Booker T. Washington had to say about politics, shall we? *"We did not seek to give the people the idea that political rights were not valuable or necessary, but rather to impress upon them that economic efficiency was the foundation for every success."*

Dr. Martin Luther King Jr. said these almost exact same words: *"The emergency we now face is economic."* We must believe that it is our birthright to partake of the riches of the world, and this is the faith that we must hold to. Dr. Martin Luther King Jr. also said, *"Faith is taking the first step even when you don't see the staircase."*

Let the words of Malcolm X ring out in your mind: *"By any means necessary."* Let's not retreat. Our forefathers did not retreat, which got us as far as we did. We must not be afraid; we must not fear. Harriet Tubman once said, *"I can't die but once."* We are in a war, and in every war there will be casualties. Sister Rosa

Parks said, "I have learned over the years that when one's mind is made up, this diminishes fear, knowing what must be done does away with fear."

Frederick Douglass had the following to say: "Without a struggle, there can be no progress." So stop talking about you being tired of fighting the system and asking why we have to fight so hard to get what's due us. Don't get tired; ask God for more strength to fight. Frederick Douglass also stated, *"If there is no struggle, there is no progress. Those who profess to favor freedom and deprecated agitation are men who want crops without plowing up the ground; they want rain without thunder and lightning."*

W.E.B. DuBois had the following to say: *"To be a poor man is hard, but to be a poor race in a land of dollars is the very bottom of hardship."*

Can we be saved on this side of the river?

The biblical characters Sampson and Hezekiah pleaded with God for another chance, and God granted them their requests. He can do the same for us if we come together in prayer, works, and faith. God is the same today as He was yesterday. II Chronicles 7:14 tells us, "If my people which are called by my name, shall humble themselves, and pray, and seek my face, and turn from their wicked ways, then will I hear from heaven, and will forgive their sin and will heal their land."

Here is what we must do: We must reflect back on what Mama Dem did. What the new generation did was this: Since they could not embrace everything about their parents/grandparents, they threw the baby out with the bathwater and started anew. They tried to bake a new cake leaving out all of Grandma's ingredients. When they got to the fork in the road, they did not want to travel the roads that Grandma had traveled. They took a new path—and here we are tore up from the floor up, in a ship without a sail, in a boat without a paddle, in the dark without a light.

We must move from being consumers to being producers. We must endure being inconvenient via going out of our way to do business with Black folks or with folks who hire Black folks. As Dr. Claud Anderson has said, "The drain of wealth and disposable income from the Black neighborhood will destabilize the neighborhood."

We must restore family and cultural values. We must take control of our children and community. We must reach out to our young folk, teach and show them the proper way to live in America where all odds are stacked against them, and let them know that if God is for them, He's more than all the world against them. We must immunize, vaccinate, and inoculate our people with the words of truth about their history. They are not just descendants of slaves but indeed, ascendants of kings and queens. We must give them their booster shot along the way to protect them from vicious racism and from the media's attack of demonization that has depicted them as being less than human.

When our children are told that Blacks do not have the ability to do math, tell them about Dr. Charles Drew who invented blood plasma; Granville T. Woods, an engineer who patented the telephone transmitter as well as over 150 electrical and mechanical inventions; and Lewis Howard Latimer who was a pioneer in the development of the electrical lightbulb, just to name a few. You cannot do those things if you have not mastered the skills of mathematics. Tell them to google Black inventions and Black patents or read Francella Henderson's book, *Hidden Secrets About Black History*.

If they tell you that Blacks don't know how to run successful businesses, tell them about Little Black Wall Street which was likened unto a mini Beverly Hills where Blacks had created a successful infrastructure and dollars circulated 36–100 times and sometimes took a year to leave the community. This town was in Tulsa, Oklahoma, and it was destroyed by White mobs in 1921, leaving 3,000 African Americans dead and over 600 successful Black businesses destroyed. Tell them that this Black enclave community without SBA loans had 21 churches, 21 restaurants, 30 grocery stores, 2 movies theaters, a hospital, a bank, a post office, libraries, schools, law offices, six private airplanes, and a bus system. Keep giving them booster shots against miseducation and misinformation and inoculate them with the truth.

Last but not least, we must teach our children about God and get them involved in a holistic church, a church that ministers to the whole person's needs, not just his/her spiritual needs. We must pray with our children and teach them how to pray. We must pray before going to bed and pray with them daily before sending them out in the world. Ask God's blessings and protection for them. We must teach them a heart of gratitude. Teach them to bless their food before eating and to thank people when they do things for them; to say please when asking for something from others.

Even though we are far off course economically, we can fix the situation by accepting full responsibility for rearing our children. We must postpone immediate gratification and make child rearing a priority and make decisions for our children based on the future and not the present. We must forego purchasing new automobiles. Buy a used car and fix it up. It will run, and you'll have less car insurance payments. If your car is not paid for, as soon as you pay it off, put the amount you were paying into a savings account. Save that money instead of spending it. Don't buy any more clothes until the ones that you have are worn out or are no longer usable. Have your purses and shoes repaired versus buying new ones. It's cheaper, and you'll save money. Shop in thrift stores. Read the book by Helen Pearson, *Thrift Store Diva: Spending Pennies and Looking like a Million Dollars*.

Teach your young child about finances. Open a savings account for your child when he/she reaches the age of 13; teach them how to manage money. Make a family budget and have family participation. Save 10 percent of your earnings, buy life insurance for yourself and your children, prepay your burial plot or crypt or cremation if that's your choice. Start a savings account for a college education for your children or work with them to keep their grades up so they can get a scholarship.

Make plans financially for your retirement. Social Security is a supplement, and that's all it is. It will not be enough to sustain you in your latter years, and in most cases, your children will not be able to help you. Have family prayer time and hold a family meeting weekly. Prepare a Living Trust if you have real estate so that your property that you worked so hard for does not go into probate. Attorney fees and probates eat up what should be left for your loved ones. You decide who gets what's in your estate so that the family does not have to fall out with each other because if there was ever a time that we need each other it is *now*, so prevent future division by proper planning now. Get rid of your credit cards accept for one and do not use it unless it's totally necessary.

We can turn this situation around if we take heed. Elders, you need to step up to the plate. You have an obligation to offer wisdom and to teach your loved ones. And the adults and children need to listen to their elders. The older generation has been where you are trying to go. They may not know how to use a computer or surf the Internet, but they know enough to help you to be better and to live better if you listen. As elders, we learn from you and you can learn from us, so let's go for a marriage. Our forefathers shed a great deal of blood and fought too hard to be delivered from the hands of slavery and because for that reason, we should fight to not return to slavery conditions—economic slavery. At this time, we are close to returning if we are not mindful of how we treat God and our finances.

Much love from an elder.

WHEN GOD TELLS YOU TO DO SOMETHING, DO IT, EVEN WHEN IT DOES NOT MAKES SENSE TO OTHERS

When God gives you an assignment, do it. Sometimes what God tells you to do, you may be ridiculed for doing it—but do it. In 1990, I wrote two books: *Satisfying The Black Woman Sexually Made Simple* and *Satisfying The Black man Sexually Made Simple*. God did not tell me to write these books; however, after I wrote them, He clearly spoke to me.

"I want you to develop a teaching ministry on sex, sexuality and relationships, and start with teaching in the church," God said.

"Oh, no," I said. "Talking about sex to church folk, I don't want to do that. I will talk about it, but not directly to church folk."

God then said, "The church should set the standard for the world and not the world setting standards for the church. The church should influence the world and not the world influencing the church."

At the time it did not makes sense, but I went forward and started doing it. The preachers and the church folk wanted to hang me for discussing sex. They would call me on the airways and suggest that I was going to hell for talking on these subjects. Like a child going back to their parent after an assignment went sour, I went back to God.

"God, these Christians don't want to hear me talking/teaching about sex. In fact, they are suggesting that talking about sex will surely land me in hell."

God then said, " It's not what you say about sex that causes problems, it's what you do about sex that causes problems and destroy families and nations."

I got it.

Reverend Cecil Murray, the former pastor of the famed F.A.M.E. Church, was the first minister in Los Angeles, California to embrace my ministry of educating the church on issues regarding sex. As a minister of the gospel, I have had speaking engagements cancelled after a member of the congregation went to my web site and saw the books that I have authored on sex. I got a little discouraged with trying to teach Christians. Once I asked a mother of the church, "Don't Christians have sex and if not how did these little babies running around in the church get here?"

In 1990, I warned the churches and the nation about what would happen to our society if we failed to address the topic of sex. The church didn't want to address it. And parents couldn't teach what was never taught to them. SEX HAS BECOME A WEAPON OF MASS DESTRUCTION and I have been admonished to get back to my assignment—educating the church on sex and relationship because sexual turmoil is the leading cause of divorces, and the divorce rate is far too high, especially among Christians.

During every presidential election, a candidate has had to bow out due to sexual encounters, alleged or true. Sexual encounters have been the downfall of pastors of mega ministries throughout the United States of America. If you think I am just blowing off smoke, don't take my word for it; Google "political sex scandals" and "church sex scandals" to see for yourself. The names are too numerous to mention.

I am going to do what God tells me to do because He woke me up this morning, not my alarm clock. He kept me from losing my mind. He dried my eyes when I thought the tears would never stop flowing. He healed my body when the doctor diagnosed me with Lupus forty years ago and my prognosis was poor. I can no longer be concerned about what man thinks that I should be doing or saying. I am taking my marching orders from God, and I am suggesting to you, the readers, to do the same and watch the peace of God that will overtake you.

I am back on track and I am going to get back to my ministry of teaching on Sex and Relationships. For confirmation, God woke me up this morning at 2:00 A.M. and had me to look through my file box—not knowing what I was looking for—and the first thing I paid attention to was a letter addressed to me. It was a letter dated August 6, 1991, written from a minister. Below is the letter. Just think, what if I had not gotten up at 2:00 A.M. as God had instructed me to do, I may have missed this revelation. This letter was my confirmation. IF GOD TELLS YOU TO DO SOMETHING, JUST DO IT. WE TEND TO LISTEN TO EVERYBODY, BUT GOD.

Having Her Say

8-11-1991
Sunday

Dear Dr. Milligan:

On Tuesday Aug. 6, 1991, I heard you on the Christian Information Show. I must tell you that your topic is what the church needs counseling in. Many couples are separating and divorcing over these very issues. I believe it was God's will that I heard your show. I believe this because before I turned on the radio I had been lying in bed trying to communicate with my wife some of my inner feelings concerning our marriage, the ministry and other topics because I am a person who needs stimulating conversation, however my wife did not want to be bothered as she has done several times before. Therefore I became frustrated again as I have done before.

So I went into the living room and begin to pray and talk to God about my feelings and my relationship. After I finished praying I went back to the bedroom and turned on the radio before I got back into bed. That is when I heard the host of the show discussing your topic on sex issues and relationships. After the host mentioned that he was holding a survey and to call in, I immediately did so. Matter of fact, I was the first caller and I won your book, Satisfying The Black Woman Sexually Made Simple. I got off the phone and continued to listen to your show. It downed on me that this did not occur by accident. After all, I do not listen to this show consistently. Therefore, Dr. Milligan I encourage you to be steadfast in this teaching because just knowing that I am not the only person going through these situations helped me. Also Dr. Milligan if I was younger or less mature this situation would most likely destroy my marriage. After all it isn't a wonderful feeling to be denied or rejected by your mate. However, Dr. Milligan I want you to know that my wife and I are in love, but like many Christian couples when they become married and they are "SAVED," they treat sexual relations as being taboo. This is how my wife feels. The only exception to this rule is when she is in a good mood. Sometimes I can't tell when that mood will present itself.

Dr. Milligan, I want to thank you for your book in advance and I believe it will help the both of us. Also I will share it with another couple and inform them of your address in case they want a copy. P.S. I will be praying for you and this teaching ministry and you have my blessing to use this testimony if it will be of any use to you.

Sincerely,

Rev. L. Campbell

www.ingramcontent.com/pod-product-compliance
Lightning Source LLC
Chambersburg PA
CBHW080456110426
42742CB00017B/2908